JAZZ IN AMERICAN CULTURE

Jazz in American Culture

PETER TOWNSEND

University Press of Mississippi
Jackson

Jazz is not about any one thing or one style. Like bolero or flamenco, jazz is a way to see life.

Paquito D'Rivera

Edinburgh University Press Ltd

22 George Square, Edinburgh
Published in the United States of America
by University Press of Mississippi,

2000

Typeset in Monotype Fournier
by Bibliocraft, Dundee, and
printed and bound in Great Britain
by The Cromwell Press, Trowbridge

ISBN 1-57806-323-x (hardback)
ISBN 1-57806-324-8 (paperback)

Contents

Preface

Jazz is one of the great musical cultures of the world. This is the underlying premise of this book. It is necessary to make the statement in this comparative, global way because, within the society in which it has emerged, jazz can have the kind of familiarity that breeds contempt without being familiar enough to be accepted on its own terms.

The statement also reasserts the centrality of music in jazz. This might seem a truism or a tautology, but like most manifestations of culture in a mediatized late twentieth-century society, jazz is and has been subject to a variety of representations that somehow fail to encompass the values, in this case musical, that lie at its heart. At the same time jazz, as a musical culture which has usually been that of a minority, has not been able to articulate itself to a wider audience. The scheme of this book is to describe the foundations of the musical culture of jazz, and then to show the shift that occurs as jazz is refracted through these other representations. The first half of the book deals with the 'Jazz' part of the title, the second half with 'in American Culture'.

Statements about jazz beg questions of definition. Jazz is often thought of as being mysterious, elusive and hard to define. But since the meaning of a word is its use, jazz is no harder to define than anything else (try defining 'popular music', for example), provided one has decided how to use the word. The preferred definition of jazz in this book stays close to the musical basis, for the reasons already stated. But jazz can be defined relatively narrowly or relatively broadly. Some writers have restricted its usage to the musical styles they prefer, like the 1940s revivalists who denied the word 'jazz' to any of the post-New Orleans styles. On the other hand, some recent exponents of 'Jazz Studies' have expanded the term to include the entire phenomenon of jazz including all its representations, derivatives and social implications. These shifts in the meanings of the word could be made transparent by other signals, such as marking them 'jazz (1)' 'jazz (2)', 'jazz (3)' and so on. It is probably wiser

vii

to accept Krin Gabbard's conclusion that jazz is 'the music that large groups of people have called jazz at particular moments in history',[1] and then to use the word in the sense that emphasizes the qualities that one considers important.

A related premise of this book is that what is called jazz is in any case a certain segment or area selected out of a continuous terrain of American musical styles. It has no precise boundaries, and at its fringes it shades off into a range of other musics. The territory of jazz touches 'pop' music, 'country' music, the blues, 'classical' music, rock and roll, and so on, and at times can hardly be distinguished from them. There are styles and artists that pose questions about boundaries and classifications: was Frank Sinatra a jazz singer? Was Louis Jordan a jazz musician? Was 'Western Swing' part of jazz or of country music? The idea of the limits of a music like jazz, of its boundaries, should be reassessed in the way that Gregory Nobles proposes for the idea of the 'frontier': as an area characterized by a 'complex pattern of human contact', not simply as a cut-off point between well-defined separate entities.[2]

Jazz is more like a region than a nation. Nevertheless, it is still possible to state some positive characteristics that mark out the region. For positive definitions, one can refer to a useful brief version by Lewis Porter: 'Jazz is a form of art music developed by black Americans around 1900 that draws upon a variety of sources from Africa, Europe and America.'[3] Jazz as a segment of American music is, by a consensus of most writers, identifiable by reference to its rhythms, its repertoire, its use of improvisation and its approach to instrumental sound and technique, and these features are reflected in the description of jazz as a music in Chapter 1.

This book is partly directed to an audience of students of American Studies and American Literature, who may not be conversant with jazz, but it is hoped that it also presents a distinctive view of jazz that will be of interest to those who are already well versed in it. During the time of writing of this book, there has been a wave of publications on jazz that have to some extent changed perspectives on it, and some of these new views are represented here. The selection of literary texts in Chapter 4 is canonical rather than a complete treatment of jazz in literary forms, but I have assumed that a discussion of prominent writers such as Morrison and Kerouac would be useful.

There are other interpretative methods than the ones used in this book that might have been relevant: Bhabha's idea of 'hybridity' from postcolonial criticism, some of Bakhtin's concepts, and those of Harold

Bloom on influence (especially as, having been a fan in the 1940s at a time when internal wrangling about the nature of jazz was going on, it is possible that Bloom was influenced by jazz itself). However, I did not want to burden jazz with the apparatus that fills literary criticism for the sake of a few insights that in any case would serve to translate jazz out of its own language into that of a generalizing academic discipline. The subject of jazz could also be approached within an 'African-diasporic' perspective, as it is in projects like the Centre for Black Music Research in Chicago, but one of the contentions of this book is that the cultural position of jazz is anomalous: as well as being ultimately an African product, it has lived all of its life in Northern America, and is deeply contitioned in all aspects by that fact.

I owe thanks to many people for their help and support during this project: to my colleagues at the University of Huddersfield, and especially to Professor Brian Maidment and Colin Graham (now of Queens University, Belfast) who took time off from Victorian and Irish Studies respectively to read some early chapters; to David Oliphant of the University of Texas, Michael Green of Birmingham and Philip Davies of De Montfort for support and encouragement at an early stage; to staff at a number of archives in the US who helped during brief but productive research visits, including Michael Cogswell and Deslyn Downes at the Louis Armstrong Archive at Queens College; Dan Morgenstern, Don Luck and Vincent Pelote at the Institute of Jazz Studies at Rutgers University; and staff associated with the Duke Ellington Collection in the Smithsonian. In the UK, David Nathan at the National Jazz Archive in Loughton was very helpful during a number of useful visits.

I owe thanks also to friends in the USA and Britain, including Larry Rafferty of Hit & Run Press, and Jim Burns, poet and jazz writer, for ideas and information on a variety of subjects. George Mackay of the University of Central Lancashire gave very valuable editorial advice; and I am grateful to Edinburgh University Press, especially Nicola Carr, for their help and occasional gentle pressure.

My thanks, as always, to my family, above all to Sue Clarke, for her support and patience. Also to Paul and Emilie McSloy, of New York, for hospitality and a great deal of information; to all my music-loving relations, especially my mother; and lastly to my late father, Bill Townsend,

drummer in The Swingtime Band (Herefordshire, England, c.1940), to
whom this book is dedicated.

Peter Townsend

The University of Huddersfield

October 1999

Notes

1. Krin Gabbard, *Jammin' at the Margins: Jazz in the American Cinema* (Chicago: University of Chicago Press, 1996), p. 8.
2. Gregory H. Nobles, *American Frontiers: Cultural Encounters and Continental Conquest* (London: Penguin, 1998), p. xii.
3. Lewis Porter, *Lester Young* (London: Macmillan, 1985), p. x.

CHAPTER I

The Language: Jazz as Music

Throughout the twentieth century the American musical idiom known as jazz has undergone regular, sometimes radical, changes of style. It has telescoped into a few years a cycle of harmonic development that in European music took several centuries. Its rhythmic basis, its instrumentation, the nature of its ensembles and its repertoire, have constantly changed. Jazz has never enjoyed the long-term stability typical of folk musics – since its origins lie at the beginning of the century, it is hardly old enough for that. Its rate of change has been comparable with that of other forms of art and entertainment in the twentieth century, subject to pressures of the market and responsive to changes of technology and public taste, as well as to the explosive creativity of its performers.

There are other dimensions of variation: the musical style of jazz has never been homogeneous at any one time. Outside the dominant style of any period, there have always been distinct traditions and ways of playing, some of these based on regional differences within the USA, or particular instruments: for example the 'Harlem stride' piano tradition, which never became a dominant jazz style, but continued as a sometimes separate stream of development alongside the group or orchestral jazz of the day.

Jazz has been a democratic music, in which innovations have been accepted regardless of where they originated, and in which there has never been a sense of central control, through academic or other institutions. A high level of ability has been widely distributed, with hundreds, or even thousands, of musicians achieving distinctive personal styles. The change and diversity within the music are comparable to the variations within a language: there are innumerable variations of time, place, function, dialect, idiolect. At the extremes of the music there are styles between which the variation is so great that there are few common components left. It is a long stretch stylistically from the jazz pop songs of Clarence Williams in the 1920s to the fractured atonal improvisations of Cecil Taylor half a century later.

To sum up the characteristics of such a rich and diverse music is to try to reduce the complexity of a natural phenomenon to the simplicity of a formula. A large part of the picture is inevitably left out of any general description, and the reader can be left with the impression that what is being described is a single, unchanging style. In the case of 'jazz', a term that covers music produced over almost a century in a wide diversity of times and places, for different purposes and in different cultural settings, this generality is particularly misleading. What 'jazz' is and has been exemplifies Wittgenstein's explanation of the meanings of a word: rather than an 'essential' jazz that a definition should try to isolate, what there has been in actuality is a 'family' of musical styles closely related enough for one generic term to be applied to them all.[1] The failure to accept the limitations of the term 'jazz', and to allow for the diversity that it conceals, is responsible for the problematic nature of some studies of the subject and some of the arguments that have sprung up about it.

Accounts of jazz as music, however, usually agree on the importance of a number of musical features that in general distinguish jazz from other musical languages and traditions. These stylistic continuities within the jazz tradition can be established by sampling music produced across the decades of its existence. The common elements in jazz performance between a recording made by Louis Armstrong in 1927 ('Wild Man Blues') and one made by Miles Davis in 1959 ('All Blues') are at first hearing hardly more apparent than the differences. Jazz is not a single, homogeneous style of music in all times and places. Its history is relatively brief, but the sum total of innovation and stylistic change across that period has been enormous. As well as following a developmental curve, the music has received all the inflections that locality, ethnicity and individuality have brought to it. One may in the end agree that Louis Armstrong and Miles Davis are shown by these two recordings to be jazz performers, but arriving at that view is a result of a balancing of similarities and differences, and not as obvious a fact as many writers on jazz have assumed.

This chapter will concentrate on some of the features of jazz as music that are found in most of the definitions that have been written, and which make jazz an identifiable sector within the spectrum of American musical cultures. These are improvisation, rhythm, repertoire, and instrumental sound and technique. Where an instrumentalist is improvising on a certain repertoire, with a certain approach to rhythm, instrumental sound and technique, the result is likely to be what a majority of listeners would agree to call 'jazz'.

Jazz Styles and History

To retell the story of the development of jazz is not an aim of this book, partly because the job has already been done thoroughly elsewhere.[2] But the character of the music, and the manner of its change, are inextricable from the historical circumstances in which it has been practised. Again, it is necessary to be aware of the simplification that is implied by telling the story of a single entity, 'jazz'. What is, and what is not, part of the history again raises issues about boundaries and definitions. To a large extent, also, its history has become entangled with myth, and with the reshapings of the story that correspond with various interpretations of what jazz is.

As in many other areas of cultural life, the history is a contested area, with different conceptions of jazz being bolstered by different versions of how and why it came to be as it is. These different narratives of the life of jazz have sometimes had ideological overtones. One example of this is in the value which is sometimes given to the idea of collectivity: some critics have had an ideological preference for collective playing which caused them to regard the post–1920s emphasis on the soloist as a loss from which jazz has never recovered. The same argument came to the fore among some proponents of 'free jazz' in the 1960s, who saw a return to musical collectivity as the ideologically radical act that jazz had long needed.[3] Although, as these examples show, its history can be itself a contested area, it is difficult to address these issues without at least an outline of jazz from its beginnings. What follows is a brief history mainly in relation to changes in musical style.

It appears that jazz came into being around 1900, by the coalescence of a number of existing popular musical styles, primarily ragtime and the blues. These were both in origin black musical idioms. Ragtime reached a high level of popularity in all sectors of the American population from the 1890s onwards. It was a rhythmically lively style of solo piano performance which made use of patterns of syncopation that had long been known in black American music, perhaps even in its African origins. Ragtime depended upon a certain level of musical literacy: a lot of ragtime music was written down, and played without improvisation. However, there is evidence that improvisation was an element in the musical culture surrounding ragtime. In other musical and non-musical activities, improvisation was already an important characteristic of African-American culture. The blues, which had come into being late in the nineteenth century, was a simpler, looser, primarily vocal idiom, based on a three-line verse form, with a simple repeated harmonic sequence. Its performers were improvisatory and individualised in approach: the music allowed scope for the rewriting of words and melodies and a wide range of vocal and instrumental effects and variations.

The earliest forms of what present-day listeners would recognize as jazz resulted from a blending of the materials and the approaches primarily of these two idioms. As ragtime and blues drifted towards jazz, what was produced combined the musical discipline and relative complexity of ragtime, the individualized and improvisatory property of the blues and the musical materials of both forms. A third component was the more formal and European brass-band tradition, which influenced the instrumentation and the repertoire of early jazz. An early performer like Jelly Roll Morton played a repertoire largely made up of ragtime-like and blues-based compositions, resulting in a looser form of ragtime and a more formalized and musically varied type of blues, with occasional march-like and Latin American influences.

Morton is one of many musicians associated with the city of New Orleans, which was, in the first two decades of the century, the first of the major American urban settings where conditions were favourable for advances in the development of jazz.[4] Until the middle of the First World War, sections of the city were given over to places of entertainment where, alongside sex and alcohol, music was in demand. The city's strong and ethnically diverse musical traditions produced large numbers of performers able to supply that demand. New Orleans supported a rich set of musical subcultures that reflected its population: elements of Spanish and French music, as well as indigenous styles, entered into the musical vocabulary of men like Morton, King Oliver and later Sidney Bechet and Louis Armstrong.

Some histories represent jazz as originating specifically in New Orleans and then appearing elsewhere only by transmission from this original source. It is clear, however, that although New Orleans was pre-eminent in this process, other areas were producing their own distinctive developments in the first decades of the century. Forms of jazz-like music were already being performed before 1920 on the West Coast and in other urban areas.[5] The chief point of arrival for musicians migrating from New Orleans and the South was Chicago, where another suitable milieu existed for musical activity. As well as a large and rapidly growing population of black migrants from the southern states, Chicago had other conditions required for jazz culture: a pool of available musical talent and an active night life. A characteristic of the social history of jazz has been its development in sectors of the entertainment economy away from the mainstream. Because of its marginality, a frequent characteristic of the kind of setting in which jazz operated was a relaxed attitude towards legality, overseen in some cases by urban machine politics and organized crime.

The New Orleans jazz style was initially polyphonic, based on collective improvisation by 'front-line' instruments, normally trumpet (or cornet), trombone and clarinet (or saxophone), supported by three rhythm players. The commercial potential of this music became evident at the end of the First World War. There was a massive broadening of the jazz audience in what F. Scott Fitzgerald named the 'Jazz Age' of the 1920s. Firstly Chicago, and later New York, became influential new centres of jazz activity. As we shall see in Chapter 2, the last of the great New Orleans innovators, Louis Armstrong, was largely responsible, through the impact of his own virtuosity during these years, for a new emphasis on the improvising soloist, which has since become an almost invariable feature of jazz performance. At the same time, under the influence of the more highly trained musicians entering jazz and of the tastes of the wider urban audience, group performances moved away from improvised polyphony towards pre-arranged formats, based in large part on written scores, with improvisation delegated to featured soloists who would improvise in turn.

From the mid–1930s, this movement towards the larger, organized ensemble led to an elevation of jazz in popularity to a point where a form of jazz became the mainstream popular music of the United States. This was the 'big band' period in which certain band leaders and soloists, such as Benny Goodman and Artie Shaw, became national celebrities, and these and numerous other orchestras broadcast their music through the new media of cinema and radio as well as on phonograph records and in public performances. The generic term for the music associated with this period is 'Swing'. The style of the large ensembles of the period was highly organized, but an important place was left for improvising soloists. In these and in the less formalized small groups of the 1930s there was produced a string of improvisers who followed Armstrong in developing the art of jazz with an increasing emphasis on individual improvisation. In the playing of such soloists as Coleman Hawkins, Lester Young and Art Tatum there was a continued exploration of the harmonic and rhythmic resources of jazz.

The big bands declined rapidly from the mid–1940s onwards. By then a new dominant jazz style had been synthesized by a group of adept and sophisticated younger musicians who had become disenchanted with the conservatism (as well as the economic and racial inequities) of the big band system, but were also driven by a general progressivist desire to develop the musical idiom.[6] The new style was referred to as 'bebop' (after the rhythm of one of its favourite phrases). Bebop introduced new repertoire, a more exacting standard of technique, and a new asymmetry of rhythm and phrasing, and it greatly advanced the complexity of jazz harmony.

Movements in jazz since bebop have tended to involve some simplification of or withdrawal from its complexity. The 'free jazz' associated in the 1960s with musicians like Ornette Coleman made the most complete break with the harmonic stringency of bebop. Free jazz used its own principles, varying from atonality to the complete abandonment of set themes and procedures. It represented a liberation of a kind, but was never in a position to gain acceptance by a mass audience. A number of its practitioners have had to endure spells of almost total rejection both within the jazz community and by the public.

The late 1950s were also the moment of another simplification. With the appearance of albums such as Miles Davis's *Kind of Blue* in 1959, musicians began to use 'modal' forms. The harmonies over which soloists improvised became simpler, at times almost static. Instead of having to formulate their solos over strings of changing chords, soloists were now improvising for long spells within a single scale of notes. Davis's composition 'So What' allows the improviser to play for twenty-four of its thirty-two bars over the single chord of D minor seventh. The only movement away from this occurs when the harmony temporarily moves a semitone higher, before returning to the D chord. The improviser has a slower rate of harmonic change to deal with than in the sometimes hectic sequences of chords in bebop harmony. The use of modal forms enabled jazz to draw closer to rock, which has always made use of simpler materials. Jazz and rock players could now meet on the common ground of modal harmony. In the 1970s this movement came to be called jazz-rock or 'fusion', and it provided one way in which jazz musicians were able to gain access to a popular music market.

The period of jazz history since the early 1980s has been variously described as one of conservatism, pluralism or fragmentation.[7] A number of influential younger musicians, most notably Wynton Marsalis, have espoused a disciplined, tradition-conscious re-examination of older styles, and this aspect of the scene has presented the most prominent public image of the music. But the spectrum of styles of music being performed under the title of jazz has been wider in the 1990s than ever before. One development seems likely in the long term even to challenge the idea of jazz as an American music. To the jazz foundation of rhythmic improvisation, musicians of other traditions and nationalities have added elements of their own folk musics, and a specifically American jazz has been subsumed in a worldwide panorama of improvised music which is still usually categorized as jazz, but which sometimes strains the elasticity of the term to its limits.

At the same time, the full range of old and new jazz styles continues to be played. There are, throughout the USA and in practically all other industrialized societies, groups of musicians who have taken it upon themselves to recreate and keep alive all of the past styles of jazz, from turn of the century ragtime to 1970s jazz-funk. Among these are many renowned professional players, but many are exemplars of what James Lincoln Collier has called 'local jazz', musicians whose non-professional, non-institutional, practical involvement with the music helps to maintain the past styles of jazz as active musical idioms at the end of the century.[8]

Improvisation and Form

We may state the task before the jazz musician as follows: Given some predetermined materials ... and a knowledge of jazz styles, compose a coherent musical statement spontaneously.   Lewis Porter

'All the Things You Are' has been played thousands of times; yet, if a musician is playing it again, he is putting his own life through it.
                                                            Clint Eastwood[9]

Improvisation is often taken to be a defining and unique feature of jazz, but neither of these adjectives is strictly justifiable. Firstly, there is music generally accepted as jazz that does not contain improvisation, and secondly there are many other musics in which improvisation is equally important. One of the peculiar features of Western music during the last 200 years has been its exclusion of improvisation. In earlier times, composers and performers, among them Mozart, Beethoven and J. S. Bach, were accomplished improvisers. Improvisation of one kind or another has been endemic in the folk musics of the world. In some 'classical' forms, such as Indian music, improvisation is central to the musical culture. European 'serious' music of the nineteenth and twentieth centuries is an ethnomusicological exception in its complete severance from improvisatory methods.

Against the background of this culturally prestigious 'serious' music, and the popular forms that stem from it, the improvisatory ethos of jazz has been seen as exceptional or aberrant. Jazz exists in an intellectual-artistic climate in which improvisation is liable to be seen as compensation for a deficiency (the inability to read written music), or as a freakish kind of gift (the jazz musician as the spontaneous, innocent, 'natural' player). Improvisatory music is close to a worldwide norm of musical practice. Nevertheless, the marginal status of improvisation in Western music reinforces the notion of the jazz musician as a 'primitive', 'instinctual' performer, and this meshes with the racial identification of the music as African American and the stereotypes of the 'instinctive', 'natural' musician that this drags in its wake.

Each idiom of improvised music throughout the world has its own methods and musical materials related to the cultural situation that formed it. The procedures of jazz are strikingly different from those of, say, Indian classical music. One of the most important factors in these differences is the material that musicians improvise *on*. Provided that improvisation is based on *something* (unlike the 'free' jazz practised by some musicians from the early 1960s on), it takes an imprint from the material used. So, in jazz, the nature of the vehicle for improvisation, of the song forms that make up its repertoire, partially determines the nature of the improvisation. What improvisers do is done within a framework provided by certain kinds of song form.

The repertoire of song forms that have been used by jazz musicians is enormous. In principle any song can be improvised on: there are instances of musicians improvising on 'Jingle Bells' and 'La Marseillaise'.[10] The repertoire of materials includes, in addition to any popular song published in the past century, a large corpus of compositions by jazz musicians and traditional songs from various American and European sources. Over the decades of the music's development, however, there has been a shakedown effect that has perpetuated some favoured songs and ignored or rejected others. The result has been that most jazz improvisation has used basic material drawn from a core repertoire of songs. This core, however, is still large. Levine, for example, gives a list of 965 songs as a model repertoire for jazz players.[11] However, he highlights only 248 of these as being essential, while the full repertoire is reduced for particular styles: a bebop player is unlikely to find the chord sequence of 'Jazz Me Blues' of practical use, whereas a 'traditional' player could not function without it. Skilled musicians in each established style will normally have a working repertoire of between fifty and 100 songs that can be played and improvised on from memory and at will. Some songs are expected to be known by all players working in post-Swing idioms, and there is a short list of about fifty numbers that operate as a jazz *lingua franca*. The guitarist Jim Hall commented: 'I've played with guys in little towns in Italy where I couldn't get through a sentence with them, but they could play "Stella" and "Autumn Leaves"'.[12]

The constituents of the repertoire for any jazz style are drawn from three main categories: popular songs, blues and jazz tunes. Jazz has always made use of whatever material the popular music industry has provided, especially from the 1920s on. The first jazz versions of some pop songs were recorded very soon after the songs were first published. Artists like Louis Armstrong and Billie Holiday were, in effect, enlisted into the publicity effort for some songs. In the postwar period, artists such as Charlie Parker recorded versions of numerous songs by Kern, Gershwin and Porter. Ian Carr has shown how Miles Davis's choice of material on his mid–1950s sessions was related to a series of popular recordings issued by Frank Sinatra a few years before.[13]

The properties of popular songs that have made them vehicles for jazz have to do with the apparently contradictory values of simplicity and complexity. A song can be good material because it is simple enough to be improvised on fluently, or, on the other hand, because it is unusual or difficult enough to be interesting to improvise on. Some commonly used themes have notably difficult chord progressions: 'Stella By Starlight', referred to by Jim Hall as part of the internationally known repertoire, passes through a number of distinct phases of harmony in its 32-bar sequence. Jerome Kern's 'All the Things You Are', part of the staple diet of improvisers for fifty years, progresses through five changes of key. The Ray Noble composition 'Cherokee' has been of interest to jazz musicians largely because of the challenge of its harmonically tricky middle section. On the other hand, there are simple popular song forms which allow for a more expansive kind of improvisation and have their natural home in older styles of jazz and in the jam session: such tunes as 'Lady Be Good', 'Honeysuckle Rose' and 'Sweet Georgia Brown'. The master example of this kind is George Gershwin's 'I Got Rhythm', which has been improvised on in some form by every jazz musician who has played a note since the song was published in 1930. Its harmonic sequence is the base for innumerable other tunes, including at least eight written by Charlie Parker.[14] Musicians refer to it generically as 'rhythm changes': the universally known harmonic sequence of the song, rather than the song itself.

The only song form more productive than 'rhythm changes' is the blues. Jazz musicians of all styles and periods improvise on the blues form. The blues is a folk form that by the early part of the century had crystallized into a specific 12-bar harmonic and lyrical sequence. The simpler forms of the blues are still played today by rock, rhythm-and-blues and early-jazz artists. For the most part, jazz has moved towards a more complicated set of blues harmonies, adding subsidiary chordal movements and making alterations to the existing ones, increasing the level of challenge to the improviser and guaranteeing a more harmonically complex outcome. The variations on the blues are innumerable, and yet the best improvisers, even within the more advanced styles, still maintain contact with the emotionality and directness of the form.

The fundamental form of the blues is, as Kernfeld suggests, a matter of conjecture and abstraction, 'something like reconstructing the Indo-European language'.[15] However, the structure that can be assumed is a 12-bar sequence that moves from the tonic chord to the subdominant, back to the tonic, then to the dominant and finally back to the tonic again. In the key of C the chord sequence reads like this:

C /C /C /C7 /F /F /C /C /G7 /G7 /C /C

Even this simple pattern has a strong narrative structure, a 'plot' that contains elements of tension and release held in balance. The 'home' tonality is established in the first four bars, but the alteration to C7 in bar four anticipates a move away. The next two bars pull the tonality away from home, and then release this tension again in the bars following, with a return to C. Then there is another, stronger pull of tension in the bars based on the dominant G7, and this is finally resolved with a return to the home tonality in the last two bars.

Alterations to the blues have evolved and ramified with each historically successive style. In the 1930s, the blues was commonly played with an added chordal movement from the eighth bar onwards, with a series of dominant chords creating further harmonic options for improvisers:

C7 /F7 /C7 /C7 /F7 /F7 /C7 /A7 /D7 /G7 /C7 /C7

Further elaborations were introduced by bebop players. By the time of Charlie Parker's blues compositions of the 1940s, the blues had moved from its original configuration of three chords to sequences as complex as the following:

C6 /Bmin7 E7 /Amin7 D7 /Gmin7 C7♯5 /F6 /Fmin7 B♭7 /C6 / E♭min7 A♭7/ Dmin7 /G7 /Fmin7 Amin7 / Dmin7 G7

In this, the sequence for Charlie Parker's 'Blues For Alice', the improviser has, in the space of twelve bars, to find a way through eighteen changes of chord, including six different minor chords, two different majors and six different dominants.

Later styles have moved away from this level of complexity. Miles Davis's 'All Blues', for instance, has a sequence that allows modal improvisers to play the entire piece using three minor scales. The blues form, in all its historical guises, also has something transcendent about it that can exempt it from some technical considerations. A very experienced player can be so thoroughly 'inside' the form that the blues can be played in a completely intuitive fashion, relying on the emotional atmosphere of the form and the player's familiarity with it. The blues is a small structure. At a moderate tempo of forty-eight bars a minute, an improviser completes the 12-bar chorus four times per minute. In an single evening a soloist might well play thirty or forty choruses. But despite this intimacy of acquaintance with the form, and the constant use that is made of it, the blues pattern seems inexhaustible. No style of jazz has yet been constructed in which the blues does not have an important place, and players continue to produce variants on it, to improvise on it more frequently than any other form, and to consider it one of the main tests of the core values of jazz musicianship.

The third branch of the jazz repertoire is what has been called here the jazz song: the large body of material composed by jazz musicians and normally played within that context. Many musicians known primarily as improvisers have also been responsible for composing melodies and harmonic sequences that have become part of the repertoire. Sidney Bechet, Lester Young, Earl Hines, Dizzy Gillespie, Miles Davis, Charlie Parker and John Coltrane are among the most highly regarded improvisers in the jazz tradition, and all have also contributed compositions that are still current in their respective styles. Others are primarily composers, and some have achieved a level of acceptance in this role that gives them a status close to that of the composer in 'serious' music. Duke Ellington and Thelonious Monk are the best examples of this: their bodies of compositions are generally played by jazz musicians with an awareness of the composer, and of the need to respect the idiom that the composer has created.

At an extreme, jazz songs, like some of the popular songs mentioned above, can be valued for technical and emotional challenges that they present, as in the case of a 'test piece' of John Coltrane's:

> Improvisers of different eras have challenged themselves by designing compositions with dense chord movements and performing them at extremely fast tempos. In the sixties and seventies, musicians considered John Coltrane's 'Giant Steps' to be the 'tour de force'. In its harmonic setting, they would have to negotiate through tonalities with unusual relationships at a tempo of approximately 285 quarter-notes per minute and a rate of harmonic change exceeding one hundred chords per minute.[16]

The jazz song provides one response to the perceived lack of jazz-viable contemporary popular song since the 1960s. Rock and the other harmonically simple popular forms have not generally been perceived by jazz players as providing good material for improvisation. It has become common among jazz musicians starting their careers since about 1970 to use self-composed material for improvisation. This reflects an ethos which is similar to that prevailing in contemporary popular music: it is almost expected of contemporary performers that they compose a proportion of their own material. To do this at least ensures that the material for improvising on is congenial to the performer, since the performer and the composer are the same person. A consequence of this has been, however, to increase fragmentation within the community. The idea of a 'jazz standard' was in recession from the 1960s until the 'neoclassicism' of some musicians in the 1980s encouraged the rediscovery of a common repertoire. During the 'free jazz' era of the early 1960s, the jazz repertoire was subject to radical criticism because of its connection with the popular music industry, and, at a more fundamental level, by its orientation towards the harmonic system. Such theorists of free jazz as Amiri Baraka argued that the popular song form, and Western harmony in general, were repressive of the essentially African spirit of jazz.[17] Numerous jazz players, among them John Coltrane, exemplified the force of this movement away from the traditional materials of jazz. By the 1990s, however, the notion of a central jazz repertoire, or a *lingua franca*, has been more or less rehabilitated.

When we look at improvisation in jazz comparatively with improvisation in other cultures, it appears a perfectly normal musical activity, in contrast to its reputation at home as something musically deviant. In its repertoire of basic material, jazz shares the structural principles stated by the ethnomusicologist Bruno Nettl:

> We may take it that each model, be it a tune, a theoretical construct, or a mode with typical melodic turns, consists of a series of obligatory musical events which must be observed, either absolutely or with some sort of frequency, in order that the model remain intact.[18]

The distinctiveness of jazz against other musical cultures is explained by Nettl in terms of what he calls 'density'. Musical structures contain various points of reference (in jazz these would be, for instance, changes of chord), and structures within various traditions differ in terms of how many such points there are, and how closely together they occur. For this measure Nettl uses the term 'density': 'In comparing various types of model, we find that those of jazz are relatively dense, those of Persian music of medium density, and those of an Arabic *taqsim* or an Indian *alap* relatively lacking in density.'[19]

The jazz repertoire provides material which imposes on its players greater 'density' than the repertoires of other improvisatory musical cultures. This is essentially a historical accident, resulting from the speed of development of jazz, its place within a modern system of cultural innovation and distribution, and the complexity of its influences. The measure of density says nothing about the quality of the musical culture itself, but it provides a useful perspective on the dynamics of the jazz repertoire: for example, the move in the 1950s from the superdense chordal structures of bebop to modal forms was a lessening in musical density, in a musical culture which had for forty years been moving in the opposite direction. More significantly, it emphasizes the syncretic nature of the basic materials of the music, and its place at the meeting point of a complex cultural mixture.

The Processes of Improvisation

Another Persian musician stressed the importance of never repeating himself, of never playing or singing a piece the same way. As an example, he cited the nightingale, which is respected by Persian musicians because it is thought never to repeat itself in this way.

Bruno Nettl

I try not to be a repeater pencil.   Lester Young[20]

The repertoire provides the framework for improvisation. But the use of this material does not in itself make jazz. Jazz improvisation has a character that differs from that of other improvisatory musics, and this has more to do with the manner in which improvisation is produced and performed than with the repertoire itself. In principle, the goal of improvisation is to respond creatively to the musical environment in which the improvisation is taking place. This means responding to the ways in which other musicians are playing, to mood, to levels of energy, but primarily to the specific musical context generated by the source material. The musical choices made by improvisers in most jazz are made against a background of a particular set of harmonies, and improvisers are obliged to take account of them even if, temporarily, the choice is made to override them or clash with them.

To take an example: a common jazz vehicle is 'All of Me', a popular song written in 1931, by Simons and Marks. As a jazz vehicle, it was recorded at least six times by Billie Holiday, and three times each by Louis Armstrong and the Count Basie orchestra, as well as featuring in the repertoire of such artists as Lester Young and Erroll Garner. The first chord of 'All of Me' is the 'home' chord of C major, which is held for the first two bars. This establishes the C tonality clearly, and while those two bars last, the improviser can stay in the right harmonic area by playing the notes of the scale of C (the white notes of the piano). In bar three, however, there is a harmonic shift. The underlying chord for this and the following bar is A dominant seventh (A7). This chord, which will normally be played in the accompaniment by pianist, guitarist and bass player, contains the notes A, C♯, E and G. The C♯ is alien to the previous home key of C, and if the improviser continues to play in that key, the result in bars three and four will be discordant and intuitively 'wrong'.

The tune has temporarily changed its key – A7 is one of the chords (the fifth, or 'dominant') belonging to the key of D, and the notes the improviser plays must be chosen from the D scale instead of the C scale. The same thing happens again in bars five and six: the chord at this point is E7. Like the previous A7, this is a dominant chord of a new key, that of A major. This again introduces a new scale, made up of notes different from those of the previous two keys: in this case A, B, C♯, D, E, F♯ and G♯. The improvising soloist has had to make two harmonic adjustments within the space of five bars, and to respond by shifting to a different 'pool' of available notes each time. And this sort of movement occurs, of course, throughout the 32-bar structure of the song.

This is the situation of the improviser stated in the abstract. There are, however, many ways of approaching the task of improvising over a tune such as this one. Some players conceptualize it in the way suggested above, thinking in terms of changing 'key centres', and new pools of notes. Closely related to this is the scalar approach, which conceives of the changing chords of the tune as cues into various available scales. These procedures assume that the improviser wants to play *within* the given harmonies. In practice, musicians throughout the history of jazz have devoted some of their creative effort to extending their area of choice, and discovering the musical effects that follow the deliberate stretching of the given harmonic base. Musicians even as long ago as 1940 would often not have restricted themselves to playing only the notes of the C scale in the first two bars of the tune. In the so-called 'bebop scale', the raised fifth was a regularly occurring extra note over major chords (in this case, the black note G♯ between G and A).

Dominant chords like the A7 and E7 in 'All of Me' are particularly suited to having harmonic extensions and alterations built on to them. In jazz playing in the 1930s, chords like A7 were liable to be 'extended' to become A9, by the addition of another note, B natural, which then became part of the harmonic context, the available pool of notes, for the soloist to draw upon. In the bebop period and afterwards, the dominant chords were given a complex array of modifications. The simple A7 might become A7♭9 (containing the B♭ rather than B natural), or A13, A13♭9, A9♭5 or A7♯9. The latter chord, for instance, introduces the note

C natural to the harmony, which can now be played together with the C♯ which is in the basic A7 chord, creating a tensely dissonant and idiomatically blues-like sound. Each of these modifications of the harmony will, if followed in the note-choices of the soloist, tend to produce a harmonically more complex improvised line. This is one of the most important forms of innovation in the bebop style in the 1940s: soloists like Charlie Parker and Dizzy Gillespie systematically expanded the complexity of their harmonies and widened the choice of notes for the improviser.

Since jazz improvisation has become a subject in many university programmes in music, the theoretical understanding of the methods that soloists have developed during the history of jazz has been codified more thoroughly than ever before. Musicians at an early stage of their careers in jazz may be introduced to the full range of musical complexities deployed in improvisation by previous generations of jazz players, and originated in untheoretical, pragmatic ways. One approach that is now part of the jazz curriculum is improvisation using 'alternative scales'. Faced with improvising over bars three and four of 'All of Me', the theoretically aware player will confront, in addition to the previous options, a whole series of possible alternative sets of note choices. In addition to the fundamental A dominant 7, or Mixolydian, scale, the soloist might consider using various alternative scales: B♭ melodic minor, B♭ diminished, G melodic minor, D harmonic minor, and so on. Each of these alternatives, used in improvisation, will result in a melodic line containing permutations of notes not in the original chord or scale. The scale derived from the basic A7 chord is

A B C♯ D E F♯ G

A scale-based improviser who chooses to substitute B♭ melodic minor at this point will be using a scale made up of

B♭ C D♭ E♭ F G A

which has only three notes in common with the A7 scale. Played over the A7 chord, the improvised line based on the new scale will inevitably create its own flavour of dissonance.

Most jazz improvisers throughout the history of the music, however, have received little or no systematic education in music theory, even as applied to jazz. The learning of improvisation has been done, on the whole, practically and through a piecemeal process. Within these pragmatic ways of conceiving of improvisation there are various stylistic tendencies. Some musicians habitually reflect the structure of the chords themselves, rather than the scales associated with them, in their improvisations. The most obvious form of this is 'running the changes': improvising a line made up of notes selected from the successive chords. Some musicians use a 'vertical' style of improvisation, in which the improvised line is designed to include all the notes that make up the chords, usually resulting in a style that is relatively dense and complex. Among musicians in pre-bebop styles, the saxophonist Coleman Hawkins was admired for the complex improvisations in which he made melodic use of the notes in each chord of the sequence of popular songs such as 'Body and Soul'.[21]

The opposite tendency is represented by Hawkins's contemporary Lester Young. Young's method was oriented to the shaping of a continuous melodic line rather than to reflecting the structure of each successive chord.[22] In order to reconcile his melodic impulse with the unavoidable demands of the chord sequence, Young tended towards note choices that were harmonically neutral, so that, in effect, he kept out of the way of the changing harmonies. In playing through a chord change like the one between C and A7, Young might, as one possible strategy, shape a melodic line that emphasized the notes common to both chords. A soloist following this approach could, for example, use the notes of A, E and G in the improvised line: all of these are in the home scale of C, and when the harmony changes to the A7, they are still acceptable as constituent notes of the A7 as well.

This description of improvisatory processes has stressed the technical demands of working within song forms. The process as experienced by improvisers, though, is not always so consciously theoretical. The song form and the improvising options can be so completely internalized as to be accessible to the player without conscious thought. Soloists may think of what they are doing as simply 'playing the song'. It appears that Lester Young, for example, preferred not to know the harmonies of some songs, so that he could give full concentration to improvising a melodic line by ear. The musical environment in which the improvisation is taking place is not, in any case, restricted to the vehicle for improvisation and its harmonies. The environment also includes the other players, the emotional atmosphere, the physical setting, and the presence and the demeanour of an audience. The content of an improvisation can be determined by any or all of these things: other musicians can give melodic or rhythmic prompting that become part of the solo, moods and atmospheres suggest strategies, affect dynamics, even influence levels of inspiration.

Improvisation can be 'on' the sense of the song or can allude to well-known previous versions of it, or to an artist's own earlier interpretations. Jazz players often work with a particular song over a period of years, and find nuances within it that spring from a continual re-evaluation of the piece. After the 1941 recording of 'All of Me' that features Billie Holiday and Lester Young improvising vocally and instrumentally on the theme, Holiday reduced the tempo of the piece for a more serene version eight years later. Young played the song in a recording made in 1956 in which the tempo was similarly reduced and the mood strikingly different.[23]

Barry Kernfeld has suggested that jazz improvisation follows three main strategies: 'paraphrase' and 'formulaic' and 'motivic' improvisation.[24] Paraphrase involves staying close to the original melody of the piece, and modifying it by slight reshaping and embellishment. This approach was seen by André Hodeir as one of the evolutionary steps in the genesis of jazz improvisation.[25] Early performers in pre-jazz idioms presumably began the improvisatory tradition by relatively slight ornamentations of melodies, and there are solo styles that even today seem to recapitulate this development, moving within a single performance from theme statement to paraphrase to the next type of improvisation, which Kernfeld calls 'formulaic'. When a soloist is improvising formulaically, the theme, the basic melody or tune, has been set aside, and the 'subject' of the improvisation is the harmonies of the piece – 'All of Me' considered purely as a sequence of chords, rather than as a song with a tune and a set of lyrics.

Kernfeld emphasizes the soloist's re-use of musical fragments or formulae, small units of musical material picked up out of the common fund of such devices or from other players' or the soloist's own favourite phrases.[26] Studies like those of Lewis Porter on the improvising style of Lester Young, or Thomas Owens on Charlie Parker, show the recurrence in the work of these artists of particular combinations of notes and phrases. Such insights into the methods of creative musicians can seem a little disappointing if one has previously bought into the mystique of jazz creativity as an instinctive, spontaneous outpouring of musical expression. However, the use of formulae allies jazz with other art forms in which improvisation is required (oral epic poetry, for instance), and there is no reason to expect jazz improvisation to transcend the limitations that affect these other arts. Formulae can be highly personal: there are phrases in solos by which we recognize Charlie Parker, or Lester Young, or their influence on other players, or a *hommage* to their styles. Owens notes that in the work of Charlie Parker the formulae are combined in numerous ways and are interspersed with freshly improvised phrases. There are other processes going on than the mere repetition of formulae: the formulaic phrases themselves may be continually varied, and the 'newly invented melodic material' may actually make up the majority of what the improviser plays.

Kernfeld's third type, 'motivic' improvisation, has a place in all styles of jazz, but motivic development in improvisation is more characteristic of 'free' and modal styles. It involves the elaboration of a melodic motive through the structure of a solo, adapting it to the changing context as the piece unfolds. This is much easier to do in a form in which there is little or no change of harmony, than in the standard song form. Miles Davis's 'So What', with its solitary change from a D scale to an E♭ scale, would be more amenable to this approach than 'All of Me' or 'Blues for Alice', where the motive would continually have to be modified to fit in with the changes of chord. There are examples of improvisations in which motivic development is effectively carried on against shifting harmonies (Parker's 'Klactoveedsedstene' and Sonny Rollins's 'Without a Song', for instance[27]), but this is a more important strategy for the improviser in styles of jazz that do not provide too many structural constraints.

Ways of categorizing improvisational methods are useful, both for listeners and, in a practical way, for learning musicians, who might want to consider the strategic options in a clear perspective. But any general approach to describing jazz improvisation is only an opening upon what must end up by being a highly complex picture. The depth and variety of jazz improvisation is best appreciated by extended listening, by experiencing actual musical examples. This would also be the best way of getting a sense of the radical individuality that is the most important criterion for judging the artistic success of a player, and a typifying value of jazz culture as a whole. The recognition of generalities in jazz can only be a prelude to the appreciation of its profusion of individualities.

Outside of the procedures that can be learned, and the specifics of any theoretical system, there is always a place for the lawless, unprescribed response to the musical situation. Some moves in improvisation are lateral. The soloist in these cases is not improvising simply in relation to forms and structures, but is driven by something in the dynamics, in the drama, of the moment. A famous example is the delicate, bell-like piano solo that Jess Stacy interposes in amongst drum solos and a blazing brass section in the Goodman band's 'Sing, Sing, Sing' at Carnegie Hall. In a live recording by the Thad Jones–Mel Lewis orchestra, the trombonist Garnett Brown enters his solo by playing the same slurred, rasped note on every one of the first sixty-four beats. This is such a pleasantly rude surprise in the context that the audience are provoked into wondering what the soloist is doing, how long he will dare to keep it up, and what will come next.[28]

What happens on a specific occasion and in a given solo is, in any case, only one of the possible frames for looking at the achievement of the improvising soloist in jazz. The here-and-now nature of the experience is, of course, central to the aesthetic identity of the music. Spontaneous composition in the moment, against the background of a music often characterized by speed and energy, can be represented as an existential adventure, and to this idea attaches a large part of the romantic mythology of the jazz musician, as we shall see, in Chapter 4, in looking at some of its literary versions. Nevertheless, improvisation can be, and is by many practising musicians, considered on a much longer time-scale. For many musicians, as is demonstrated in Paul Berliner's *Thinking in Jazz*, it is a lifelong enterprise, any moment of which is only a partial draft of a piece of work that will never be considered finished. Berliner's remarkable book details, in the words of many musicians, the multiple stages and cycles of performance, study, analysis, reconsideration and restructuring that musicians go through in their progression towards the goals of the art of improvisation.[29]

Rhythm

Rhythmic energy is like improvisation in being a discounted, even a dubious, value within the system of Western music. It has a lower position in the hierarchy of musical elements than harmony, melody and form. Rhythm is the least cerebral, the most bodily of the components of music: it can have an implication of the automatic, the involuntary. It was an easy matter for some of the early moral objectors to the new music, or for a theorist of social control like Theodor Adorno, to elide the prominence of rhythm in jazz with its supposed corrupting or hypnotizing effects upon young people, or on 'the masses', or on social morals in general.[30]

These views, which have been expressed throughout the century, and which continue to be applied to post-rock popular music, often carry racial implications. In the more extreme forms, the racial message is explicit: black rhythms corrupt white youth. More usually, rhythm in music is taken to be a 'primitive' value as compared with the principles on which Western music is founded. The rhetorical connection with race is explained by the drummer Andrew Cyrille: 'People think drums are *primitive*. They relate to primitive societies and savage peoples, of course they can't be musically *sophisticated*.'[31]

The provenance of the rhythmic language of jazz is from black music, and ultimately from African traditions. The shadow of nineteenth-century imperialism still hangs over those styles of music in which rhythmic energy is a positive value. Rhythm in jazz has the reputation of being race-specific, and of having little to do with technique and learned expertise. It is relegated to the 'mystery' of black performers, and, by extension, of black culture in general. Black people are understood to be genetically predisposed towards expression through rhythm, which is therefore felt to be a domain best not ventured into, or not worth venturing into, by Western musical theory. Its interest for some scholars is anthropological rather than artistic, one of the ways in which African otherness is manifested in music.

The earliest Europeans attempting to write down African-American music found it formidably difficult. Lucy McKim Garrison, writing in 1867, cited the notational problems posed by 'the odd turns in the throat and the curious rhythmic effect produced by single voices chiming in at irregular intervals'.[32] Some early writers on jazz were aware of the impossibility of notating jazz rhythm accurately using ordinary Western musical notation: 'Hot jazz rhythm may contain other peculiarities of an imponderable nature, peculiarities which cannot be expressed in musical notation or any similar form of measurement.'[33] With the increasing publication of transcriptions and analyses of improvisations, this kind of caveat about the non-notatability of jazz rhythm has become standard. Some transcribers prefer to write out the notes in 'straight' rhythm and to rely on the reader's feeling for the idiom, or reference to a recording, to make up for the differences.

Jazz culture itself has not produced an alternative system of notation in which these subtleties of rhythm can be captured, but it has its own language in which to express fine distinctions in this domain. Rhythmic strength and skill in rhythmic expression are considered to be absolutely basic musical values, even more so than the capacity for original improvisation, and a vocabulary has grown up around this crucial set of abilities and perceptions. The two master terms that express the issues for the player and the listener are 'swing' and 'time'. These can sometimes come to the same thing: it can be said that a player does or does not 'swing', does or does not 'have good time'.

Hodeir, Schuller and Collier, among many others, have tried to define and to explain the mechanism of 'swing', but a consensus exists among writers and analysts that no satisfactory explanation has yet been given.[34] Some writers are happy to settle for describing swing as 'undefinable', others as 'elusive' and 'mysterious'. What cannot be denied, even without an accurate account of the mechanism, is the fact that perception of, and pleasure in, the element of swing has been an overwhelmingly important experience for listeners and audiences throughout the history of the music.

Hodeir and Schuller provide diagrams to represent models of how swing operates. Schuller has used computer-aided acoustic measurement, and Collier psychometric tests, to examine the acoustic profile of a swinging melodic line, or to give a scientific check to notions held about jazz rhythm. Hodeir cites five conditions necessary to swing, including relaxation and what he calls 'vital drive'. Schuller lists the factors of a regularly reiterated beat, the musician's unconscious internalization of that beat, the way in which notes are attacked, and a complex factor which he calls 'maintaining a perfect equilibrium between the 'horizontal' and 'vertical' aspects of musical sounds'.[35] The acoustical diagrams in Schuller's *The Swing Era* suggest that what is characteristic of the attack and the decay of a note played by a jazz musician, as distinct from the same note executed by a 'classical' player, is its contribution to continuity: the note is sustained fully, with as much as possible of its energy carried over into the next note, so that, in Schuller's words, 'the notes almost link up with one another in a continuous musical line'.[36] The emphasis is on the carrying forward of the note, or the beat. In contrast, the notes played 'classically' remain separate, the energy of each being allowed to die away before the next is begun. 'Swing' in jazz, in this account, is seen as happening because each beat of its metre transfers energy to the beat that follows. The line of beats becomes a steady flow of rhythmic propulsion, which the guitarist Emily Remler thought of as being like 'a sine wave in relation to which she varies the phrasing of her melodies'.[37] The feeling of the rhythm is one of moving kinetically onward. One of Hodeir's descriptions is echoed by many musicians' accounts: 'the beat, though it seems perfectly regular, gives the impression of moving inexorably ahead (like a train that keeps moving at the same speed but is still being *drawn ahead* by its locomotive)'.[38]

This forward-orientation of jazz rhythm has led to explicit links being drawn between the music and the kind of society in which it has had its being. The onward-flowing force of jazz is likened to the restless energy of American life; its liking for fast tempos is the correlative of the society's addiction to speed in its behaviours; the excitement it generates is the excitement of a modern, dynamic culture. Many writers have been willing to find ways of turning jazz rhythm into a metaphor for aspects of American twentieth-century life. The songwriter Irving Berlin, for example, spoke of jazz as being 'the rhythmic heart of our everyday lives. Its swiftness is interpretive of our verve and speed and ceaseless activity.'[39]

Jazz rhythm, however, has never remained fixed in a single form. Like the other musical elements of jazz, rhythm has varied from one period to another, seeming to follow certain tendencies along a developmental curve. Jazz did not 'swing' in the same way in 1945 as it did in 1925 or in 1935. The overall direction of change seems to have been towards a levelling out of the beat. Early jazz, up to about the mid–1930s, used a rhythmic style, the 'two-beat' rhythm, based on a strong accentuation of the second and fourth beats in the bar. By the late 1930s, the four beats of the bar were being sounded more or less equally, and the standard procedure for drummers was to mark all four beats on the bass drum. In bebop, the marking of beats shifted to the top cymbal, played with the drummer's right hand, a lighter sounding of the beat that made it less emphatic. If the beat in jazz is thought of as a kind of oscillation, what has happened progressively in jazz rhythm is that the depth, the amplitude of the oscillation has become shallower. In early jazz there was a relatively big difference between the stressed beat and the unstressed one. This difference is levelled out in the thirties and then again in the bebop of the 1940s and 1950s. The rhythmic principle of later styles has been described as a further movement along the same line. The effect is smoother: there are fewer and slighter rises and falls in the path the improviser rides on. The Stearns' history of jazz dance implies a link between this tendency of rhythmic change and the development of dance forms such as the Lindy Hop, which 'flowed more horizontally and smoothly' than earlier styles.[40]

Musicians make fine discriminations concerning the quality of the beat. Paul Berliner quotes the pianist Fred Hersch as claiming that 'there should be ten, fifteen kinds of time. There's a kind of time that has an edge on it for a while and then lays back for a while. Sometimes it rolls over the bar, and sometimes it sits more on the beats.'[41] Particular rhythmic qualities of the beat or the 'feel' or 'groove' can be the products of particular occasions, or the rhythmic fingerprint of specific performers. Players differ in terms of their sense of the beat and their own playing in relation to it. Charlie Parker, for instance, generally phrased well behind the beat, while rhythm section players Art Blakey and Charles Mingus 'are admired for their aggressive, driving style, which involves playing on top of the beat without rushing the tempo'.[42] Miles Davis expressed his admiration for the rhythmic sting the drummer Tony Williams brought to his group in the mid–1960s: 'Tony played on top of the beat, just a fraction above, and it gave everything a little edge because it *had* a little edge'.[43]

Some players have rhythmic styles that are as individual as their improvised lines. The improvisations of Lester Young were typified by an extremely relaxed approach to the beat, seeming alternately to push the rhythm forward and then to step back from it, while Coleman Hawkins's improvisations seemed to press continually forward, forcing the phrases up against the rhythmic pulse. Miles Davis made use of strong contrasts in rhythmic phrasing, and went further than most jazz musicians in the use of spaces or silences in the rhythmic pattern. Erroll Garner derived the great rhythmic energy of his playing from the slight retardation of phrases in his right-hand line behind the on-the-beat chords in his left.

'Time' is personal, and the individual sense of the beat is an accomplishment or a possession of the musician that should be preserved at all times:

> I began to argue with them about the fact that, if you are playing, the tempo should be in your head, don't depend on me. Depend on yourself, because if you're playing music, the tempo that you're playing in is in your head ... You keep your tempo yourself. Because you can play the music without anything, alone. You can play your part.[44]

Learning musicians are encouraged to practise drills and exercises to develop a sense of time that can be relied upon in the situation referred to here, when other musicians are 'breaking up the time', or deviating from a regular statement of the beat. This inner time sense is thought of as being metronomic, though Collier has shown that in actual performances the beat is liable to fluctuate by several percent, often for good musical reasons.[45] Some musicians have said that their time sense was developed by the communal handclapping that is a feature of black church music:

> There was something about the rhythm of jazz that I equated exactly with the gospel. I mean, the way we used to sing and clap our hands in church was just like the jazz drummer playing cymbals. It was the same swing feeling.[46]

Instruction books and courses in jazz often contain exercises in hand-clapping or beat-counting, in order to establish a firm sense of the beat and to enable the player to handle complex counter-rhythms:

> In Barry Harris's workshops, students learn a store of patterns with short figures of eighth notes and sixteenth notes occasionally embellished with eighth-note triplets, as well as figures including sustained rhythmic values with alternating on-beat and off-beat characters.[47]

Highly skilled and experienced players, such as Miles Davis, can develop a dogmatic confidence in their own sense of the beat: 'I can hear when the time drops one beat ... It's just something I've always had. I mean, I can start my tempo off and go to sleep and come back and be at the same tempo I was in before I went to sleep.'[48] Within the community of jazz musicians, the ability to handle time has an almost ethical aspect to it. It is expected of players that they should possess the internalized time sense that allows them to keep their own time and provides a reliable grounding for their own rhythmic expression in improvisation or in rhythmic variation.

It is in this sense also that the musicianship of the individual touches directly on the needs of the group. A musician whose time sense is perceived as uncertain may be open to criticism from other players. Miles Davis's autobiography reports on his constant preoccupation with the rhythmic competence of his group members. Davis eventually sacked his own nephew from one of his later bands because: 'He was always dropping the time, and if there's anything I can't stand in a drummer it's to drop the time.' Davis sees his decision as being governed by a sense of integrity higher than family loyalty: 'I had to do it for the music.'[49]

Michael Zwerin recalls a remark made to him by Davis: 'You got good time for a white cat.'[50] Some musicians and writers have been convinced that there is a qualitative difference between the rhythmic skills of black and white musicians. Martin Williams argues against easy rejection of the '"liberal" bugaboo of "natural rhythm"', and concludes that 'Negroes as a race do have a rhythmic genius that is not like that of other races and... this genius has found a unique expression in the United States'.[51] Ben Sidran, writing during the period of black militancy of the early seventies, was equally open to the rehabilitation of 'the old bromide: "Negroes have a natural sense of rhythm".' In this context, the racist stereotype is reinterpreted into a claim for the distinctiveness of black culture, in which rhythm performs the function of an 'inside' language.[52]

This, however, is not necessarily to regard rhythmic skill as a 'natural' attribute of a particular ethnic group. It points to a cultural tradition which stretches back to African origins, but which is nevertheless a cultural rather than genetic inheritance. Rhythmic skill, 'swing' or 'good time' is also the product of a learning process and a discipline, a technical achievement of the same order as good intonation or instrumental technique. Zwerin records Miles Davis's reaction to a performance by his own rhythm section (universally regarded as one of the greatest in the history of jazz): 'He looked furious. "What the hell is Paul doing with the time?" The time sounded pretty good to me, but I said nothing.'[53] Rhythmic performance is an aspect of jazz musicianship that has to be maintained, and, even in the advanced player, is always open to criticism.

This view, as with the more pragmatic view of how improvisation is learned, militates against some of the more mythic versions of jazz as music. Rhythmic skill, 'swing' itself, is a function of learned musicianship rather than of any genetic endowment or of the unconditioned spontaneity of the jazz performer. Swing does not occur any more 'naturally' than playing in tune, or hitting the right keys. Yet it is significant that it is so often conceived of in this way. The identification of the black performer with 'natural' rhythmic skills, coupled with the image of the jazz milieu as a place where a special experience of spontaneity and improvisation occurs, produces a myth that applies to other aspects of jazz musicianship as well: in the jazz world, remarkable feats are achieved without conscious thought or without what anyone would think of as training. Jazz music comes into existence as an emanation of the jazz musician's being: blacks and culturally deviant whites alike simply give off this music as an effect of their identities.

Rhythm remains the area in which jazz has its strongest distinguishing features as a music. Some reference to rhythm occurs in all definitions of jazz. André Hodeir discovers the 'essence' of jazz in a specific rhythmic feature, the interplay between tension and relaxation.[54] Ira Gitler speaks of responding to the radical new styles of the forties because he could recognise in them 'the qualities it had maintained from the previous jazz styles I had been brought up on and loved so much', first among which he names 'rhythmic propulsion'.[55] Rhythm has also provided the most fruitful area for the finding of correlatives with the wider culture: 'The '40s was a period when we had airplanes that could really move, and Charlie Parker had a number called "Constellation". Whether or not that was on purpose, it typified the speed of that mode of transportation of the day.'[56]

Instrumental Technique and Sound

Individuality is valued very highly in jazz. This valuation shows up nowhere more fully than in the diverse instrumental techniques that have been devised by musicians within the successive jazz styles. Technique in an absolute sense has been developed to remarkably high levels by many musicians, especially in the later styles. But this has largely been achieved in a musical culture without a system of formal schooling in technique, at least until the recent growth of jazz instruction in schools and universities.

For most of the historical span of the music, the typical jazz player has received only a minimal formal grounding in the rudiments of music. There have also been many instances of musicians who were completely self-taught, but for players of all types of prior education, the most important learning experience has come in the looser framework of the jazz world itself. This experience has consisted of a range of unpredictable influences such as peer pressure, occasional informal advice and instruction, and the accidental outcomes of personal practical experience.

Jazz players of all instruments have been relatively free of the pressures that exist in the classical field to acquire orthodox techniques and standard instrumental tones. The spectrum of acceptable sounds on any given instrument is very wide. The jazz clarinet, for instance, has been used to produce sounds as distinct as the gutty, vibrato-laden tone of Edmond Hall, the darker sound of Sidney Bechet, which Duke Ellington described as 'all wood',[57] and the 'classical' sound of Jimmy Hamilton and Benny Goodman. These alternative sonorities reflect influences as well as personal inclination: the more highly schooled background of Goodman against Bechet's immersion in the indigenous New Orleans clarinet tradition.

These and still other clarinet tones are personal and highly identifiable. Players like Hall, Bechet, Barney Bigard and Pee Wee Russell each project a sonority which is the unique acoustic of the player, the instrumental voice-print. The same is true of other instruments: the trumpet sounds of Louis Armstrong and Bix Beiderbecke, the saxophone tones of Johnny Hodges, Lee Konitz and John Coltrane, are just as highly individualized. In principle though not in practice, the sonorities of all jazz musicians are distinguishable from those of all others. In reality, those whose sounds are unmistakable are comparatively few, but complete distinctiveness of sound represents an ideal towards which all instrumentalists are understood to be striving. Practice is directed not towards a received ideal of sound, but towards the fullest development of personal individuality.

The techniques that have been developed in the loose, unsystematic and individualistic matrix of the jazz world vary from the well-schooled to the home-made. Personal innovations, some of them quite radical, are not uncommon. Guitarists, for example, have displayed a variety of personal initiatives in the handling of the instrument, even in matters as fundamental as ways of striking the strings. The jazz guitar has usually been played using a plectrum, but many guitarists have used finger techniques, and some have developed methods of using the thumb. Wes Montgomery's account of how he arrived at the latter conclusion is indicative of the highly circumstantial causes of some technical solutions. Montgomery explained that when practising at home with the guitar amplified

> the sound was too much even for my neighbours, so I took to the back room of the house and began plucking the strings with the fat part of my thumb. This was much quieter. To this technique I added the trick of playing the melody line in two registers at the same time, the octave thing; this made my sound even quieter.[58]

Montgomery's recourse to a thumb technique determined some of the characteristics of his playing style: a round, muted sound, a tendency towards slurred rather than individually struck notes, a liking for long passages played in octaves. Other guitarists have devised even more radical approaches: some, like Carl Kress and Stanley Jordan, have redesigned the tuning of the instrument for their own technical purposes.

Players not infrequently arrive at techniques that are classically 'incorrect', ways of addressing the instrument such as some trumpeters' habit of placing the trumpet off-centre against the lips, or Lester Young's eccentric tilting of the saxophone. For some musicians, the search for solutions to practical problems results in extensions of the known potentials of the instrument, as in Jack Teagarden's discovery of some non-standard configurations on the trombone, or Beiderbecke's still-mysterious trumpet fingerings:

> By the time he began to play in public, Bix had worked out a fingering system which appeared to other brass players to be no system at all. Sometimes he'd use his second valve to play a written B, as they did, but sometimes, depending on the passage and the key, he would use one and three and 'lip' the note into tune. Sometimes fourth-line D came out with just valve one, sometimes with one and three.[59]

Concentration on the technical possibilities of the instrument results in further individualization, personal styles being characterized by favourite devices: the use of half-valving by the trumpeter Rex Stewart, Thelonious Monk's dissonant piano voicings, some saxophonists' exploration of the instrument's artificial harmonics, glissando effects that depend upon the slide construction of the trombone. Brass players such as Clark Terry and Joe Nanton have developed special, and in some cases unduplicable, methods using mutes.

For many musicians, the personal style arrived at, especially in improvisation, is a result of a complex combination of influences. As well as whatever formal musical instruction the individual may have received, there is the direct, informal learning that comes from encounters with other musicians in what Paul Berliner has called the 'educational system' of the jazz culture.[60] There are numerous accounts given by musicians of formative technical advances that were due to hints or pieces of advice handed out by others. Personal ways of playing are in part a function of the other players that the individual has listened to, watched, spoken to, or been advised by. A player is also likely to be partially a product of what Daniel Neuman has called 'micro-traditions'.[61] In jazz, this can mean an allegiance to one of the subtraditions based upon a certain instrument, or a particular locality or region, as in the 'Texas Tenor' style of saxophone playing, or upon an admiration for a particular player. Instrumentalists define their own styles by closeness to or distance from the various exemplars of their instrument, seeing themselves as 'descended from' a particular musician in a quasi-familial pattern, or as modelling themselves upon a chosen example.

The history of the tenor saxophone in the years around 1940 has been represented by many musicians as a matter of making a choice between the two influences then prevailing: Coleman Hawkins or Lester Young. This kind of elective affinity affects the instrumental sound the player ends up producing: in the Hawkins/Young dichotomy the choice was between a heavier and a lighter tone, as well as between vertical and horizontal approaches to improvisation, and between different inter-pretations of rhythm. Players negotiate these stylistic choices in indi-vidual ways and continue to add further influences to them, including those of their own practical experience with the instrument and the music. A player like Illinois Jacquet can be seen as blending a Hawkins tonal quality with a phraseology deriving from Young, and supple-menting this with his own qualities of energy and rhythmic buoyancy. The 'dialects' of the broader tradition break down into the 'idiolects' of each player, and the central values of the music have always included the preference to let this individuation flourish.

Instrumental techniques and sounds can still be evaluated on certain criteria: considered, for example, as simply weak or inadequate. Tech-nique and tone remain attributes that require work and development. But the jazz tradition has tended to validate sounds and techniques that are idiosyncratic, and to regard them as integral to personal expression. The sound that Charlie Parker produced on the alto saxophone, while it paid little regard to received ideas of tonal beauty, nevertheless came to be perceived as having its own aesthetic rightness in the medium of his style, indeed its own kind of beauty. A large part of the literary effort of writers on jazz has gone into attempts to describe instrumental tones. Whitney Balliett, for example, describes Teagarden's trombone tone as 'nasal, bright-gray', Bill Coleman's trumpet as possessing a sound that 'sometimes suggests light bells, sometimes lucent silk', and (not the first to resort to an elaborate image in this case) Bix Beiderbecke's cornet as sounding like 'a carillon playing on a dry morning'.[62]

The breadth and the depth of jazz as a music is far from exhausted by examining the dimensions of it that have been discussed in this chapter. Jazz as a music is not exhausted by extensive and detailed studies of its products and procedures such as those of Paul Berliner and Gunther Schuller. Even the entirety of its history on records, enormous as those resources are, does not represent the full extent of its possibilities. Jazz is still in the process of being created, over a sizeable portion of the globe and on a nightly basis, and the parameters of its musical definition change gradually but inexorably within that unceasing practice.

The aspects of jazz discussed here – repertoire, improvisation, rhythm and individual technique – were chosen as being the stable elements in any consensus as to its musical definition. As we shall see later, there has been a tendency to read these features of jazz symbolically, and to relate them directly to features of American culture. Improvisation, for example, has served as a metaphor for types of action other than the practice of jazz. The individualism which is valued in jazz expression can be represented as symbolic of social individualism. The untheorized nature of jazz music, its creation in practice, can be interpreted as a case of the wider American tradition of pragmatism. The diversity of the jazz repertoire can be seen as a metaphor for American social diversity.

One of the themes of this book, however, is the complex and indirect nature of the relationship between jazz and American society. These symbolic readings of the musical parameters of jazz inevitably oversimplify both the nature of the music and the modality of its supposed links with general features of the society as a whole. If jazz is 'pragmatic', as are some American schools of philosophy, this is not necessarily because of any real and demonstrable connection between these two phenomena. 'Improvisation', in some sense of the word, may characterize some areas of American culture some of the time, but this does not entail any real resemblance or link between these practices, whatever they are, and the art of improvisation as developed in the specific cultural matrix of jazz music.

This first chapter has also been dedicated to a proposition about jazz which seemingly remains one of the most difficult ideas to assimilate about it, and one of the most resisted: that it is first and foremost a *music*, that it answers to the imperatives common to other musics of the world, and that it exists as a culture of music before it is pressed into use as a symbol for some social idea, or as a counter in some other argument. In order to make this point, emphasis has been placed in this chapter on its musical complexity, on knowledge, on discipline, on the sheer *difficulty* of the skills it requires. Before jazz becomes a second-order term in some other cultural matrix, it is, especially within the constituency of those who choose to play it, a music. It has generated, as the next chapter will discuss, a historical succession of musical cultures of its own.

Notes

1. Ludwig Wittgenstein, *Philosophical Investigations* (Oxford: Blackwell, 1968).
2. Major jazz histories seem to be written every twenty years: Marshall Stearns, *The Story of Jazz* (New York: OUP, 1956); James Lincoln Collier, *The Making of Jazz* (New York: Delta, 1978); Ted Gioia, *The History of Jazz* (New York: OUP, 1997).
3. For a discussion of the importance of collectivity in the context of the general ideology of jazz in the early 1960s, see Peter Townsend, 'Free Jazz: Musical Style and Liberationist Ethic, 1956–65' in Brian Ward (ed.), *Beyond Martin Luther King: Media and Culture, Race and Resistance in the Civil Rights and Black Power Eras* (Gainesville: University of Florida Press, forthcoming).
4. For discussion of the musical life of New Orleans in the formative period of jazz, see Martin Williams, *Jazz Masters of New Orleans* (London: Macmillan, 1967) and Alan Lomax, *Mister Jelly Roll* (London: Jazz Book Club, 1956).
5. Charles Nanry points out 'the "popular and over-simplified historical conception" that 'jazz "went up the Mississippi"' and that the 'facile conception of the New Orleans-Chicago-New York jazz axis does not wholly account for the history of jazz in the United States' (Charles Nanry, *The Jazz Text* (New York: Van Nostrand, 1979), p. 21 and p. 26). Studies of particular locations, such as Kenney's on Chicago, also indicate the presence of plenty of proto-jazz musical activity in the very early years of the century.
6. Two good books on the background and nature of bebop style are Scott DeVeaux, *The Birth of Bebop: A Social and Musical History* (Berkeley: University of California Press, 1997) and Thomas Owens, *Bebop: The Music and its Players* (New York: OUP, 1995).
7. Ted Gioia dates the fragmentation of jazz styles back to the bebop period (*The History of Jazz*, pp. 277–335).
8. James Lincoln Collier, *Jazz: The American Theme Song* (New York: OUP, 1993), Chapter 10, pp. 263–75.
9. Lewis Porter, *Lester Young* (London: Macmillan, 1985), p. 56; Clint Eastwood, quoted in *Jazz Times*, September 1995, p. 32.
10. 'Jingle Bells' was recorded by the Duke Ellington and Count Basie bands in 1962 and by Benny Goodman in 1935. A version of 'La Marseillaise' was recorded by Django Reinhardt and Stephane Grappelli in London in 1946.
11. Mark Levine, *The Jazz Theory Book* (Petaluma: Sher, 1995), pp. 439–58.
12. Bill Milkowski, 'Jim Hall and Mike Stern: Six String Rapport', *Jazz Times*, August 1994, p. 38.

13. Ian Carr, *Miles Davis* (London: Paladin, 1982), Appendix B, 'Notes on Repertoire', pp. 315–16.

14. Levine, *The Jazz Theory Book*, pp. 237–43, gives a general account of 'rhythm changes'. He mentions Parker's 'Anthropology', 'Moose the Mooche', and 'Steeplechase' as compositions based on this progression.

15. Barry Kernfeld, *What to Listen for in Jazz* (New York: Yale University Press, 1995), p. 44.

16. Paul Berliner, *Thinking in Jazz: The Infinite Art of Improvisation* (Chicago: Chicago University Press, 1994), p. 90.

17. LeRoi Jones [Amiri Baraka], *Black Music* (New York: Quill, 1967). In a 1965 essay reprinted in the book, Baraka states (p. 105) that 'Coltrane seeks with each onslaught to completely destroy the popular song.'

18. Bruno Nettl, 'Thoughts on Improvisation: A Comparative Approach', *The Musical Quarterly*, Vol. LX, No. 1, January 1974, p. 12.

19. Ibid., p. 13

20. 'Another Persian musician . . .' is from Nettl, ibid., p. 8; Lester Young's remark was made in an interview with François Postif in 1959, reprinted in Martin Williams (ed.), *Jazz Panorama* (New York: Da Capo, 1979), pp. 139–44.

21. Hawkins's most famous version of 'Body and Soul', recorded in 1939, is discussed extensively in DeVeaux, *The Birth of Bebop*, pp. 98–115.

22. Young's improvising style is analyzed in Porter, *Lester Young*. For detailed accounts of Young's recorded solos, see Frank Büchmann-Møller, *You Got to be Original, Man!: The Music of Lester Young* (New York: Greenwood, 1989). Several versions of 'All of Me' are analyzed on pp. 162–5.

23. The version with Holiday and Young was recorded on 21 March 1941. The date of Young's 1956 version was 13 January .

24. Barry Kernfeld, 'Improvisation', in Kernfeld (ed.), *The New Grove Dictionary of Jazz* (New York: St Martin's Press, 1994 edn), pp. 554–63.

25. André Hodeir, *Jazz: Its Evolution and Essence* (New York: Grove, 1956).

26. Porter, *Lester Young*, especially Chapter 4; Owens, *Bebop*, 'The Parker Style', pp. 28–45.

27. For a discussion of 'Klactoveedsedstene' in the context of Parker's style, see Hodeir, *Jazz*, Chapter VII, pp. 99–115. Rollins's 'Without a Song' is featured on the album *The Bridge*, recorded in 1958.

28. Stacy's solo was recorded on 16 January 1938; Garnett Brown's solo with the Jones–Lewis orchestra was recorded in April 1967 and appeared on the album *Thad Jones and Mel Lewis Live at the Village Vanguard*.

29. Berliner, *Thinking in Jazz*, especially 'Epilogue: Jazz as a Way of Life', pp. 485–504.

30. Theodor Adorno, 'Jazz – Perennial Fashion', in *Prisms* (London: Neville Spearman, 1967), pp. 121–32. For a discussion and analysis of Adorno's view of jazz, see Peter Townsend, 'Adorno on Jazz: Vienna versus the Vernacular', *Prose Studies*, Vol. 11, No. 1, May 1988, pp. 69–88.

31. Cyrille quoted in Kitty Grime (ed.), *Jazz at Ronnie Scott's* (London: Robert Hale, 1979), p. 106.

32. Quoted in James Lincoln Collier, *The Making of Jazz* (New York: Delta, 1978), p. 29.

33. Winthrop Sargeant, *Jazz Hot and Hybrid* (London: Jazz Book Club, 1959), p. 111.

34. André Hodeir, *Jazz*, pp. 195–209; Gunther Schuller, *The Swing Era: The Development of Jazz 1930–1945* (New York: OUP, 1989), pp. 222–5 and Appendix II; James Lincoln Collier, *Jazz: The American Theme Song*, pp. 71–88.

35. Schuller, *The Swing Era*, p. 224.

36. Ibid p. 855.

37. Quoted in Berliner, *Thinking in Jazz*, p. 176

38. Hodeir, *Jazz*, p. 198.

39. Quoted in Kathy J. Ogren, *The Jazz Revolution: Twenties America and the Meaning of Jazz* (New York: OUP, 1989), p. 144.

40. Stearns quoted in Ogren, *The Jazz Revolution*, p. 81.

41. Berliner, *Thinking in Jazz*, p. 151.

42. *The New Grove Dictionary of Jazz*, p. 86.

43. Miles Davis, with Quincy Troupe, *Miles: The Autobiography* (London: Picador, 1990), p. 264.

44. Kenny Clarke, quoted in Ira Gitler, *Swing to Bop: An Oral History of the Transition in Jazz in the* 1940s (New York: OUP, 1985), p. 55.

45. Collier, *Jazz: The American Theme Song*, pp. 81–4.

46. Carmen Lundy, quoted in Berliner, *Thinking in Jazz*, p. 149.

47. Berliner, *Thinking in Jazz*, p. 150.

48. Davis, *Miles*, p. 387.

49. Ibid., p. 367, and p. 373.

50. Michael Zwerin, *Close Enough for Jazz* (London: Quartet, 1983), p. 4.

51. Martin Williams, *The Jazz Tradition* (New York: OUP, rev. edn, 1983), p. 8.

52. Ben Sidran, *Black Talk* (London: Payback, 1971), p. xx.

53. Zwerin, *Close Enough for Jazz*, p. 41.

54. Hodeir, *Jazz*, pp. 237–8.

55. Gitler, *Swing to Bop*, p. 5

56. Ibid., p. 311.

57. Mark Tucker (ed.), *The Duke Ellington Reader* (New York: OUP, 1993), p. 337.

58. Adrian Ingram, *Wes Montgomery* (Newcastle: Ashley Mark, 1995), p. 47.

59. Richard Sudhalter, Philip Evans, *Bix: Man and Legend* (London: Quartet, 1974), p. 476.

60. Berliner, *Thinking in Jazz*, Chapter 2, pp. 36–59.

61. Daniel M. Neuman, *The Life of Music in North India* (Chicago: Chicago University Press, 1990), p. 232.

62. Whitney Balliett, *Dinosaurs in the Morning* (London: Jazz Book Club, 1962). Balliett's descriptions of Teagarden, Coleman and Beiderbecke are on pp. 209, 132 and 159 respectively.

CHAPTER 2

'A Marvel of Social Organization': Jazz as a Culture

Jazz and its history is coming to be looked at in greater detail and greater depth. Such writers as Kathy Ogren, William Howland Kenney and Scott DeVeaux have in recent years published research on locales and periods of jazz history which have set the music within contexts that are much more clearly defined than previously. Kenney's work, for instance, provides a clear picture of the circumstances in which Chicago jazz musicians worked in the 1920s and 1930s. DeVeaux's study of the emergence of bebop pays special attention to the economics of the music profession in the early forties. Where research of this kind is published, it can have the effect of overturning some of the casually promulgated myths about the origins of jazz and its development. A more general but important effect has been to change the currency of writing about jazz. It becomes more difficult to issue generalized statements about the music, to speak of its 'essence', or of characteristics which are unrelated to time and place. In a word, writing about jazz, and after that the understanding of jazz, are becoming more realistic.[1]

As with many other phenomena, the more closely one looks at jazz, the more the variations within it become apparent, and the more provisional the generalizations that one can make. An analogy can be drawn here with linguistic studies, especially with dialectology. 'Jazz' and 'jazz culture' can be seen as broad labels equivalent to a linguistic term like 'the Southern accent'. A dialect map may have lines drawn on it around the 'Southern accent' area, but a closer look at the detail reveals how unpredictable and irregular the defining features actually are: supposedly 'southern' features occur out of place, and 'non-south-ern' features occur within the 'southern' area; every place you look at, in or out of the designated zone, has its own combination of features that do not necessarily conform to the pure definition. It is the same with jazz culture: everything overlaps; there are no boundaries other than those imposed on reality by the language used.

These comments can be applied, as was argued in the Preface, to the problems of defining jazz itself; in this chapter, they indicate the sense in which 'jazz as a culture' is being defined. We should not expect the culture of jazz to have an unchanging essence, without concern for differences of time and place. The culture of jazz is differently constituted in New York City in 1999 than it was in Chicago in 1929, than in Kansas City in 1939, and so on. All kinds of conditions differ: the professional context the musicians work in, the nature of their audiences, the ethics and the aesthetics of performance, the technologies available. These contexts have different 'ecologies', to use Daniel Neuman's term.[2] Neuman mentions four components of the 'ecology of music' additional to the music itself: the producers of music, the consumers of music, the context of music events, and the technology of music production and reproduction. Each of the historical sites of jazz has a different configuration of these factors. 'Jazz culture' is therefore a different thing at different times.

Rather than attempting a context-free, universal description of 'jazz culture', this chapter will look instead at a particular 'moment' of jazz in relation to these ecological factors: at one of the successive cultural formations into which jazz has arranged itself during its history. The formation in question has been chosen as having a special importance, in being an occasion when jazz moved in the direction of autonomy, when at a particular cultural moment the music was being created in a context which owed relatively little to outside influences; when jazz, in so far as is possible, was developing its own practices and values. The cultural formation in question is that of the informal 'jamming' or 'blowing' musical world of the 1930s and 1940s.

It was during this period, through the intensive development of certain skills, that the basis of future jazz styles was determined. The jam session, though a group event, pushed into the foreground the performance of the individual improviser, in a playing situation in which everyone, barring some rhythm-section players, had the opportunity to develop these skills. Techniques and stylistic details within the solo became the point of the exercise, and this tended to promote discovery and innovation. The hierarchy of players within jazz came to be based on progress in improvising skill and the gradual stylistic advances that accompanied it. Jazz style has since the 1940s never lost this concentration on the improvised solo. The overall musical style of any given period has been defined in response to the output of soloists:

rhythm, harmony, phrasing, group interaction and even written composition have reflected the influence of the major improvising soloists from Charlie Parker onwards. Influential players like Parker, Lester Young and Miles Davis very largely formed their approaches to improvisation within the setting of the jam session.

It could be argued that the 'jamming' culture of the 1930s and 1940s determined the nature of jazz post-Second World War, by abstracting a particular element and making it the central purpose of the musical form. During this period jazz became a 'pure' form of musical activity, placing an overwhelming emphasis on the art of the improvising soloist, while at the same time being relatively unconcerned about group organization and positively hostile to any entertainment function. Solo improvisation was pursued intensely, with a continual mobilization of new musical methods and knowledge in support of this one central activity. The jazz performance, like the jazz ensemble, became a setting for the presentation of successive soloists' abilities. Jazz performance has been typified ever since by the format of the 'string of solos' which is the product of jam-session culture.

This movement was both a refinement and a narrowing: the amount of creative effort expended on the individual art of improvisation carried jazz to some unforeseen levels of inquiry and development, and ensured that jazz was capable of being appreciated as a music detached from extraneous factors; on the other hand, it left other possibilities for the most part unexplored. The insistence on pure musical values also tended to reduce the size of its audience. It was during this period that the typical polarity in jazz discourse between musical values and commercial values, a motif in many literary versions, was first expressed. From bebop onwards, performers concerned themselves predominantly with improvisational skill, and musicians whose presentation included other kinds of crowd-pleasing behaviour, such as Dizzy Gillespie's on-stage 'clowning', were viewed as indulging in displays that were irrelevant or even inimical to what jazz performance is about.

For musicians half a generation earlier this separation of the pure musical function is harder to maintain: as in the case of, among many others, Lionel Hampton, Fats Waller and especially Louis Armstrong, in whose work it is impossible to draw lines of demarcation between 'music' and 'entertainment'. Nevertheless, jazz culture did make this act of separation or abstraction, and came to regard the extra-musical elements of the performance of men like Waller and Armstrong with disdain or embarrassment. Part of the reason for this is that for postwar African-American musicians, the self-presentation of these earlier artists enacted the stereotype of the black man as clown, and also distracted from the achievements of progressive jazz musicians, as measured in purely musical terms. But the change of attitude also reflected a longer-term historical movement, which is the emergence of jazz as a distinct musical style, rather than as an ingredient in a mixture of popular entertainments. The rise of the semi-autonomous jam-session culture was one of the indications that an identifiable jazz community, with its own values centring upon music, was coming into being. In these years, jazz musicians as a group separated themselves from the world of entertainment in which their musical activities had historically been embedded.

Jazz and Entertainment

Accounts of jazz history have tended to describe jazz as a sort of musical creed that has somehow kept itself intact in hostile environments, sometimes being forced to compromise with commerce and show business, but passing the flame on from hand to hand in a permanent detachment from the rest of the world. Especially with regard to the early years of the century, this appears to be a retrospective projection of the postwar autonomy of the form on to a very different set of circumstances. Rather than having a sense of a distinct set of 'jazz values' that needed to be safeguarded, it is clear that many players did not even think of themselves as jazz musicians, in the sense that became established later. Many saw their own activity as musicians as being continuous with the entire spectrum of performance and public entertainment. In musical terms, few early jazz musicians were aware of a categorical difference between 'jazz' styles and the others that formed part of their professional involvement in providing music for public consumption.[3]

Many musicians now regarded as carriers of a specifically jazz tradition had early careers in quite different milieus. William 'Count' Basie, known to jazz history as the august leader of one of the great jazz orchestras, had his professional beginnings in the broadest kind of entertainment spectacle:

> Basie had gone to the West with a show. He couldn't play the blues then. He was an 'actor' when I first saw him. They would ballyhoo in front of the show, take a band and play a number, and have fellows singing. They would be out in the street, and Basie would explain the

show as a crowd gathered around. We'd stand through all the ballyhoo until Basie would play. 'That guy's crazy' we'd say, because he played so good.[4]

Basie's 'act', in this mid-1920s sighting, consisted of a lot besides music, and even the musical part of his performance was not necessarily in a jazz style. Another Kansas City musician, Buster Smith, speaks of his own early experience as an entertainer, in an account that also shows the developmental link between this kind of musical performance and what was coming to be called jazz:

I'll tell you, a lot of it started around here on these medicine shows. We used to have them all over town here. A medicine show used to have four or five pieces: trombone, clarinet, trumpet, and a drummer, every man blowing for himself as loud as he could to attract a crowd for the 'doctor'. Then there would be a couple of comedians clowning a little bit, then the doc would have the boys blow again to attract another crowd after he's sold the first crowd . . . Then the boys would get up and blow again to attract another bunch of suckers. That's how that jazz started in these parts.[5]

From the early 1920s, jazz orchestras were presented, in theatres like those of the TOBA circuit, as stage attractions alongside the usual range of vaudeville performers, and the packaging of jazz performers together with other kinds of entertainers continued into the 1930s and throughout the 'Swing Era'. The roster of performers booked for the Apollo Theater in Harlem included (for the week of 5 October 1934) the impeccable jazz orchestra of Duke Ellington on the same bill as Bee Footz and the Patent Leather Kids. The bill for 30 March combined another of the great jazz ensembles, the Luis Russell orchestra, with Red and Struggie, Jelli Smith and Bits Turner. Fletcher Henderson's orchestra topped a bill that advertises 'a great Revue cast' including the 3 Lang Sisters and others, and a 'Mystery Drama' entitled 'The Man Who Cried Wolf'.[6] In later years, motion pictures often made up part of the evening's entertainment in the theatres in which jazz bands were booked.

The kinds of performance situations in which jazz musicians worked were, by the mid-1930s, extremely varied. The larger American cities in which there were significant black populations offered a wide range of opportunities to play for all kinds of musical and entertainment events. In the view of historians like Kathy Ogren and William Howard

Kenney, the influence of these experiences upon jazz styles was decisive. Ogren writes that 'professional entertainment networks for blacks had already begun to shape performance styles before World War I and before jazz began to reach white audiences'.[7] Kenney's study of the jazz and popular music world of South Side Chicago gives a detailed description of the settings in which the professional musician operated: to the established circuits of minstrelsy, circuses, tent shows and medicine shows, the Chicago urban scene added night clubs and cabarets, in which the musicians' role might be to accompany blues singers, to provide music for dancing, to be a 'turn' in their own right:

> Professional jazz performers also studied instrumental expression, tinkering with techniques in order to develop a performance specialty, a distinctive sound or instrumental 'act' that would make what cabaret performers called an 'up' (vaudevillians spoke of a 'turn') during floor-shows. A featured entertainer earned between $15 and $35 a night in the early twenties, considerably more than sidemen in the orchestras.[8]

Even in strictly musical terms, many artists were skilled in a variety of idioms that might include only a small proportion of the elements of jazz. The bandleader Andy Kirk worked in the early 1920s in the orchestra of George Morrison, one of the leading black bands of the day, which toured the USA from New York to San Francisco. Kirk described the band's repertoire as 'schottisches and waltzes, one-steps and two-steps', and he contrasts their style with that of another touring band from Texas that played music 'built on the structure of the blues'.[9] The Kansas City pianist and bandleader Jay McShann remembered that the featured song of the blues singer Jimmy Rushing, later the vocalist in the Count Basie orchestra, was a sentimental waltz entitled 'When the Trees Bid the Leaves Goodbye'.[10] Mary Lou Williams, recalling the early days of the Midwestern touring band of T. Holder, emphasized their versatility as professional entertainer-musicians: 'They did little acts and they did everything. They could play for proms and then go to an all black dance and be just as good.'[11] The repertoire of the Louis Armstrong band included stock arrangements of tunes like 'The Anniversary Waltz' and 'We'll Gather Lilacs',[12] and Armstrong's admiration for the 'sweet' music of Guy Lombardo (often cited by jazz players as the antithesis of their own artistic values) was well documented. Even though, as we shall see later in this chapter, Armstrong was viewed by others as the model for a purely jazz aesthetic, it is clear that, as Gerald Early puts it, 'Armstrong saw himself as an entertainer who must, by any means, please his audience.'[13]

Their function as musicians, or as players of jazz, was for many of these early figures indivisible from their function as participants in a world of professional entertainment. Many of these players enjoyed a high degree of what Ingrid Monson has called 'polymusicality'.[14] In the absence of a developed jazz aesthetic, individuals later identified as jazz performers shared part of their musical range with other cultural worlds than that of jazz, or of black music in the broad sense. Monson argues that this polymusicality 'should not be seen as a liquidation of cultural identity but rather as an important component of a group in contact with multiple cultural others'.[15] Histories of jazz, which have all been written after this period, have tended to represent black jazz musicians' exposure to other repertoires as compromise or frustration, as if an integral jazz aesthetic already existed, and jazz players were sometimes compelled against their will to cross the boundary that divided it from other popular musics. But as Charles Nanry has written, 'jazz musicians have always had to articulate their expression within the larger world of entertainment'.[16]

For musicians and critics in the post-Second World War era, this articulation has been a process of separation, even opposition: jazz exists as a coherent set of musical practices and values, as a separate musical culture which defines itself against the culture of entertainment and popular music. But for this to be possible, for an alternative culture to be articulated, jazz has had to become self-conscious, to think of itself as a distinct cultural entity. This essential step, of a body of musicians and listeners considering themselves as cultivating a specific form, or being involved in a collective shaping of a musical culture, only occurred in jazz from about the mid-1920s onwards.

Even then, there are qualifications to be made to this: not all of those within jazz culture would necessarily have expressed an identity in those terms (Mary Lou Williams, for instance, says that 'The only bad thing about it is the name'[17]), and for a long time afterwards the boundary between jazz and the other popular musics, between jazz and the entertainment business, would not be strongly drawn. Performers like Armstrong, Waller, Hampton and some others remained professionally identified as entertainers inseparably from their musical careers. Even as late as the mid-1940s, as Ted Gioia explains in his study of the jazz scene in Los Angeles, a distinct jazz culture had not separated itself out from the popular entertainment business:

> Entertainment was just one small part of what Central Avenue was about, and jazz was just one small part of the entertainment picture, coexisting over the years with R&B, song-and-dance, comedy, blues, revues, shake dancing, vaudeville and the like. The Club Alabam, the best known of the nightspots that dotted the landscape, is sometimes spoken of by jazz writers as a West Coast Birdland or Village Vanguard, but it was both more and less. The Alabam featured lavish revues that covered the gamut of the entertainment spectrum, and though the jazz might be spectacular – with Charles Mingus, Dexter Gordon and Art Pepper playing in the house band, it no doubt was – jazz was still just a small part of the show.[18]

Individualism and the Soloist

For the emergence of a semi-autonomous jazz culture to take place, certain conditions were necessary. The economic circumstances and the working conditions in which the prospective jazz performers operated had to be favourable, to the extent of making jazz activity sustainable for a sufficiently large number of participants. Secondly, jazz had to reach a certain level of self-consciousness, at which there existed, for a community of players, a sense of a well-defined activity in which their own contributions could have a definite meaning against a set of communal standards.

In the mid- to late-1920s, this second condition was met, as the community of players responded to a rapid change in the orientation of jazz performance, from an emphasis on the ensemble to an emphasis on the individual soloist. At the same time, there was a qualitative change in the instrumental skill required of the musician. It was no longer sufficient, at the higher levels of the culture, for an instrumentalist to be able to sustain a part in collective improvisation and to carry out the duties of the jobbing musician. The individual player was separated out from these collective contexts and put in a spotlight in which what was required was the ability to improvise musical statements, to project individuality, and to be original.

The main impetus for this change seems to have come from the arrival of a generation of players who were capable of the sustained musical invention that would make this soloistic art possible. Without subscribing entirely to the 'great man' theory of history, it can be argued that much of the change was brought about by the effect of one musician, Louis Armstrong, while some historians would also cite another New Orleans player, Sidney Bechet, who had developed solo skills to a comparable level a few years earlier than Armstrong. There are several reasons for doubting the simplicity of this theory. One is that many explanations of the history of jazz have had a mythological rather than a real basis, and the story of the intuitive genius who changes everything would play well to the same constituency. Another is that improvisation of a more rudimentary kind was already wide-spread in the playing of jazz and related music, and might have been developed to a higher level even without Armstrong and Bechet. A more far-reaching cultural explanation would point to the repeated appearance in black American culture of improvisatory forms, from the verbal contests of games like 'the dozens', to hip hop music, to a current dance form like 'stepping', which has many parallels in its attitudes and distribution to jazz itself.[19]

However, there is evidence that Armstrong's arrival in Chicago and New York in the mid-1920s, and his example as a consummate improviser, had an enormous impact upon the attitudes and aspirations of other musicians. James Lincoln Collier points out that in the six years of jazz recording from its beginning in 1917 up to mid-1923, among several hundred recordings made, there was only one single significant jazz solo, King Oliver's three choruses on 'Dippermouth Blues'.[20] The musician learning jazz before that time was, as Collier points out, concerned with learning to play a part in an ensemble-based music. The only places for solo improvisation in the earlier style were the 'breaks', usually two-bar or four-bar gaps in which the more skilled players could interpolate brief improvised passages. According to Gunther Schuller, 'these breaks were what every interested listener waited for'. Schuller's interpretation of the development of the solo proper is that the 'break' became expanded when instrumental skill reached a high enough level: 'greater fluency and instrumental skill were inevitable, and for this reason alone the polyphonic collective style was doomed to extinction'.[21]

Bechet and Armstrong were the first instrumentalists to be capable of raising the stakes for improvised solo playing. Armstrong's playing on the recordings he made over a three year-period with a group called the Hot Five are generally seen as having broadcast to jazz players, and to a wider public, the advances in improvisational standards. There are numerous accounts by contemporary players of the reception of these recordings. The drummer Zutty Singleton spoke of a cross-country car journey in the late 1920s in which 'every big town we'd come to, we'd hear Louis' records being played on loudspeakers'.[22] A few years earlier, according to the clarinettist Buster Bailey, Armstrong had 'upset Chicago' with his 'execution ... and his ideas, his drive. They got crazy for his feeling.'[23] The impact of Armstrong's recordings was more than matched by the response to his live performances. Singleton describes an early appearance by Armstrong as a stand-in for the Duke Ellington band at a theatre in the Bronx: 'Louis played the *St Louis Blues* and I saw something I'll never forget as long as I live. When he finished, even the band in the pit stood up and applauded for him.'[24]

The qualities of Armstrong's improvised playing that so enthused contemporary audiences have been described by many musicians and writers. Schuller's book *Early Jazz* sets out four features: his choice of notes, tone quality, rhythmic sense and inflection of notes.[25] While all of these features are frequently mentioned in other accounts, it is Armstrong's rhythmic sense which is most often marvelled at. Rex Stewart writes that Armstrong could 'take one note and swing you into bad health on that one note. His rhythmic concept is *that* profound.'[26] The pianist Teddy Wilson speaks of Armstrong as embodying 'the essence of the jazz rhythm.'[27] Armstrong also carried sheer instrumental technique to higher levels. One of his bravura stage routines was to astonish the audience with a succession of 100 high C notes (at a time when 'to hit or play over C made the player exceptional') and then to top it off with a prodigious high F. 'He blew a searing, soaring, altissimo fantastic high note and held it long enough for every one of us musicians to gasp. Benny Carter, who has perfect pitch, said "Damn! That's high F!"'[28]

The improvisational solo style that Armstrong displayed from the mid-1920s, in these galvanic live performances and in his wonderfully expressive playing in recordings like 'West End Blues', elicited much direct imitation. Numerous trumpeters in the 1930s borrowed Armstrong's phrases and devices. But the more general emulation that players like Armstrong, Bechet and others set off was the idea of the solo itself. Instrumental playing in jazz was increasingly seen as having its main purpose in individual expression through improvised solos. Armstrong and Bechet were the first to have strong enough musical personalities and a high enough level of invention for their individual improvisations to be the central focus for the listener. Their example set the achievement of improvisation as the main standard by which jazz players measured their own work. It was only through Armstrong and Bechet that improvisation became impressive enough to serve as a goal for the jazz community to take as the basis for its future activity. As Gunther Schuller has written, Armstrong 'established the general stylistic direction for jazz for several decades to come'.[29] The pianist Sammy Price expressed a consensus among musicians about the effect of Armstrong in the mid-1920s: 'It was Louis who liberated the music. You must remember that in the early days of Ma Rainey and Bessie Smith, instrumental solos were just beginning – he liberated the jazz musician.'[30]

From the time of Armstrong and Bechet – James Lincoln Collier sets an approximate date of 1927 for this – jazz has, in his words, 'become the soloist's music'.[31] Collier sees this direction of development in jazz as being an expression of a deeper social and cultural change during the 1920s. 'The call was no longer for community, but for individualism, for self-expression.'[32] Collier portrays this shift as taking place simultaneously in all the arts: he cites the movement from the nineteenth-century novel of 'social systems' to the individualised, isolated protagonists of Hemingway, Joyce and Fitzgerald, and analogous shifts in music and in dance. As 'the soloist emerges from the Dixieland ensemble', so impressionist art and music privilege the perspective of the individual over that of a common artistic language.

> It cannot be only coincidence that jazz changed swiftly from an ensemble to a solo art in precisely those years of the mid-1920s when the new spirit of the new age was catching hold of the young American generation, which would be the primary audience for jazz at the time. Given the cry for individualism, there was no way that the dixieland ensemble could stand up against the romantic hero, trumpet against the sky, flinging his feelings to the midnight air.[33]

Collier's coupling together of a procedural shift in various art forms besides jazz seems more relevant to an explanation of the public response to jazz than to the dynamic operating within the emerging jazz community itself. It also explains the appeal of the music for an audience approaching it from the mythologized and romanticized perspective which caused the romantic fatalist F. Scott Fitzgerald to name the 1920s 'The Jazz Age'. This was the first appearance of a romantic myth of the jazz musician which has never been superseded.

For the jazz musician, and for the immediate audience for the music, it became the case after the mid-1920s that, as the clarinettist Tony Scott said three decades later, 'We always have to depend on the soloist to point to new developments in jazz styles.'[34] Within the community of players that became conscious of itself as such in the late 1920s, the work of solo improvisation was the nodal point, the locus of the continuous development of the musical language. From that time on, given the example of players like Armstrong and Bechet, and the working environment which made it possible, the development of solo improvisation became the overriding purpose of a continuous collective creative effort, taking place in a wide variety of locations, primarily in the major cities of the United States. This collective effort, with its combination of collectivity and individualism, co-operation and competition, informality and seriousness, purpose and play, became over the next twenty years the central act around which a jazz culture formed itself.

Jam-session Culture

The origination of the term 'jam session' is claimed by the clarinettist and writer Mezz Mezzrow, who traces it to some 'impromptu concerts' held in a basement in State Street, Chicago in the early twenties, but Mezzrow makes it clear that similar events had long taken place, in fact if not in name, 'among the colored boys'.[35] He distinguishes between the competitive nature of the sessions among the black musicians and the more co-operative mood of his colleagues' activity. This dichotomy between the jam session as sociable music-making and as competitive event ('cuttin' contest' in black slang) runs throughout its history. The jam session has been idealized as a vernacular academy of musicianship, dramatized as an arena for trials of strength, politicized as a model of collective endeavour. Like so many other features of the cultural positioning of jazz, it seems to stand between a number of familiar antinomies, between individual and group, competition and co-operation, formality and informality, commercialism and autonomy, order and freedom.[36]

The practice of 'jamming' among professional jazz musicians had a very wide distribution in the United States in the approximately twenty-year period in which it was at its height. There were reports in contemporary sources of widespread activity in places far away from the main population centres: *Metronome* magazine reports in mid-1941 that 'Tacomans are so excited about jazz that groups of them may be found jamming at any and all hours of the night.'[37] It can be assumed that musicians behaved in a similar way wherever the conditions were right, but in general the greatest flourishing of this informal sector of the musical world took place in cities where there was a sufficient critical mass of working musicians, audiences and places to play in.

The culture took root typically in black entertainment districts, away from but within reach of mainstream entertainment outlets. In these districts rents and running costs were lower, and night clubs and cabarets could be set up quickly and cheaply. The main centres from the 1920s through to the 1940s were Harlem in New York, the South Side of Chicago, and a small but influential section of Kansas City. On the West Coast, the main focus was the area around Central Avenue in Los Angeles. 'It was a big city', says the trumpeter Benny Bailey, 'but the scene was pretty small. All the musicians knew each other, jazz musicians.'[38]

The scene in New York was the most extensive and, in the long run, the most important; but the Kansas City music scene became enormously productive and influential during the 1930s, providing a setting that exposed and encouraged the talents of players such as Lester Young and Charlie Parker, and so indirectly affecting the course of jazz over the following decades. The Kansas City jazz musician's world was for the most part compressed into a section of the city six blocks square between Twelfth and Eighteenth Streets, in which, according to Mary Lou Williams, there were as many as fifty clubs or cabarets that provided work for musicians.[39]

But this semi-autonomous activity of the jam session operated at one or more remove from the professional sector. The term 'jam session' itself is flexible, referring to a spectrum of different playing situations, from a group of friends getting together in someone's house, through unpaid playing which depends upon earning a living in other jobs, to sessions which are almost indistinguishable from ordinary public concerts. Gunther Schuller, in the *Grove Dictionary*, defines the jam session as 'an informal gathering of jazz musicians playing for their own pleasure',[40] but the pleasure principle was in many situations moderated by monetary needs. The purest kind of example of the session based on sociality and musical sharing is given in Louis Armstrong's account of Bix Beiderbecke visiting him after working hours in Chicago in the 1920s:

he would haul it out to the Sunset where I was playing and stay right there with us until the last show was over and the customers would go home. Then we would lock the doors. Now you talking about jam sessions ... those were the things ... with every one feeling each other's note or chord, et cetera ... and blend with each other instead of trying to cut each other ...[41]

Many musicians speak of long hours of playing for which they were not paid, in after-hours, private or semi-private jamming, or 'sitting in' or taking part in semi-organized sessions in clubs. Teddy Wilson expressed the motivation of the musician moving between clubs to sit in and jam: he 'sat in on thousands of jam sessions and would play until daylight for nothing', because for him 'the jam sessions would have been pay enough'. Wilson described spending time with the great pianist Art Tatum, who 'could play for 12 hours a day', and the succession of clubs and houses they would seek out in order to continue playing until 'nine o'clock in the morning, or noon – as long as we could stay up and physically play the piano'.[42]

The prospect of a large pool of highly talented musicians asking to play for next to nothing must have been an inspiring sight for club owners. In Kansas City, as Ross Russell comments,

> The practice of jazzmen floating about the district from one club to another and sitting in as the spirit moved them was a matter of great convenience for the club operator. Once a club was established, it was necessary to hire only a few key musicians who might serve to attract others. Sometimes only a good rhythm section was necessary or, as was the case at the Sunset Club, a drummer and a top piano player.[43]

The club operator could, in this fluid after-hours world, acquire a band of ten or more players while paying only two or three. Russell names, as two of the most 'persistent and indefatigable cabaret-hoppers',[44] Lester Young and Charlie Parker, who were in effect giving away for nothing services which in later years could be worth hundreds of dollars a night.

Much jam-session activity took place in a shadowy sector of the economy, in locations sometimes controlled by gangsters. This was certainly the case with many of the Kansas City clubs, which had grown up in an economic microclimate dependent on alliances between the city administration, under Mayor Tom Pendergast, and organized crime. Mary Lou Williams, who worked as a pianist on the Kansas City scene, spoke with awe of some of her employers:

> It was during the Prohibition and a little bit of everything was happening in Kansas City. Certain people did exactly what they wanted to do ... I've heard people speak of gangsters in New York. Well, they were kids to the ones I've worked for.[45]

Robert Altman's 1996 film *Kansas City* is based upon this co-existence of the world of the jazz musician with that of organized crime. According to the saxophonist Bud Freeman, there were advantages to working for the gangsters: 'at least we could play what we wanted.'[46]

Many players in effect subsidized their after-hours, voluntary, jam-session participation through wage-paying jobs in more conventional musical outlets. This was probably the most common pattern during the period. There are many accounts of musicians in the big cities working in dance-halls, cabarets and theatres, and then joining the population of itinerant jazz players after midnight to play unpaid in one of the jam-session locations. The total amount of playing time logged by some of these players was enormous, to judge by this not untypical account, by the drummer Max Roach:

> In those days, you worked seven nights a week. And then you worked six weeks straight and had a week off. You didn't have a night off. So we were working from nine to three downtown at George Jay's 78th Street Taproom. Then we'd pack up our gear and run uptown to the Uptown House, and we worked from four till eight, seven days a week.[47]

Roach's position on his 'downtown' job was a conventional assignment in a white club, and at Monroe's Uptown House he backed up the lengthy jam sessions. As a rhythm section player, Roach would have played more or less continuously throughout his ten hours' nightly session. In these conditions, as Roach himself comments, a great deal of musical learning could go on. The playing hours could be severe on the Kansas City scene:

> The schedule at the Reno Club called for the band to back up four floor shows, lasting about an hour each ... the first of the floor shows starting at nine and the last at four the following morning. In addition to the floor shows, the band was expected to furnish music for the

'dancing pleasure' of the Reno clientele. The musicians were given a ten-minute break every hour, but were otherwise on from nine to five. There was no night off. On Sunday mornings, the weekly breakfast dance and jam session, a popular feature with the sporting life crowd that frequented the club, lasted until ten and sometimes noon. Jesse Price estimates that approximately sixty hours each week were spent in actually playing.[48]

The format of the jam session itself was variable, according to the setting and the relationship between the musicians and the audience. The playing situation typical of the after-hours world of New York, Chicago and Kansas City did, however, develop a certain regularity of format. The saxophonist Cecil Scott describes how the Capitol Palace cabaret on Lenox Avenue in Harlem, where his band were resident, became in the mid-1920s the rallying point for musicians looking for jam sessions:

> When the other clubs closed, one by one their band members and patrons would drift into our spot, and musicians from such places as the Cotton Club, Club Alabam, Roseland, Paradise Inn, used to vie for the chance to sit in with us. We usually had a waiting line holding their horns against the far wall waiting turns. Fellows like Johnny Hodges, members of Fletch Henderson's gang, Fats Waller, Earl Hines, and fellows from Charlie Johnson's band, Luis Russell's band – all these and many others. They were eager to blow since on their regular job they were restricted from righteous playing because they would have to play stock arrangements to floor shows.[49]

Once admitted, the player would be allowed a turn in the long exchanges of improvisation that made up the session. In order to take part, the player would need some instrumental skill and knowledge of the material being improvised on. Among the jam-session repertoire were innumerable versions of the blues and the short list of popular songs that were the common currency, including 'I Got Rhythm', 'Lady Be Good' and a few others. The player might be thrown into the midst of a protracted round of improvisation on a single tune. The Kansas City club owner Milton Morris gave a description of a night when Lester Young, Ben Webster and Charlie Parker, three of the greatest improvisers in jazz, were present together in a session at the Novelty Club:

On this occasion, as Morris recalls, the competitive spirit fostered by jamming had led to long solos by each of the three saxophonists, some of them lasting twenty or thirty minutes and a single number by the band two hours, so that the non-players would adjourn to the bar for drinks, drifting back to the huckster's wagon when they sensed the soloist was running out of ideas.[50]

Kansas City jam sessions seem to have been given to lengthy improvisational displays. Ross Russell recounts an experience of the pianist Sam Price, who one night left the Sunset Club around ten o'clock:

> After a drink Price went home to rest, bathe and change clothing. He returned to the club around one. The bandstand was more crowded than before, and the musicians were still playing the same tune. They had been playing it without interruption for over three hours.[51]

These are extreme examples, but the jam session typically involved a large number of players, each of them seeking an opportunity to stretch themselves, and the typical performance would tend to run to some length.

An incidental but variable feature of jam-session culture was a degree of racial mixing. There are reports of white musicians even in the early 1920s frequenting clubs where virtuosos like Armstrong and Hines could be heard, and later of white musicians participating in sessions together with black musicians. Russell, for example, gives a list of roughly equal numbers of black and white visiting players at the Subway Club in Kansas City in the 1930s,[52] and the sessions involving Beiderbecke and Armstrong have already been mentioned. To a large extent the racial composition of sessions reflected the demographics of the city districts, so that the population of an after-hours club in Harlem, for example, would be predominantly black. But it is apparent that a good deal of meeting and playing together went on between black and white players, at a time when it was still unacceptable for players of both groups to appear together on a theatre stage or in a conventional music job. Even the bandstands in clubs like Minton's and Monroe's in the 1940s, where the expression of black identity was part of the agenda, were not closed to white players.

The early 1940s jam sessions at Minton's Playhouse, a club run by the bandleader Teddy Hill on 118th Street in Harlem, are more celebrated than any others. They have achieved a historical status in which, as the novelist Ralph Ellison puts it, 'the dry facts are easily lost in legend and glamour'.[53] Russell describes Minton's as a 'battleground' where older and newer styles of playing struggled for supremacy. Another frequent description is of Minton's as a 'laboratory' where 'experimentation' was going on. These metaphors oversimplify the kind of action and interaction that Minton's (and, less famously, Monroe's) supported. The reading of Minton's as a laboratory, especially, puts it too straightforwardly into the familiar discourse of Modernism, representing the aggregate of a collection of diverse motives as artistic experimentation in the sense in which that was known in literary fiction or in the visual arts.

The radical developments which came out of Minton's were arrived at through the usual interactive dynamics of the jam session, but Minton's gradually gained an institutional status among New York musicians. The Monday night jam sessions were regularly attended by a majority of the significant players in jazz, and became the focus for the energies of virtually the entire jazz community. Minton's was the successor to earlier New York venues such as the Clef Club and the Rhythm Club, which were social centres for the black New York musicians. Minton's musical policy was also built around, as it happened, the participation of a group of younger players who approached the sessions in a more programmatic frame of mind, wanting to bring about certain changes in jazz style. These were the circumstances in which the effect of Minton's could amount to what some writers have called a 'revolution'.

For many of the participants, however, it was, in the words of the singer Carmen McRae, 'just a place for cats to jam'.[54] What was soon to be called 'bebop' may have been constructed there, but this occurred through an acceleration of the processes of learning that would occur in all jam-session playing. Minton's combined and concentrated the creative energies of a large number of talented players in the raising of jam-session culture to a new intensity at which far-reaching changes were likely to result. While remaining, in its casualness, its sociality, its competitiveness, its marginality, entirely typical, Minton's represents the metamorphosis of the jam session into a different form of life.

At Minton's as at many other jam sessions, the musicians were in large part also the audience: not that others were excluded (although Ellison comments that 'customers who were not musicians were crowded out'[55]), but musicians were the essential audience for the communication going on. The performances of individual players were monitored by the rest of the musical community (especially by those who played the same instrument), and were variously evaluated or learned from. The trumpeter Joe Newman commented of the audience at Minton's that 'The people that came in there really came to hear music',[56] rather than to use it for any of the other functions of the nightclub. Whether made up of musicians or not, the jam-session audience was required to be committed and knowledgeable.

A distinction made by players of classical music in North India is applicable here: Daniel Neuman notes that Indian musicians 'distinguish essentially two kinds of listeners: those who are connoisseurs (*samajdhar log*, "people who understand") ... and those who are musically unsophisticated, for which there are a variety of epithets'[57] (in jazz slang of the period the relevant epithet might be 'square'). In the ecologically quite different musical culture of India, there is a similar relation between player and audience, and an analogous sense of an 'inside' communication of musician to musician, as in the jazz jam session: 'Another kind of *samajdhar* audience is one made up of other musicians. It is perhaps the most discriminating audience and one for which the artist will presumably do his best.'[58] Or, to revert to the language of the jazz musician, in this case the saxophonist Sonny Criss, speaking of racially mixed jam sessions in Hollywood in the 1940s, 'it was such an *in* thing. The audience were special people. They were artists, writers, actors and so forth. They were very into the music. They inspired all the musicians to play their asses off.'[59]

From the mid-1940s onwards, the jam-session culture of the cities began to lose its coherence. The rapid commercial decline of the big bands created employment problems for jazz musicians, taking away the essential economic prop that had supported the informal sector of the jam session. There was no longer the steady flow of musicians into and around the major cities that produced the required concentration of talent and energy. In some cases jam sessions became formalized and were presented in a more professionalized format. From 1946, sessions involving top-ranking soloists were presented in public arenas by promoters such as Gene Norman and Norman Granz. Larger audiences were admitted to displays of jam-session musicianship in a way that had not been possible before. In the view of some writers and musicians, this large-scale public performance changed the nature of the jam session to its detriment. Musicians might find themselves playing for the kind of audience 'for which there are a variety of epithets'. In this setting a premium might be placed on those musical skills that translate best to the stage, such as loud, fast and spectacular playing. Whatever the merits of the kinds of musical interaction that stage presentation produced, it was no longer fulfilling, within the community of musicians, the same function as the vernacular jam session.

Nevertheless, the jam session has continued to exist, and to exert an influence over the ways in which jazz is played. Informal playing, in settings as various as hotel rooms, rehearsal studios and nightclubs, is so inherent in the practices and the ethos of jazz that it is inconceivable that it should not continue in some form. There is, however, no longer an identifiable, localized culture of the jam session in the sense in which such a culture existed through the 1930s and 1940s. The scene lacks that sense of a community with its own network of times and places, its belonging in its own territory, its own loose but visible social organization. A writer reporting for a British jazz magazine in 1985 reported that regular sessions in the Blue Note club in New York City were attracting large numbers of players who 'come from far and near for a chance to sit in – because jam sessions are virtually a thing of the past these days'.[60] Lewis Porter, the biographer of John Coltrane, stresses the importance of the jam-session experience that Coltrane acquired in his early years on the Philadelphia scene, but comments pessimistically on the situation in the 1990s:

> When I was a young player in the Bronx around 1972, there were many such sessions, but primarily in black neighbourhoods, and I believe that they are still common at local clubs in black neighbourhoods and thus escape the notice of most writers and educators. However, it is probably true that there are fewer open jam sessions than there used to be.[61]

The jam session still exists, and still figures largely in the experience of most players, but it is diffused, even on a worldwide scale, and can no longer be the community phenomenon that it was in the 1930s and 1940s in New York, Chicago, Los Angeles, Philadelphia, Detroit, Pittsburgh and other American cities. It is a long way back from the current economy of jazz to the Chicago scene of the forties:

> In those days Chicago was a jamming town. Loosely knit cadres of musicians would travel around like roving bands, looking for places

to blow. They'd always have their horns with them ... if the bartender, or manager, were agreeable – after all, they were getting free entertainment for the club – you have an instant session.[62]

The Jam Session and Jazz Values

The jam session dealt in the skills of the soloist. A typical occasion presented the talents of a large number of soloists in succession, sometimes matched instrument by instrument, and giving an account of their improvising abilities using the same musical materials. Comparison between players was inevitable, both for audiences and other musicians. An element of competition was implicit in the jazz jam session, as it is to varying degrees in all improvisatory cultures. Daniel Neuman gives a description of a North Indian *jugulbandi* ('a duet with, in this case, the overtones of a duel') featuring two famous players of the *sitar*:

> As this was the first time these two giants had performed together in something like fifteen years, the atmosphere was electric. The concert had barely begun when the tabla player, Pandit Shanta Prasad, who was sitting between them, said to the audience 'I feel like a lamb sitting between two tigers'. The audience laughed, acknowledging the now public definition of this contest as a duel and the role of the tabla player as performing mediator.[63]

There are jazz-like overtones to this classical Indian jam session: it is a nocturnal, though not 'after hours', event, with soloists, backed by rhythm, improvising on common themes in an attitude compounded of mutual respect and competitiveness. The dichotomy between the sociable and the competitive functions of the improvising session is apparent here, as it is throughout the literature of the jazz jam session.

In discussing the cultural values of the jam session of the 1930s and 1940s it is essential to place this kind of event within a context that makes clear both its likeness and its unlikeness to comparable events in American, African-American and other cultures. The issue of competitiveness in jam-session culture, for example, should be seen within a wide cultural and historical frame of reference. Writers, critics and musicians have deployed a range of culturally very specific imagery in speaking of it. It is useful, however, to look at jazz culture from the point of view of the neighbouring creative world of African-American dance.

Jacqui Malone, in her study of black dance in America, claims that dancers, singers and musicians alike used improvisation in the same way: 'They inspired each other and pushed the evolution of their art forms along through improvisation, competition and hard work.'[64] Malone's term for this culturally characteristic process is 'competitive interaction', which she calls

> the driving force that keeps African American dance, music and song in the avant garde worldwide. We see it, for example, in the jam sessions of jazz musicians, cutting sessions of tap dancers, challenge matches of break dancers, colorful parades of black social aid and pleasure clubs, and the 'sing-offs' of blues shouters of the twenties, gospel quartets of the thirties and forties, and doowop vocalists of the fifties.[65]

In this view, jazz is one of many African-American cultural practices that share the same fundamental organization, the same goals, and the same values. The element of competition within the form takes on a different sense when placed within this frame of reference, as against the ways in which it is usually represented within mainstream discourse.

Within jazz, there were precedents for the competitive use of musical skill, among them the 'battles of bands' which existed in New Orleans early in the century, and which recur up to the 1940s. The reputation of a Midwestern band like the Blue Devils was based upon their competitive record in these events. 'Such battles', Ross Russell comments, 'were a southwestern institution, welcomed by the public, and exploited by bookers and ballroom operators.'[66] The Blue Devils, according to one of its members, 'was a great band for a battle of music. Every time we'd find another band we'd grab them and give them a hard time.'[67] Rex Stewart writes of his own band, the Fletcher Henderson orchestra, being unexpectedly 'cut' by a 'Johnny-come-lately white band from the sticks', the Jean Goldkette orchestra.[68] One of the most famous mid-1930s battles was between the Chick Webb band, defending their own turf at the Savoy Ballroom in Harlem, and the Count Basie band, newly arrived in New York from the Midwest. Musicians shared a consensus about the ranking order established through these contests. Teddy Wilson, for instance, comments that 'They said Duke could blow Chick out, he's the only one, that's what I heard, and I would have loved to have heard a battle of music with Duke and Chick.'[69]

As the competitive focus shifted from the ensemble to the soloist, accounts were given of legendary occasions featuring star players, and a notional score was kept of who had beaten whom. There were reports, for example, of the saxophonist Coleman Hawkins, top of his profession on his instrument, having to defend his primacy in an all-night contest against some unexpected talents cropping up in Kansas City; another of Hawkins returning from a trip to Europe and cruising the New York clubs to check on any likely competitors that had emerged during his absence.

Ted Gioia's account of the Los Angeles scene of the 1940s speaks of the 'pressure-cooker atmosphere of Central Avenue' in which players like the tenor saxophonists Dexter Gordon and Wardell Gray acquitted themselves especially well.

> The proceedings would just get started around midnight and often continue until close to dawn. 'There'd be a lot of cats on the stand' Dexter Gordon explains, referring to the Basket battles. 'But by the end of the session it would wind up with Wardell and myself.'[70]

Gioia's reading of these events deploys a range of metaphors that recurs in many other accounts: 'Borrowing pugilistic parlance, one sees their battles as a classic match-up of puncher against boxer'; 'Being acknowledged as the top saxophonist is not a little like being known as the fastest draw in a Wild West town: soon every challenger wants to match up with the top gun.'[71] This last image finds an echo in the pianist Allen Tinney's description of a competitive meeting between two alto saxophonists at Minton's: 'a guy named Earl Bostic used to come in and watch [Charlie Parker]. You know it's like gunslingers, and one night they hooked up ... .Bostic had been scouting him, and they really hooked up.'[72]

The language here is that of the Western movie shoot-out, and the imagery of boxing, fights with swords and knives (hence 'cutting contests'), 'duels' and 'battles' are also common in many accounts. There is an undoubted machismo involved in this and in some other aspects of jazz culture. 'Women instrumentalists', according to the Los Angeles trumpeter Clora Bryant, 'no matter how well known, steered clear of the jam sessions.' Bryant often found herself 'the only female that would get up and play' in the Central Avenue jam sessions.[73]

The agonistic aspect of improvisation in these environments may simply have to do with male competitiveness, and it clearly also has, in a market economy, a bearing on individuals' employment prospects and rates of pay. A younger musician attempting to enter the competition might be exposed to failure or even humiliation if shown up or out-played by others, as in the teenage Charlie Parker's experience of trying to jam with members of the Count Basie band: the drummer Jo Jones showed his low estimation of Parker's ability by detaching one of his cymbals and throwing it across the dance-floor (a gesture used as the central image of *Bird*, Clint Eastwood's 1988 film biography of Parker). In the sessions at Minton's, experienced players sometimes used tactics such as choosing difficult keys, or repeatedly changing keys, in order to raise the height of the hurdles that faced their competitors.

The jam session as ordeal, or as showdown, or as trauma, is the version that possesses the greatest dramatic and mythological potential. For a mainstream audience outside of the 'interpretative community' of the jam session's participants themselves, these familiar cultural models provide the easiest means of making narrative sense of an event which, as Scott DeVeaux points out, 'offers few clues to the uncontexted outsider'.[74] Without the immediacy of the original context, or Jacqui Malone's perspective across a range of cognate African-American improvisational forms, the jam session can be understood by the ana-logy of a sports event, or a contest of physical bravery, or represented as a psychological challenge putting self-respect, manhood, or even the integrity of the personality at risk. Fiction about jazz shows many examples of this kind of interpretation, as we shall see in Chapter 4.[75] Narratives of this kind grow out of the model of simple competitive individualism, but this model only appears appropriate to the jam session because it isolates a single aspect of the activity and overlooks the wider and longer-term context.

The model derived by Malone from other African-American cultural settings stresses the coexistence of competition with other functions, 'improvisation, competition and hard work', in the pursuit of goals which are manifested at the community as well as at the individual level. It is noticeable that in some of the accounts given above of head-to-head contests between instrumentalists, a comment is appended about the overall artistic quality of the occasion, which is perceived as being more important than a competitive result. In the classical-Indian sitar recital, 'The concert, which began at nine in the evening and ended at three in the morning, was so outstanding that there was no talk about the superiority of either soloist.'[76] Similarly, in the 'gunslinging' encounter between Bostic and Parker, 'I don't really know who won because it was too tremendous.'[77] The event witnessed as a whole may or may not settle the relative rankings of the competing players, but what it certainly does is to display the overall level of performance in the community of musicians. It is for this reason that Malone sees individual improvisatory competition as having an evolutionary purpose in the vernacular forms of music and dance: emulation raises the standards in the art form as a whole.

Competitiveness in these skills can coexist with recognition of and respect for the talents of others. The final comment of the saxophonist Hal Singer on the Parker–Bostic contest is 'Both of them were great and had a great feeling towards each other. There was a great admiration for each other's drive and technique.'[78] The processes of earning and maintaining respect within the community of players are frequently mentioned in jazz writing and in oral accounts. Ralph Ellison, for example, explains how the criteria of musicianship within the improvising situation overrode the incipient racial exclusivity of the Minton's sessions: 'White musicians like Tony Scott, Remo Palmieri and Al Haig who were part of the development at Minton's became so by passing a test of musicianship, sincerity and temperament.'[79]

Malone's third term 'hard work' also enters into the value system that leads to the evaluation of musicians and the earning of respect. In North Indian music the practice habits, or *riaz*, of an improviser are prominent among the professional virtues: 'In the public media, for example, accounts of famous musicians will characteristically include descriptions of their extensive *riaz* habits.'[80] Jazz culture has not usually foregrounded practice in this way, but there are well-known accounts, for example, of Charlie Parker's period of dedicated work following his failures in Kansas City:

> Charlie's summer schedule was a full one. He worked the dance jobs with George Lee by night, snatched a few hours sleep and arose early to study harmony with Powell and Ware. Additional time was devoted to scales, arpeggios and saxophone drills. According to Gene Ramey, the Ozark summer lasted three months; according to Jay McShann, six months.[81]

This 'woodshedding' is the equivalent within jazz culture of the *chilla* in Indian music, a period, usually forty days, of dedicated practice. Part of the respect, bordering on reverence, in which the saxophonist John

Coltrane is held is related to his reputation as a prodigious student of scales and harmonies and an almost compulsive practiser on his instrument.

Musicians are valued, again in apparent contradiction of the competitiveness of the form, for their contributions to a collective creation. Of the early 1940s Minton's scene, Allen Tinney comments that 'A lot of people contributed. It wasn't just something that you turn the page, and it was there.'[82] Jazz improvisation, the foundation skill of jam-session culture, was an accomplishment of some complexity. Ralph Ellison writes that he 'learned from the jazz musicians I had known as a boy in Oklahoma City something of the discipline and devotion to his art required of the artist'.[83] Ellison's account also lays a much greater stress on the co-operative aspect of the music than on competitiveness: 'The delicate balance struck between strong individual personality and the group during those early jam sessions was a marvel of social organisation.'[84] The difficulty of acquiring and perfecting the required skills was another factor binding a community in a sense of shared endeavour. In the words of the trumpeter Benny Bailey concerning the Los Angeles jazz community: 'There was very little enmity in those days. Everybody was very friendly because everybody was trying to learn the same thing.'[85]

Within the community of jam-session musicians, an individual could achieve the kind of status attributed by a player within another improvisatory culture, that of *klezmer* music, to some of his peers:

> We were not considered to be artists. Among *ourselves*, people like Max Epstein, Dave Tarras ... people like that, were considered to be artists, but among the public, we were just serving a purpose.[86]

The jazz drummer Shelly Manne expressed this in an analogous fashion for jazz players: 'They all know who the "in" guys are, even though they're not accepted as great stars publicly or by the critics.'[87] Ellison's early Oklahoma City exemplars were, in his account, motivated by 'neither money nor fame', but by the desire 'to express an affirmative way of life through its musical tradition'.[88] Each of these explanations attributes to jazz culture, to the community of jam-session improvisers, a degree of autonomy, either in its judgements or its motivations. Jazz culture is perceived as being independent of the market economy, of the star system, of mainstream conceptions of material success. A distinct set of values seems to exist that establishes its own criteria, and awards its own measures of success where it decides that they are merited.

Ellison's examples are from around 1930, Manne's from the mid-1940s. Both of these views provide evidence of the changes that had taken place during that span of time, from a situation where jazz was hardly separable from the rest of the popular musical entertainment world, to a stage where it possessed a developed community sense not only of itself as a unique musical form, but also of its own standards and values. It was during this period, from the late 1920s to the mid-1940s, that jazz in America came closer than at any other time in its history to a self-created identity and definition. Through the long exercise of the form in the independent activity of a critical community of musicians, playing together with as little thought as possible for the pressures of economics, the jam-session culture offered, in Scott DeVeaux's words, 'the spectacle of musicians playing for their own enjoyment, capturing some of the dignity and autonomy of the concert stage without losing the informal atmosphere that tied jazz to a vernacular social context'.[89]

The historical after-effects of this cultural moment are long-lasting: from the 1940s onwards, jazz players have typically followed what they perceive as the enduring jazz values, and in so doing have separated themselves as a category from other types of musical performer. Jazz performance today retains many of the practical procedures of jam-session culture, from the minimal nature of its presentation to its overriding emphasis on solo improvisation. Jazz, in other words, is still deeply marked by the period in which conditions allowed it to generate its own musical-aesthetic values.

As this chapter has already shown, that temporary and qualified independence was itself dependent on a relation with the market economy in the form of the commercial music business. The culture of the jam session was able to develop and maintain a niche for itself during a period of intense economic activity around jazz, and existed in a symbiotic or even parasitic relationship with that activity. To put this more concretely: jam-session culture flourished because jazz had become viable in the commercial sector of the big bands and the economic activity they generated. The jam sessions were therefore exactly contemporary with a development which seemed to be taking jazz off in a completely opposite direction. Just as, on one level, jazz was able to devote itself to building an identity of its own, so on another level, it was pulled into the orbit of the powerful media which would establish a quite different sense of its identity. The next chapter will deal with this almost exactly contemporaneous development.

Notes

1. Kathy J. Ogren, *The Jazz Revolution: Twenties America and the Meaning of Jazz* (New York: OUP, 1989); William Howland Kenney, *Chicago Jazz: A Cultural History 1904–1930* (New York: OUP, 1993); Scott DeVeaux, *The Birth of Bebop: A Social and Musical History* (Berkeley: University of California Press, 1997).

2. Daniel M. Neuman, *The Life of Music in North India* (Chicago: University of Chicago Press, 1990), p. 203.

3. 'Jazz musical culture was created in a series of laborious steps, and did not reach a definitive state (in which musicians were conscious of standards and worked to preserve and advance them) until the late 1930s.' Burton Peretti, in Reginald T. Buckner, Steven Weiland, *Jazz in Mind: Essays on the History and Meanings of Jazz* (Detroit: Wayne State University Press, 1991), p. 100.

4. Stanley Dance, *The World of Count Basie* (London: Sidgwick and Jackson, 1980), p. 20. These comments are by Jimmy Rushing, later the vocalist with the Basie band.

5. Ross Russell, *Jazz Style in Kansas City and the Southwest* (Berkeley: University of California Press, 1971), p. 76.

6. Details of these programmes at the Apollo Theater are taken from material in the Schiffman collection held at the Smithsonian Institution in Washington DC.

7. Ogren, *The Jazz Revolution*, p. 40

8. Kenney, *Chicago Jazz*, p. 50.

9. Andy Kirk, as told to Amy Lee, *Twenty Years on Wheels* (Oxford: Bayou Press, 1989), pp. 43 and 46.

10. Jay McShann, transcript of interview in the Jazz Oral History Project, Institute of Jazz Studies, Rutgers University, pp. 83–4.

11. Mary Lou Williams, transcript of interview in the Jazz Oral History Project, p. 45.

12. The repertoire and scores for Armstrong's band are to be found in the Louis Armstrong Archive, Queens College, Queens, New York.

13. Gerald Early, *Tuxedo Junction: Essays on American Culture* (New York: Ecco Press, 1989), p. 297.

14. Ingrid Monson, 'Doubleness and Jazz Improvisation: Irony, Parody and Ethnomusicology', *Cultural Inquiry*, 20, Winter 1994, p. 312.

15. Monson, 'Doubleness', p. 312.

16. Charles Nanry, *The Jazz Text* (New York: Van Nostrand, 1979), p. 249.

17. Mary Lou Williams, Jazz Oral History Project interview, p. 143.

18. Ted Gioia, *West Coast Jazz: Modern Jazz in California, 1945–1960* (New York: OUP, 1992), pp. 4–5.

19. Jacqui Malone, *Steppin' on the Blues: The Visible Rhythms of African American Dance* (Urbana: University of Illinois Press, 1996).

20. James Lincoln Collier, *Jazz: The American Theme Song* (New York: OUP, 1993), p. 27.

21. Gunther Schuller, *Early Jazz: Its Roots and Musical Development* (New York: OUP, 1968), p. 79.

22. Singleton quoted in Nat Hentoff and Nat Shapiro (eds), *Hear Me Talkin' to Ya* (London: Penguin, 1962), p. 172.

23. Ibid., p. 108.

24. Ibid., p. 172.

25. Schuller, *Early Jazz*, p. 91.

26. Rex Stewart, *Jazz Masters of the Thirties* (London: Macmillan, 1972), p. 42.

27. Teddy Wilson, transcript of Jazz Oral History Project interview, Reel 1, p. 31.
28. Stewart, *Jazz Masters*, p. 47.
29. Schuller, *Early Jazz*, p. 89.
30. Price quoted in Max Jones, John Chilton, *The Louis Armstrong Story 1900–1971* (London: Studio Vista, 1971), p. 99.
31. Collier, *Jazz*, p. 36.
32. Ibid., p. 42.
33. Ibid., p. 47.
34. Scott quoted in Hentoff and Shapiro, *Hear Me Talking' to Ya*, p. 371.
35. Mezzrow quoted in Ibid., p. 131.
36. For further discussion of cultural antinomies, see Chapter 6.
37. *Metronome*, July 1941, p. 10.
38. Quoted in Ira Gitler, *Swing to Bop: An Oral History of the Transition in Jazz in the 1940s* (New York: OUP, 1985), p. 163.
39. Williams quoted in Hentoff and Shapiro, *Hear Me Talkin' to Ya*, p. 281. For the Kansas City scene in general, see Ross Russell, *Jazz Style in Kansas City*.
40. *The New Grove Dictionary of Jazz*, (New York: St Martin's Press, rev. edn, 1994), p. 577.
41. Armstrong quoted in Hentoff and Shapiro, *Hear Me Talkin' to Ya*, p. 161.
42. Teddy Wilson, Jazz Oral History Project interview, Reel 1, pp. 30 and 34.
43. Russell, *Jazz Style in Kansas City*, p. 20.
44. Ibid., p. 20.
45. Mary Lou Williams, Jazz Oral History Project interview, p. 89.
46. Bud Freeman, *Crazeology: The Autobiography of a Chicago Jazzman* (Oxford: Bayou Press, 1989), p. 33.
47. Roach quoted in Gitler, *Swing to Bop*, p. 77.
48. Russell, *Jazz Style in Kansas City*, p. 135.
49. Scott quoted in Hentoff and Shapiro, *Hear me Talkin' to Ya*, p. 173.
50. Russell, *Jazz Style in Kansas City*, p. 20.
51. Ibid., p. 27.
52. Ibid., pp. 17–18
53. Ralph Ellison, *Shadow and Act* (London: Secker and Warburg, 1967), p. 205. For the Minton's scene see, as well as Ellison's essay 'The Golden Age, Time Past' from which this quotation is taken, Chapter 3 , 'Minton's and Monroe's', in Gitler, *Swing to Bop*, pp. 75–117.
54. McRae quoted in Hentoff and Shapiro, *Hear Me Talkin' to Ya*, p. 325.
55. Ellison, *Shadow and Act*, p. 209.
56. Newman quoted in Gitler, *Swing to Bop*, p. 82.
57. Neuman, *The Life of Music in North India*, p. 69.
58. Ibid., p. 69.
59. Criss quoted in Gitler, *Swing to Bop*, p. 169.
60. Mike Hennessey, *Jazz Journal*, April 1985, p. 2.
61. Lewis Porter, *John Coltrane: His Life and Music* (Ann Arbor: University of Michigan Press, 1998), p. 311fn.
62. Gitler, *Swing to Bop*, p. 267.
63. Neuman, *The Life of Music in North India*, p. 75.
64. Jacqui Malone, *Steppin' on the Blues*, p. 3.
65. Ibid., p. 5.

66. Russell, *Jazz Style in Kansas City*, p. 79.

67. Buster Smith quoted in Russell, *Jazz Style in Kansas City*, p. 80.

68. Stewart, *Jazz Masters*, p. 11.

69. Teddy Wilson, transcript of Jazz Oral History Project interview, Reel 2, p. 21.

70. Gioia, *West Coast Jazz*, p. 28.

71. Ibid., pp. 41 and 44.

72. Tinney quoted in Gitler, *Swing to Bop*, p. 75.

73. Danica L. Stein, 'Clora Bryant: Gender Issues in the Career of a West Coast Jazz Musician', in Jacqueline DjeDje, Eddie S. Meadows (eds), *California Soul: Music of African Americans in the West* (Berkeley: University of California Press, 1998).

74. DeVeaux, *The Birth of Bebop*, p. 203.

75. See in particular the very intense version of the jam session ordeal presented in John Clellon Holmes's *The Horn*, as discussed in Chapter 4, below.

76. Neuman, *The Life of Music in North India*, p. 75.

77. Gitler, *Swing to Bop*, p. 75.

78. Ibid., p. 76.

79. Ellison, *Shadow and Act*, p. 212.

80. Neuman, *The Life of Music in North India*, p. 42.

81. Russell, *Jazz Style in Kansas City*, p. 183.

82. Tinney quoted in Gitler, *Swing to Bop*, p. 81.

83. Ellison, *Shadow and Act*, p. 189.

84. Ibid., p. 189.

85. Bailey quoted in Gitler, *Swing to Bop*, p. 163.

86. Klezmer musician Peter Sokolow, speaking in a programme in the BBC documentary series *Rhythms of the World*, 1992.

87. Manne quoted in Gitler, *Swing to Bop*, p. 100.

88. Ellison, *Shadow and Act*, p. 189.

89. DeVeaux, *The Birth of Bebop*, p. 202.

Plate 1 Louis Armstrong, whose outstanding performances and recordings in the mid-1920s raised the stakes for jazz improvisation (see Chap. 2).

At The 125th STREET

APOLLO

AMERICA'S SMARTEST COLORED SHOWS!

THEATRE
125th Street
Near 8th Av.

Telephone
Un. 4-4490

ONE WEEK ONLY — Beg. FRIDAY, OCT. 29th

FLETCHER | With The Greatest! |

HENDERSON

and his **GREAT ORCHESTRA**
with **CHUCK RICHARDS**
in a
Clarence Robinson
Revue Hit
with a Great Revue Cast:

**3 LANG SISTERS
ALICE HARRIS
RED & CURLEY
SHAW & MEAD
JOHN MASON
GEORGE WILLIAMS
JOHN VIGAL
VIVIAN HARRIS**

16 — LOVELY ROBINSON GIRLS — 16

also "THE MAN WHO CRIED WOLF"
Mystery Drama

| MIDNIGHT SHOW SATURDAY | AMATEUR NIGHT WEDNESDAY |

Week Only Beginning FRI., NOV. 5th | **COUNT BASIE** and his ORCHESTRA

BUTTERBEANS and SUSIE

Plate 2 Jazz still embedded in the world of professional entertainment: the Fletcher Henderson band featuring in a variety show at the Apollo in Harlem in the 1930s.

Plate 3 The two top competitors in the Los Angeles jam sessions, Wardell Gray (left) and Dexter Gordon, here advertising a recording that excited, among others, Kerouac's Dean Moriarty.

Plate 4 The typical composition of the classic 'big band', shown here in a photograph of the Count Basie band in the studio in 1940 (see Chap. 3).

Plate 5 Charlie Parker, most frequent model for the narrative of the tragic, 'self-destructive' jazz life (see Chap. 4).

Plate 6 A study of Billie Holiday, one of the visual images credited with representing 'the essence of jazz' (see Chap. 6).

CHAPTER 3

Rhythm is our Business:
The Swing Era 1935–45

People were dancing to that kind of music in those days so there were just hundreds and hundreds of those bands ... People were dancing.

Teddy Wilson

The music was getting better again. When I was young during the depression, it wasn't so hot ...

F. Scott Fitzgerald[1]

When we turn from the culture of the jam session to the period in the history of American jazz and popular music which has come to be known as the 'Swing Era', we are immediately in a different ethnomusicological world. The two phenomena are historically simultaneous, and we have already seen that for many musicians in the jam-session culture, employment in one of the big swing bands was the economic platform on which their informal playing stood. Nevertheless, the experience of big band playing was in many ways the polar opposite of that of the jam session participant. Instead of unrestrained improvisation there was playing from written music in disciplined orchestral teams; informality was replaced by formal organization; the ascendancy of the individual soloist was lost in the large ensemble; the primary racial identity of the music became white rather than black; and there was a shift from independence towards being part of a set of interlocking commercial enterprises.

The kind of autonomy enjoyed by jazz and its players in the vernacular settings of after-hours clubs and bars was not a possibility when the music was offered up as a commercial proposition in the emerging mass media of the 1930s. The Swing Era caused, even by its name, a fresh outbreak of confusion over what 'jazz' meant. Historians of jazz in the 1920s, such as Kathy Ogren and William Howard Kenney, have shown how broad a field the term 'jazz' covered at that time: in

Ogren's words, 'For many Americans the term "jazz" referred to all popular music.'[2] In the mid-1930s, just as, in jam-session culture, jazz was assuming a specific identity, popular music was introducing a new term 'swing', which was (and is) sometimes seen as a historical successor to jazz, sometimes as the antithesis of it. The word 'jazz' suffered a slight temporary suppression. 'Jazz' was seen by a part of the public as that older music which the more modern 'swing' had supplanted; for others, jazz remained a stylistic trace that one might hear *in* swing from time to time; or, a fundamentalist variant, jazz was the true music which would survive the age of swing.

The 'Swing Era' is understood to have begun suddenly in August 1935, when the Benny Goodman orchestra, at the end of a disastrous cross-country tour, scored a huge success at the Palomar Ballroom in Los Angeles, and was carried back to New York and to national fame on the strength of the wave. Goodman himself became 'The King of Swing', and continued to enjoy a level of fame and material reward that had been open previously only to movie stars. By 1939, Goodman's commercial success was surpassed by that of another white bandleader, Artie Shaw, and Shaw in turn was soon outdone by the most successful white bandleader of them all, Glenn Miller. All of these men, and a large group of lesser names, enjoyed huge success within and beyond the USA, with large followings of fans, high incomes from performances, recordings, broadcasts and film appearances, and broad acceptance across all social classes.

The fortunes of these market leaders, moreover, were repeated lower down the scale. Swing became a pop phenomenon that generated a living for thousands of musicians across the United States, creating a demand for live performance that could be supplied by local orchestras and performers. Swing found its way everywhere, in the manner of later popular music crazes. It has a claim to be the first of the youth-culture upheavals of the twentieth century. It was a music that found its audience primarily among the urban American young, and it was also a mass phenomenon, able to be supplied quickly to large numbers of consumers through the mechanisms of the new mass media.

Swing was almost entirely identified with the 'big band', an organization of twelve to eighteen musicians, consisting of a rhythm section and separate sections of three or four trumpets, saxophones and trombones. A few orchestras were co-operatives in which decision-making and profits were shared, but generally bands were run by and named for a leader, who might be a composer-arranger (like Duke Ellington), an outstanding soloist (like Goodman or Shaw), a figurehead (Bob Crosby) or a general organizer (Jimmy Lunceford). The leaders of many of the big bands were stars, with a very high level of personal recognition among the general public. Bands, by their very structure, required a great deal of rehearsal, co-ordination and logistical work. Musical arrangements had to be written by members of the band or bought from professional arrangers, although some bands, such as Count Basie's in its early days, were capable of improvising full-band routines ('head arrangements'). Musicians, except for the small number of specialist improvising soloists, had to be able to read music well and to keep good musical discipline within the band.

A form of jazz had been played orchestrally for twenty years before this sudden explosion of popularity in the mid-1930s. The San Francisco bandleader Art Hickman is credited with being the first to organize jazz orchestrally, and by the mid-1920s the Paul Whiteman orchestra was sufficiently famous for its leader to be referred to as 'The King of Jazz'. By the late 1920s there were many large groups playing an arranged form of the music, among them black orchestras like those of Duke Ellington, Luis Russell and Fletcher Henderson, which would have an important influence on Swing Era styles. From the point of view of black bands, the Swing Era was less of an abrupt change than it was for men like Goodman, Shaw and Miller, who had previously made a living as professionals playing in small bands and for recording sessions. Black bands shared to some degree in the surge of popularity, but many of them simply continued producing the same kind of music that they had been creating before the craze happened. Black bands like those of Chick Webb and Andy Kirk had been in existence for some years before the 1935 boom. One exception to this continuity was Fletcher Henderson, whose orchestra survived from 1924 up to 1939, by which time Henderson's own scores were being played with much greater acclaim by Benny Goodman's band.

Another kind of large popular-music ensemble had already flourished for some time: the dance orchestras such as those of Rudy Vallee, Vincent Lopez and Guy Lombardo, which during the swing period became stigmatized as 'sweet' bands. 'Sweet' became half of a dichotomy with 'hot' or 'swing' bands, and this distinction was frequently debated in the swing media. Orchestras like these claimed little or no connection with jazz or 'hot' music. They did not usually feature improvisation and did not try to generate much rhythmic effect. Their arrangements were often designed as showcases for popular singers ('crooners') like Vallee or Bing Crosby, and their instrumentation could include units alien to jazz such as string sections.

The constant opposition of 'swing' to 'sweet' makes it clear that what a young mass audience found in swing music were some of the qualities associated with jazz, particularly the dynamism of its rhythm. The arrival of swing in 1935 is in some ways comparable with that of rock and roll in the mid-1950s, where a large and predominantly young white audience made a sudden discovery of a rhythmic popular music style, of black origin, that contrasted starkly with the prevailing styles of the day. There were similar public displays of unruly behaviour: the Swing Era equivalent of the riots at Alan Freed's rock and roll concerts at the Cleveland Arena in 1952 were the riots at the Shrine Auditorium in Los Angeles in 1940, or the scenes described by John Hammond on the Goodman orchestra's engagement as guest band at the Savoy Ballroom in early 1937:

> There was an incredible sight on Lenox Avenue and 140th Street, Tuesday, May 11. Mounted police, the fire department, deputy in-spectors and a score of ordinary cops were required to keep in check a mob of ten thousand souls who were fighting to get into the Savoy ballroom to hear the battle of the century between Benny Goodman and Chick Webb's orchestras. About four thousand people managed to jam their way into the Savoy, where four or five cops were stationed on the Goodman bandstand to maintain law and order.[3]

As with rock and roll twenty years later, there was extensive investigation of the psychology and the cultural significance of the young fans, who were given the name 'jitterbugs', a term which could be neutral or unfavourable, or 'ickies', a term with a definitely negative connotation, and usually applied to the obsessive or fanatical swing enthusiast. Again as with rock and roll, swing fans provoked the law into action to deal with threats to public order: for example, *Metronome* magazine carried a report in January 1939 of a 'Jitterbug Ban in Iowa', organized by a ballroom operators consortium based in Des Moines. *Metronome* commented that the move was 'working out successfully.'[4]

Swing fandom generated its own publications: the humorist S. J. Perelman, in one of his classic *New Yorker* articles, satirized a swing-based romantic fiction magazine:

The Jitterbug is a febrile paper published bimonthly by Lex Publishers, Inc., of 381 Fourth Avenue, devoted to the activities of alligators, hepcats and *exaltés* of swing everywhere. These activities, which consist of hurling one another violently about to popular music, riding astride one another, and generally casting out devils, are portrayed in ten or fifteen pages of photographs and cartoons that need no explanation.[5]

Fans sent fan mail: Chick Webb's band, with a regular radio programme on NBC, was reported in 1937 as receiving five thousand fan letters a week. Swing fans also engaged in correspondence with magazines on matters such as the relative merits of various bands. A *Metronome* reader, Abe Fliaschnik, of Buffalo, NY, wrote in March 1939 of a recent experience of hearing the Erskine Hawkins band: '"Jack" those cats are tops. They made me blow my topper. Judging from the record crowd and the response – everybody's wig was on end.'[6]

Swing music was able to reach a wider audience than previous forms of popular music because its rise to prominence coincided with the consolidation across America of the commercial and technical infrastructure necessary to support it. It emerged in full force in the mid-1930s at a time when a small group of radio networks for the first time covered the entire country, when the recording industry was mature and looking for new product, when there were large numbers of established venues for live performance, including theatres, ballrooms and hotels, and when a small group of booking agencies had emerged to control access to these various media. The agencies were able to locate the swing bands within this complex of opportunities.

Scott DeVeaux has written that 'The Swing Era was above all a *system* of economic interdependence in which individual musicians played clearly defined roles.'[7] The role of a successful musician, for example the white bandleader Jimmy Dorsey, included the opportunity to be seen and heard in films and on radio, to be guided by a major promotional agency, to undertake tours of one-night stands or longer 'location' jobs across the country, and to be accessible to the media. The Dorsey band's activities were reported in the magazines: breaking all records in the history of the Strand theatre (June 1942), going on a Midwestern tour in December 1941, and being featured in *Down Beat* in August 1939. The feature included profiles of individual band members in which they talk about themselves and their 'pet peeves'

(Joe Lippman: 'Single, he likes baseball and detests schmaltz music').[8]
Dorsey, with his brother Tommy, was the subject of a movie biography. He also featured in advertisements endorsing Conn saxophones,
and contributed an article on the issue of the moment to *Bandstand*
magazine: 'Jimmy D. Takes a Crack at Defining Swing Music Styles'.[9]

Dorsey's affairs were handled during this time by one of the largest
booking agencies, Rockwell-O'Keefe, which also handled Glenn Miller,
Artie Shaw and Woody Herman. The MCA agency managed Tommy
Dorsey, and the William Morris agency had among its clients Duke
Ellington and Count Basie. As David Stowe comments, 'Swing as a
national fad of the late 1930s would have been impossible without the
agencies.'[10] Some of the penalties of trying to do without agency man-
agement are illustrated in the trumpeter Rex Stewart's account of the
organizational burden that fell upon Fletcher Henderson. Henderson,
with his wife's help, continued to try and set up his own band's touring
schedule: 'For Fletcher and his wife, Leora, these trips were a lot of
hard work ... the Hendersons wrote many letters, sent loads of tele-
grams, and telephoned all over the eastern seaboard to coordinate the
trips and consolidate the bookings.'[11] For Henderson, all of this came in
addition to organizing the band's music, playing the piano and writing
most of the arrangements.

By contrast, Duke Ellington's dates on tours, managed first by Mills
Artists and later by the Morris agency, were properly scheduled and the
ground was prepared by advertising material sent to representatives
situated in the various towns and cities. The advertising material on
Ellington gives a good idea of the ways in which Ellington and his band
were 'positioned' by his agents. The promotional notes sent to representatives included 'punch lines' such as 'America's Genius of Modern
Music' and 'Direct from Carnegie Hall', as well as the clear, if imperious,
instruction to refer to the performance strictly as a 'Duke Ellington
Concert': '*Do not call it a Jazz Concert*'.[12]

The most important of the components of the Swing Era 'system'
was radio. The rise of swing occurred less than ten years after the first
coast-to-coast broadcast, but by 1935 there was already an extensive
network of stations, many once independent, but now owned by one of
the large broadcasting companies CBS or NBC. The first dance
orchestra to be heard on a live 'pickup' was that of Vincent Lopez,
from Newark in 1921, and by 1924 the Fletcher Henderson band had
established a regular radio engagement from the Club Alabam in

Harlem. A white Kansas City orchestra, the Coon-Sanders Night-hawks, built up a reputation far beyond the Midwest through regular live pickups from the Muehlebach Hotel: 'Dial twisters the country over were tuning to station WDAF for the rollicking rhythms and good fellowship projected by the Coon-Sanders organisation.'[13]

Radio was also important to the Ellington band, networked from the Cotton Club in New York, and to the Count Basie band, which owed its breakthrough to being heard by the impresario John Hammond on his car radio in a live transmission on station W9XBY. The most celebrated break due to radio is that of the Benny Goodman band, whose sudden success in Los Angeles in 1935 was attributed to the scheduling of their programme 'Let's Dance' at an hour which for West Coast listeners was mid-evening prime time. Jazz and dance music publications were full of references to radio. *Metronome*, for instance, carried regular pages of radio reviews alongside record and live performance reviews. Magazines carried listings of the current radio-station locations of popular bands: the May 1942 *Metronome* told its readers that the Paul Whiteman orchestra was featured on KPAS, Pasadena, while the Jack Teagarden orchestra could be heard on KHJ from Culver City.

Radio features for bands were of two kinds, one more desirable than the other. 'Sustaining' programmes were broadcast live from a club or dance-hall which had a permanent link with a radio station. These provided the largest amount of airtime for bands, but were financially beneficial mostly to the radio stations, which often did not bear the cost of the link to the location. For bands, these broadcasts were important for the publicity they gave, which the band would hope to cash in later in the form of bookings for tours and one-nighters. More attractive to the musicians were the regular sponsored radio programmes, for which the bands were usually well paid. These engagements were usually reserved for established performers, and were sponsored by major businesses such as Nabisco, Coca-Cola and a number of tobacco companies: Camel, for instance, sponsored a Benny Goodman programme, Tommy Dorsey was sponsored by Raleigh and Glenn Miller by Chesterfield. The products linked with these popular bands were slanted towards the youth market that had a ready-made association with the music.

Recording, though an important aspect of the Swing Era system, was not as central as radio, and for most bands accounted for a smaller proportion of their income than was the case in popular music twenty years later. The typical Swing Era band made more money out of live performances than from record sales, though there were instances of hit recordings that made a big difference to the careers of some performers. The sudden success of Artie Shaw's 'Begin the Beguine' created a major upward step in his popularity, and the same could be said of the Tommy Dorsey band's 1937 recording 'Marie'. Gunther Schuller writes of being on tour in 1943 'and hearing Shaw's "Stardust" on every jukebox in every restaurant'.[14] The Andy Kirk band's unexpected commercial success with the ballad 'Until the Real Thing Comes Along' enabled them to break out of the stereotyping that restricted the repertoire of black bands and to begin to reach a wider 'crossover' audience.

Recordings became financially more significant as the Swing boom went on. A major contribution to this came from the growing popularity of jukeboxes, which from the late 1930s onwards gave a long-awaited stimulus to record sales. The recording industry had suffered severely from the Depression, but in the longer term, even from the mid-1920s, had lost a lot of ground to competition from radio. The Swing phenomenon as a whole was associated with a rise in record sales: *Down Beat* reported at the beginning of 1937 that

> during 1936 the American public played more records than during any similar period since the last really big year the industry enjoyed– 1928. In fact, one of the companies claimed to have more than tripled its total sales of the preceding year.[15]

Records of swing music are estimated to have accounted for about 25 per cent of all sales during the period of its greatest popularity.[16]

Radio and recordings made a band's name known, but the payoff from these activities for most bands came in the live engagements that they could secure across the country. Name bands were booked into 'location' jobs in hotels and ballrooms, involving a stay of weeks or months in a single venue. This kind of job had obvious advantages for the musicians, and often carried the benefit of a 'sustaining' radio network link. From a venue like the Hotel Pennsylvania in New York City, for instance, the bands of Goodman, Shaw and Miller broadcast live to a coast-to-coast audience of millions of radio listeners. Location jobs, however, were not in themselves financially attractive: bands sometimes lost money in extended engagements that were undertaken for the sake of the radio exposure. More profit was made in shorter-term, especially one-night, engagements which were consolidated into touring schedules.

Some of the tour itineraries followed by bands during the Swing Era were very arduous. This was especially true for the lower ranks of the swing hierarchy, whose journeys were longer-lasting, less comfortable and less well rewarded. The Kansas City bandleader Jay McShann, for instance, reports playing ninety consecutive one-nighters.[17] Black orchestras in particular, lacking proper opportunities in other areas of the business, tended to be dependent on touring engagements and the hard travelling that went with them. The Jimmy Lunceford band was notorious for the severity of a travelling schedule that brought its members to the point of mutiny on several occasions. Andy Kirk's autobiography is entitled, poignantly, *Twenty Years on Wheels*.[18]

In June 1941 the American Federation of Musicians imposed a limit of 400 miles on moves between engagements, but even given this, life on the road could be uncomfortable and unhealthy. The routine might include four or five hours performance each night, a long bus journey of up to 400 miles (or up to 700 in the earlier years), little chance to eat or sleep properly, and then the next performance, the next busride and so on. This relentless process might be continued for weeks or even months without a break. For black bands travelling in the southern states there were further indignities: the guitarist Danny Barker devotes several pages of his autobiography to the problems arising from not being allowed to make toilet stops in southern towns.[19]

The more successful black bandleaders such as Duke Ellington and Cab Calloway were able to provide means of transportation that insulated their musicians from some of the problems of the road, hiring private Pullman cars that carried the bands and their equipment from gig to gig in comfort and security. Many of the lesser names remained in the category of 'territory bands', with a reputation and a touring schedule restricted to a few states, most often in the Midwest. Bands such as those of Alphonso Trent, based around Texas, and the T. Holder band before Andy Kirk took it over, are typical examples of the many territory bands that existed throughout the period.

A 'name' band like Duke Ellington's had, by contrast, a nationwide geographical reach. In 1942 alone, Ellington's itinerary included every major American city except those in the South. The Ellington band's travelling schedule in that year passed through Chicago five times, Los Angeles four times, St Louis three times, Kansas City four times, and each of the other large cities more than once, among a long list of performances in smaller towns, including Madison, Waukegan,

Steubenville, Moline, Ocean Park, Stockton, Tacoma, Salem, Long Beach, Dayton, Topeka, Columbus, Bridgeport, Toledo and many others. Ellington's schedule for the year included not only 25,000 miles of travelling between short-stay engagements but also film work, recording sessions, publicity appearances, benefit concerts and the constant pressure of composing new material for his band.

The places in which band engagements were played varied greatly from city to city, from college auditoriums to armories to ballrooms, theatres and (in the South) tobacco warehouses. Two types of venue especially typified the tone and ethos of Swing Era performance, and represented an important shift in the public presentation of jazz-based music: the movie theatre and the large ballroom. In theatre gigs like those at the Paramount in New York City, bands were required to play many performances per day, sometimes beginning early in the morning in order to bring in an audience of school-age fans. In this kind of location, the music was provided as a part of an entertainment package which included a full-length movie, though the demeanour of the fans often made it apparent that the bands were the real attraction. Nevertheless, the featured movie could add to or detract from the drawing power of the bands. A March 1939 report on an occasion when the Shaw and Goodman bands were in competition in neighbouring theatres in Newark takes the movie factor into account: 'Neither side benefited greatly from the pictures, both theatres stringing along with Class B films.'[20]

It was in the theatres that some of the wildest fan behaviour was seen. One of Lewis Erenberg's first-hand informants refers to impromptu dancing in the theatre aisles and a high state of excitement leading to police being called to a Glenn Miller concert in St Louis. Similar scenes are reported in towns like Des Moines and Fort Wayne, Indiana, where a Duke Ellington performance at the Palace Theatre caused 'pandemonium, dancing in the aisles, in the orchestra pit ... we all went nuts'.[21]

Ballrooms were the other characteristic type of venue in the Swing period. Most towns of any size in the USA had ballrooms which were an important focus for local entertainment. The ballrooms that were constructed during the period or shortly before it were frequently large and aesthetically striking. Some of them were among the most celebrated locations in the entire music business. The Savoy Ballroom on Lenox Avenue in Harlem, for example, was famous for its discerning and independently creative audience, which had innovated a string of new dance styles on the Savoy's dance-floor. The Savoy served as a proving ground for new bands or those newly arrived in New York City. The Savoy ballroom itself was the largest of those in New York: it had room for two bandstands and a huge dance-floor that could accommodate 4,000 dancers at a time.

Writers like Richard Stowe and Lewis Erenberg have considered the architectural design of venues like the Savoy to be in itself a significant statement of the ethos of the new musical era of Swing. There was evidently a shift from the smaller venue described by William Kenney as typical of the setting of 1920s jazz, where intimate 'night-time worlds of exotic excitement' were offered to its public.[22] These newer locations, both the theatre and the ballroom, were, by contrast, large and highly populated. Their structures were large and open, and access to them was broadly available and cheap. The ballrooms, in particular, resembled the vast, opulent movie-houses of the same period.

As Lewis Erenberg puts it, these new settings emphasized 'inclusiveness over exclusivity'.[23] The way in which the experience of Swing fitted into its supporters' lives took on a new character: the patron of one of the large theatres or ballrooms was not going there in search of some semi-covert subcultural thrill, but more and more, as the period progressed, as an ordinary member of the American public looking for an accessible and inexpensive good time. Many writers emphasize this democratizing tendency:

> Even the architecture and décor of Swing establishments reflected a difference in the culture of Swing, one that rendered it more inclusive, democratic and culturally acceptable. Whereas the emphasis of the cabarets and nightclubs had been on intimacy and 'atmosphere', the ballroom of the swing era reflected size, grace and elegance.[24]

The critic and lyricist Gene Lees has written with eloquent nostalgia of another of these arenas for the mass consumption of dance music, the 'chain of dance pavilions and ballrooms that had grown up along the urban and interurban railways'.[25] These too were settings that offered openness and accessibility to a wide audience. Swing performance presented itself as a part of the continuum of public entertainments for Americans, costing about as much as a movie ticket (and often including a movie in the price). There was nothing about its presentation that suggested marginality, subculturalism or cultural subversiveness. Experienced in a large theatre or in a huge, grandly decorated ballroom, the music seemed to be simply one among the repertoire of experiences offered by the entertainment industry.

The music itself was assimilated into a straightforward American-ness. At the same time, any distinct ethnic identity also began to be effaced. If swing could be performed by either black or white orches-tras, and if a Duke Ellington concert could be consumed on the same bill as a Lana Turner movie, any residual ethnic distinctions that placed the Ellington concert in a separate cultural and expressive category ceased to carry much weight. A process of acculturation was going on which brought the qualities of jazz and African-American music into acceptance within popular music style.

Swing and the Black Musician

The Swing Era is often seen as a positive and progressive phase in American culture, and the greater visibility and acceptance of black musical forms is sometimes seen as part of this. Jazz, to the extent to which its influence was acknowledged in swing music, lost some of its stigmatized status. The presence in the mainstream of a form that had much to do with African-American culture tended to raise the com-mercial profile of black performers. As Scott DeVeaux puts it, 'If black musicians remained on the periphery of economic power during the Swing Era, they were nevertheless closer to the center than ever before.'[26]

As DeVeaux implies, the inclusion of black musicians among the material beneficiaries of the Swing Era was a relative matter. The interest of a large section of the American public, most especially the young, had been excited by a form of popular music that was closely linked with jazz, and black bands were able to demonstrate the ability to produce it at least as effectively as white bands. Duke Ellington, Cab Calloway, Count Basie and a few others led bands that had a place in the upper echelons of the business, even if none of these was as popular as the white bands of Miller, Goodman, Shaw, the Dorsey brothers and a number of others.

The performances of black (or 'colored' or 'sepia') bands were always liable to be criticized for limitations of musicianship, especially intonation: a review of a 1941 Cab Calloway band broadcast from the Hotel Sherman in Chicago comments 'seldom does any band relax as much as this on the air; equally as seldom does any colored band sound so crisp and clean and make so few mistakes'. A 1942 report on the

Lionel Hampton band comments that it 'plays more in tune than any other colored crew, except the Duke's of course and the Count's'.[27]

In the popularity polls that were regularly organized by the magazines, black performers rarely did as well as one might think from the perspective of later jazz history, which has had another sixty years to apply its own values to the products of Swing. It is a surprise to find, for instance, Art Tatum and Lester Young ranked twenty-ninth and thirty-first, on piano and tenor sax respectively, in the *Down Beat* poll for 1941. In the same listings, only nine of the top thirty-four, and four of the top twenty, swing bands were black. Only three black players were ranked top on their instruments in the *Metronome* poll for the same year, but this is a little better than the *Metronome* 'All Stars' selection for 1939, in which, out of sixteen instrumental and vocal categories, only one was headed by a black performer, Ella Fitzgerald being named best female vocalist.

African-American bands and individual players had to contend with a disadvantageous position inside and outside the music business. Many venues had long been segregated, either by local ordinance in the South or *de facto* in the rest of the country. Music and entertainment were areas in which African-Americans had already achieved some recognition nationally, as in the cases of the dancer Bill 'Bojangles' Robinson and Louis Armstrong. Nevertheless, the markets for black musicians tended to be confined to a black audience, because of the nature of the venues available and because of marketing policies, for example in record companies, which limited the target audience for black recordings exclusively to a black public.

This demarcation in jazz recording was not as strict as in blues and folk music, where 'race' records were produced and marketed specifically for black consumption, but, as already noted, there was a tendency on the part of record producers to stereotype both the abilities of the musicians and the tastes of their audiences. This sort of pressure is reflected in Rex Stewart's comments on his experiences of making records with Fletcher Henderson:

> Although the Henderson band played a variety of music on the tours, the record executives categorised Smack's band as a stomp band. They didn't accept the fact that a Negro band could play sweet, though, as a matter of fact, we used to get tremendous applause at Roseland and other places for playing waltzes beautifully.[28]

The experience of the Andy Kirk band with its recording of a 'sweet' ballad 'Until the Real Thing comes Along' has already been noted. Kirk observed 'We jumped from 10000 sales to 100,000. *Real Thing* was to widen our territory, open up new areas for jobs and help us to reach people of all levels.'[29] Kirk's memoirs relate the difficulty of persuading the record company to let the band make the record at all: 'We played our special ballad. He said that it was OK, but I could see it didn't really strike him. He had the race thing on his mind.'[30]

The most popular among the black bands were those of Duke Ellington and Count Basie, but even these experienced shortfalls of the kinds of opportunities that would have been routine to white performers of the same standing. *Metronome* magazine's review of 1938 relates Ellington's ongoing problems in securing adequate public exposure:

> ELLINGTON, leading the greatest dance orchestra of all time playing the best it has ever played, received almost no public acclaim whatever because he was seldom presented in the right places and received practically no air buildup whatsoever. This is the most glaring example in dancebanddom of credit NOT going where it is due.[31]

Four years on, in December 1942, in a review of a broadcast Ellington performance for servicemen at Fort Dix, New Jersey, it is apparent that the problem of radio exposure has continued to frustrate Ellington and his fans: 'For a long time, listeners in the east have been looking forward to this program. It was to be Duke's first commercial air appearance in years, his first broadcast over eastern radio in months. The expectancy was enormous.'[32] For a reader accustomed to Ellington's present standing in jazz history, it comes as a surprise to find him unable to secure regular radio programming at a time which represents the peak of his creative output.

Lack of commercially sponsored radio engagements was, together with lack of opportunities for hotel locations, the major area of grievance for black swing bands. According to Elliott Grennard, writing in 1941,

> It is in the radio field ... that Negro bands take their biggest single licking. White bands get upwards of 35 per cent of their total earnings from this source. Yet it is practically impossible for Negroes to break into big money radio.[33]

For a black band to receive the endorsement of a sponsored radio booking was clearly still news in 1942, when *Down Beat* headlined 'Teddy Wilson Lands Radio Commercial'. The report reflects on the effect that the lack of such breaks had had on Wilson's prospects:

> Teddy Wilson popped out of obscurity two weeks ago when he and his band took over musical duties on the Sanka 'Duffy's Tavern' program, heard over a nation-wide CBS network. Wilson thus becomes one of the very few colored artists to land a radio commercial . . . Teddy for more than a year now has confined his activities to playing at Cafe Society Downtown, but without airtime or records he more or less dropped out of sight.[34]

Only four years before this, Wilson had achieved national prominence as featured pianist in Benny Goodman's small group, his participation as a black musician in a well-known white band attracting a lot of attention as a significant breach of racial barriers. In 1939, in the manner of many sidemen from the 'name' bands, Wilson had tried to launch his own big band. He experienced a lack of co-operation from the booking agents which caused his initial investment, money he had saved from his employment with Goodman, to ebb away. Speaking about the event forty years later, he described his situation:

> I had to finance the band myself, you know, get the uniforms and the PA set to carry around on the road with us, and buying arrangements and the stands, and all the equipment you need to run a big band. I could have borrowed money at exorbitant interest in the band, like at 40% interest, but I had saved up money from Goodman to do it myself. But the money began to run out, and without the cooperation of MCA, the booking office, to book us in decent jobs and keep it going, the band began falling apart.[35]

The lack of cooperation that Wilson complains of here is not necessarily a result of simple racism. Wilson himself attributes it largely to the producer John Hammond's dislike of big bands and adherence to the idea of the 'authentic' black jazz of the small group. But it is striking that even when the black bandleader was Teddy Wilson, with a track record in one of the top contemporary bands, he was not in a position to call the shots. It is noticeable, too, that some white ex-Goodman employees, launching their own bands at the same time (Gene Krupa and Harry James), had much greater success.

Another black band, Andy Kirk and his Twelve Clouds of Joy, also managed to bump along just below the point of economic comfort throughout the period. The Clouds of Joy had been in existence long before the swing boom started, having made its first recordings in 1929. The Kirk band was original and versatile, and had within it the writer, arranger and pianist Mary Lou Williams, one of the most remarkable individuals in popular music. Despite this, the Kirk band was never able to secure the opportunities to free itself from a constant round of travel and one-nighters. An article by Danny Baxter published in early 1939 predicts that with the addition of Floyd Smith, the first electric guitarist in jazz, the Kirk band 'are slated to be the 1940 sensation among colored bands', but then reminds the reader that 'They said the same thing in 1937, and 1936.' Commenting on the band's sequence of successful recordings, Baxter goes on 'But that's about all that happened. Kirk still had never played a top spot for any length of time; his radio wires had been few and far between.'[36]

In the same month, *Metronome* reviewed the Kirk band's difficulties and their effects on the band's performances: 'KIRK'S men, probably plenty 'beat' from kicking around the country so much, developed a listlessness with which the band had not been cursed previously.' By this time, Kirk himself estimates, the band was travelling a total of 50,000 miles a year between engagements.[37] The band continued to receive favourable notices in the places in which it performed, drawing, for instance, 4,000 dancers to a Monday night dance in St Louis. In March 1942 the band was reviewed by *Down Beat* at an engagement in Chicago:

> This polished sepia ork still proves itself one of the most unique dance bands of the day ... In addition to their already recognized ability to play sweet tunes the equal of any ofay band, the Clouds now have a sharper brass section and an improved Kaycee style beat which is making the band jump.[38]

Notices like these were not enough to unchain the Kirk orchestra from the necessity of permanent travelling between short-stay engagements, and the orchestra continued in this way of life until its disbandment in 1949. Kirk himself, a benign, forbearing man, made a virtue out of a necessity and later expressed himself grateful for the experiences that constant travel had put in his way. There is no doubt, however, that the alternatives, radio and hotel work, would have been preferable at the time. However, it was just these prestigious and commodious jobs that were beyond the reach of almost all black swing bands.

The Swing Era has been seen as a period of positive progress for black musicians. The breaking of the 'color line' by the appointment of Teddy Wilson and Lionel Hampton in the Goodman band was followed by other hirings of black artists in previously all-white ensembles. Billie Holiday and Lips Page performed in the Artie Shaw orchestra, Roy Eldridge was featured trumpet soloist with Shaw and Gene Krupa, and Goodman went on to hire the drummer Sidney Catlett. The experiences of these individuals were mixed: Holiday quit the job with Shaw in some distress, but some of the other connections lasted well, without, however, bringing about a complete racial integration of the big bands.

During the period there was a great deal of debate in the jazz and popular music press about the black contribution to American music, and a renewal of interest in the origins of contemporary musical styles. In this inquiry, the music's roots in African-American culture were, if anything, emphasized. The leftist 'Popular Front' politics of individuals like John Hammond included the desire to achieve recognition and equality of opportunity for African-Americans, especially in Hammond's own sphere, the music business.[39] The swing phenomenon itself produced something of a reaction among a section of the American public who reconstructed the dichotomy between swing (a synthetic, commercial music) and jazz (an 'authentic' music of the people). This dichotomy identified the depth and the authenticity of 'jazz' as issuing from roots deeply embedded in African-American culture. A writer in *Down Beat* in early 1942, for instance, sees signs of a return to musical righteousness in a shift in local taste:

> Negro hot jazz is solidly warming its way into the heart of the musically conservative San Franciscan. The reversal of taste from the saccharine and sniveling ofay orchestra to the jazz of the colored artists has been almost complete.[40]

The position of black musicians within American cultural life was changed by the Swing Era. There were limited material gains, and a pressure for the breakdown of some of the barriers to employment and opportunity. Black musicians shared in the democratic optimism of the early Swing years. There was a growing general recognition of the fundamentally African-American conceptions that were embodied in the popular swing bands. At the same time, the disparity between this contribution and the limited rewards available for black bands caused some uneasiness. It was widely known, for instance, that the Goodman band owed some of its success to the very same arrangements with which the black Fletcher Henderson band had failed some years before (this is true in a literal sense: Bud Freeman, who played with Goodman, commented 'The charts were brown with age').[41]

For some critics and fans this uneasiness led to an increasing, sometimes ideological, espousal of an 'authentic', usually black, jazz in preference to the commercial product called Swing. One outcome of this tendency was the 'revivalist' movement of the early 1940s. This was an attempt to rediscover and so to 'revive' the lost virtues of the true jazz that had been blotted out by the hegemony of Swing. True jazz was identified with the music of the New Orleans ensemble of the 1920s and earlier: a small group of unschooled improvisers playing in a style which was the antithesis of Swing in its rough and spontaneous, if backward-looking, approach. Revivalists set about reconstructing the picture of the jazz ensemble as it was in the days before it succumbed to commercialism. This involved, amongst other things, locating some of the legendary black musicians of the New Orleans past, and relaunching them as performing musicians. Through the efforts and the values of this movement, black musicians benefited indirectly from the disaffection that Swing had produced in some sectors of its white audience.[42]

Swing and Cultural Value

The Swing Era found many of the musical qualities of jazz, and many of its practitioners, locked in, to use James Lincoln Collier's words, 'the embrace of show business'.[43] The polarity between a creative, autonomous 'jazz' and a regimented, commercial 'swing' was reiterated more and more frequently as the boom went on. One of the film representations of jazz during the period, the 1941 *Blues in the Night*, embodied this polarity in the characterization of its hero, Jigger Pyne.[44] In Pyne's small group setting he is impulsive, individualistic, perfectionist, a seeker after musical truth. In a contrasting sequence in which he finds employment with the Guy Hyser band (cp. the real-life Kay Kyser), we see him wearing a white satin uniform and listlessly performing a role in the orchestra.

Representations such as these have a grounding in a real difference of experience: the Chicago saxophonist Bud Freeman frequently refused big-band swing jobs because 'combos allow me the freedom to play what I want. When you play in a big band you go into an arrangement, jump up and play eight or sixteen bars, and that's it.'[45] However, not all musicians, even those who saw themselves as committed jazz players, felt this way. There were many who regarded their appointment to one of the major bands as a proud achievement in itself. Nevertheless, there was a tension underlying many players' participation in the bands, a feeling that a more thoroughgoing and fulfilling jazz-playing environment was a step or two away.

All bands risked the occasional, or persistent, accusation of being a 'Mickey Mouse' or 'Hershey bar' organization, that is, of pandering to a debased public taste for novelty effects or playing in too 'sweet' a style. The jazz press and the fans could be critical of a perceived lack of musical integrity or of questionable presentational tricks. A reader writes to *Down Beat* in early 1942 that 'J. Dorsey, Kay Kyser, Glenn Miller, Freddy Martin, Guy Lombardo, Blue Barron, Sammy Kaye, et al' are 'an unsightly blemish to an honorable profession. They depend upon a series of catch phrases and novel innovations to fire the fancy of the public.'[46] In a similar vein, a 1937 *Down Beat* column comments on a recent rash of novelty names among the bands:

> Some of the boys, inspired by the success of Shep Fields with his 'Rippling Rhythm' have gone overboard in their anxiety to create screwy names for alleged new styles of music, which in most cases they have not created. Just to mention a few, we now have Will Osborne and his 'Slide Music', Jan Savitt and his 'Stream lined Rhythm' and even Bill McCane and his 'Staccato Style'. And there are many others. Imitation seems to be substituted for originality in all branches of show business.[47]

This last sentence could have come from one of the essays written about Swing in the late 1930s by the Marxist theorist Theodor Adorno.[48] Adorno sees jazz in this form as exemplifying the strategies of the culture industry as a whole: those of standardization and imitation. In the concern among bandleaders and booking agents for a 'trademark' for each band, Adorno would see a search for product differentiation that masked the essential sameness of what was actually being offered. For Adorno, listening to music in the modern capitalist era is 'fetishistic', a neurotic attachment to, rather than an authentic pleasure in, what the music industry creates. Swing fans and audiences were in this view compulsory consumers of a limited and constantly repeated range of musical goods.

Adorno's scepticism and dissatisfaction found echoes among other observers of the American jazz scene: the poet Weldon Kees, for instance, writing in 1948:

> It is midafternoon. I come away from the window and the rooftops and turn the knob on the radio that sends a thin line cutting across the rows of numbers. I would like to hear, say, Jelly Roll Morton playing 'The Crave', but will settle for a Lee Wiley record; except for a station on which a voice not easily distinguishable from Miss Margaret Truman's is singing 'At Dawning' and another on which a programme of light classics by a feeble string group emerges oppressively distinct, all the other stations are playing record after record by big dance bands. Claude Thornhill, Kay Kyser, Tex Beneke, Charlie Spivak, Vaughn Monroe. I switch off the radio and go into the other room to pour myself a drink.[49]

In this piece, the names of Morton and Wiley stand for the values of jazz, and represent for Kees a positive and valuable alternative. As is not the case for Adorno, Kees retains the belief that a genuine and valuable musical tradition is close at hand, though screened out by the monopolistic domination of big band swing.

The same perspective is expressed in one of Otis Ferguson's articles, from 1941:

> It is pretty clear around New York that jazz has gone back to its obscure and unprofitable limbo again. And not only in New York at that, for whose are the top bands in the country? Glenn Miller, with a watered-down version of what Benny Goodman's idea was when he started it six years ago; Guy Lombardo, with a scrupulously edited version of nothing at all; Kay Kyser, a zany practically innocent of all musical knowledge.[50]

Ferguson's gloomy roll-call of ersatz bands attests to a feeling in the jazz community that, in James Lincoln Collier's words, 'what had started as an interest in a certain kind of music had become … a fad, a craze, a social phenomenon'.[51] The values that seemed to prevail in this commercial climate were not those of the informal hierarchy of merit of the jazz community, but novelty, product differentiation and name recognition. A striking example of the latter was provided when Jesse Owens, the 'colored Olympic Games star' tried to start a career as an orchestra leader at the height of the craze in 1937. In a kind of move which has since become familiar in popular music, celebrity itself became a negotiable commodity in the heated state of the market for Swing.[52]

During the Swing Era a public consciousness of jazz regrouped itself in several distinct ways. In the long term the most decisive of these was what the last chapter called the jam-session culture that was concurrent with Swing. There was also the 'revivalist' movement that formed around the idea and the practice of older, New-Orleans based styles; and there were also in the jam-session world the stirrings of bebop which became the next dominant style of jazz. All of these counter-movements to Swing can be seen as reactions to it. Bebop, for example, has been represented as in large part a revolt against the 'regimented' nature of the big band format, though Scott DeVeaux has shown how much more complex and divided its motivations were. The dichotomy which sprang up in the late 1930s between jazz values and commercial values hardened into a myth of rebellion, following the well-worn archetype of the pure artist rejecting an impure commercial world.

In some narratives of the history of jazz the Swing Era is seen as a short-lived aberration, a deviation from the true path of jazz as an autonomous music into the slough of commercialism. Jazz has to atone for the opulence and largeness of the big band era by the austerity of the bebop small group, with its single-minded interest in improvisation. From the viewpoint of many jazz narratives Swing, the highest point of its public popularity, is rarely if ever seen as its highest point of artistic and cultural achievement.

There is an opposite view of the era which approaches it instead from the angle of popular music and popular culture. From here the view of the Swing Era is much brighter. Within the narrative of the history of popular music, the big band era is often seen, in contradiction to the historians of jazz, as a peak moment. In this phase of history, a remarkable coalition of cultural and economic forces is seen as having produced music of lasting value. James Lincoln Collier's summation of the period contains some of the typical arguments for this positive view:

As the Swing period went on, the public taste became increasingly sophisticated, until in the 1940s it was ready for the more advanced harmonies of Herman, Stan Kenton and others ... American taste in popular music was much more mature at the end of the swing era than it was at the beginning.[53]

The terms of this comment, the coming together of popular taste and a music of high intrinsic quality, are reproduced in many other sources, and by musicians as well as historians. Teddy Wilson, for example, commented in an interview that 'That period was the nearest to blending a mass audience with good music. The music of the musicians and the public coming together' (to which his interviewer, the bassist Milt Hinton, replies 'Precisely').[54] Gunther Schuller's musicological study of the period has numerous comments of the same kind: 'Here at last was a happy and rare coincidence: a large segment of the public seemed to prefer the best and most advanced arrangements the band had to offer and not, for once, the worst.'[55] The critic Gene Lees comments that 'it was an era when a lot of popular music was good and when a lot of good music was popular', and, in almost identical language, a 1990s radio trailer for a swing programme runs 'when good music was popular and popular music was good'.[56]

This statement carries several implications: first, that the Swing Era stands out as a unique instance of a popular music being good, and that before and after Swing, popular music was bad. Secondly, swing is 'good music'. This raises many issues about quality in popular culture. In what sense was swing 'good' in a way in which other popular music is not? The answers to these questions are referable to some conventional definitions of musical quality: the swing band was well organized; its players required a high level of general musicianship; many of its star performers, like Goodman and Shaw, were virtuosi on their instruments; bands played material composed or arranged by a cohort of talented writers. Swing also added to these qualities a level of drive and vitality which was not manifested in the other popular music styles of its time.

Schuller's high estimation of popular musical taste from 1935 to 1945 is based on the closeness of swing to jazz. He calls the Swing Era 'that remarkable period in American musical history when jazz was synonymous with America's popular music, its social dances and its popular entertainment'. It was 'a temporary victory in jazz musicians' crusade against the commercial establishment'. Moreover, there was an especially comfortable fit between the kind of music being played and the mood of the American people: 'It is undoubtedly the only time in its history when jazz was completely in phase with the social environment.'[57] Jazz itself is seen as the beneficent element in this coming together. The fact that popular taste could be so enlightened as to be able to assimilate such a vital and creative idiom into a popular style is an indication for Schuller and others that the American public's instincts and judgement were in good shape.

The Swing Era can be said to have ended in 1946, when in the space of a few months virtually all of the top-flight bandleaders quit the business in response to a sudden downturn in popularity. The decline of swing coincided with and paralleled the sudden decline of the cinema, which hit its all-time peak of popularity in 1946. The Swing boom had threatened to fail once before, in 1941, but the outbreak of war in late 1941 gave it, along with other forms of entertainment, a resurgence of popularity. *Down Beat* reported, for instance, a 30 per cent rise in nightclub business within a few weeks of Pearl Harbor.[58] As soon as the war was over, and as the public moved rapidly into the sphere of privatized domestic entertainment offered by the television age, the Swing Era folded up almost as suddenly as it had begun ten years before.

Swing has provoked more intense feelings of nostalgia than any other style of jazz or popular music. Cultural commentators, too, look back on the period as having been optimistic, progressive, and expressive of an energized and civilized Americanism. Lewis Erenberg portrays the Swing Era as a time of social rebirth and regeneration following the Depression of 1929-35, a refocusing on the American Dream. Richard Stowe's study of the era sees its formal changes of style as related to structural change in American society during the 1930s, and especially under Roosevelt's 'New Deal' of 1935.

Stowe's approach here can be likened to that of Will Wright's study of the Western movie.[59] Both writers view their respective art forms as reflecting in their internal structures the contemporary shifts in social and political relations. For Wright, the change from the 'classical' Western to the 'professional plot', post-1960, mirrors the shift from an individualistic to a corporate economy. In Stowe's reading of Swing, this form of music 'did more than symbolise' the New Deal: 'Swing was the preeminent musical expression of the New Deal: a cultural form of "the people", accessible, inclusive, distinctively democratic and thus distinctively American.'[60]

The formal structure of the swing band and the swing musical arrangement is seen by Stowe and others as being an example of New Deal politics in action: 'Swing's much-noted quality of enabling the individual voice to contribute to the collective whole also accords well with the notion of a co-operative commonwealth central to Franklin Roosevelt's vision of America.'[61] An analogous argument, though in a quite different historical and musical context, has been put forward by Charles Hersch, in a discussion of the 'free jazz' of the early 1960s. Hersch sees Ornette Coleman's collectively improvised piece 'Free Jazz' as 'combining unprecedented individual freedom with group coherence', as representing 'a musical enactment of the ideas of freedom put forward in the growing civil rights movement'.[62] Both Stowe and Hersch are arguing from the formal structures and the group structures of jazz to models of relationship within society.

Both, as it happens, are referring to progressive phases in American social history. In both cases, too, the achievement of cohesiveness within the jazz ensemble is seen as realizing within its own domain what Erenberg, speaking of Swing, calls the 'utopian potential'.[63] The jazz ensemble itself becomes the site of a prospective, or an actual, social utopia. For Hersch, despite the jazz community's eventual rejection of the 'Free Jazz' model, 'its performances show that the redemptive community is possible.' For Stowe, summing up the ideologies of the Swing Era, while its political ideals 'were at times imperfectly fulfilled in the broader society, they achieved their highest expression, according to its proponents, in the musical realm of swing'.[64]

Swing, unlike jazz in many of its other manifestations, has been consistently represented as American, as embodying the nation and its spirit at a particular moment. Lewis Erenberg regards the entry of Swing into the concert halls (as in the widely publicized Benny Goodman performances in Carnegie Hall) as representing the triumph of 'a true American music rooted in democratic culture' over 'European and hierarchical cultural forms'.[65] Thus swing's preeminence was another cultural declaration of independence comparable to those of American literature in the mid-nineteenth century, embodied in such consciously democratic and consciously American writers as Whitman and Twain.

Swing music was never culturally marginalized as were other forms of jazz both before and after it, despite the jitterbugs and the wild scenes in movie theatres. American society as a whole was prepared to 'own' Swing and to regard it as a legitimate cultural expression of the nation.

This was especially the case in wartime: Erenberg and Stowe have written about the US government's enthusiastic 'conscription of swing' into the war effort as a means of propagandizing American values. In Stowe's words, 'swing found itself transformed into a galvanising symbol of national purpose'.[66]

Even before the commencement of the Second World War, this valorization of Swing as a representative product of America is observable in popular cultural representation. Nowhere is this more comprehensively shown than in the finale to the 1940 film *Strike Up the Band*, in which Mickey Rooney, as the musically precocious hero, conducts a huge orchestra through a medley of popular styles. The sequence climaxes with a swing performance in which Rooney impersonates a swing drummer of the Gene Krupa type before reappearing in an admiral's uniform saluting the flag. Swing is presented here as one of the ways of expressing patriotic pride in America, as well as showing the kind of 'youthful enthusiasm' that will 'keep the future of our country in safe hands'.

Jazz, in its most popular derivative, Swing, had moved a long way from its roots in African-American culture (not one black face is seen among the hundreds of musicians appearing in the film's Busby Berkeley spectacle), and from its suspect status of the 1920s. As jazz, initially in the form of swing, moved from the margins to the mainstream, so it moved into range of the kind of representations that Hollywood and other mass cultural forms were liable to give it.

Notes

1. Wilson from transcript of interview for the Jazz Oral History Project, reel 3, p. 44, F. Scott Fitzgerald, *The Last Tycoon* (London: Penguin, 1960), p. 84.
2. Kathy J. Ogren, *The Jazz Revolution: Twenties America and the Meaning of Jazz* (New York: OUP, 1989), pp. 101–2.
3. John Hammond, *Down Beat*, June 1937, p. 2. For the Shrine riot, see David W. Stowe, *Swing Changes: Big Band Jazz in New Deal America* (Cambridge: Harvard University Press, 1994), p. 31.
4. 'Jitterbug Ban in Iowa', *Metronome*, January 1939, p. 31.
5. Collected in S. J. Perelman, *The Most of S. J. Perelman* (London: Eyre Methuen, 1978), p. 106.
6. *Metronome*, March 1939, p. 8.
7. Scott DeVeaux, *The Birth of Bebop: A Social and Musical History* (Berkeley: University of California Press, 1997), p. 118.
8. *Down Beat*, August 1939, p. 8
9. *Bandstand*, June 1939, p. 1.

10. Stowe, *Swing Changes*, p. 105.

11. Rex Stewart, *Jazz Masters of the Thirties* (London: Macmillan, 1972), p. 24.

12. The publicity material on Ellington, produced by his agencies in the Swing period, is held in the Duke Ellington Collection in the Archives Center at the Smithsonian Institution in Washington, DC.

13. Paul F. Karberg, liner note to *'Radio's Aces' – The Coon-Sanders Nighthawks*, LP on RCA-Victor RD-7697.

14. Gunther Schuller, *The Swing Era: The Development of Jazz 1930–1945* (New York: OUP, 1989), p. 704.

15. *Down Beat*, January 1937, p. 15.

16. Stowe, *Swing Changes*, p. 113.

17. Jay McShann, transcript of interview for the Jazz Oral History Project, Side 5, p. 13.

18. Andy Kirk, as told to Amy Lee, *Twenty Years on Wheels* (Oxford: Bayou Press, 1989).

19. Danny Barker (Alyn Shipton, ed.), *A Life in Jazz* (London: Macmillan, 1986), pp. 166–9.

20. 'Goodman, Shaw Battle to Swing Draw', *Metronome*, March 1939, p. 11.

21. Lewis Erenberg, *Swinging the Dream: Big Band Jazz and the Rebirth of American Culture* (Chicago: University of Chicago Press, 1998), p. 47.

22. William Howland Kenney, *Chicago Jazz: A Cultural History 1904–1930* (New York: OUP, 1993), p. xiv.

23. Erenberg, *Swinging the Dream*, p. 41.

24. Stowe, *Swing Changes*, p. 45.

25. Gene Lees, *Singers and the Song* (New York: OUP, 1987), pp. 83–4.

26. DeVeaux, *The Birth of Bebop*, p. 119.

27. The Calloway notice was in *Down Beat*, July 1941, p. 16, the Hampton review in the May 1942 issue, p. 12.

28. Stewart, *Jazz Masters*, p. 26.

29. Kirk, *Twenty Years on Wheels*, p. 87.

30. Ibid., p. 85.

12. *Metronome*, January 1939, p. 51.

12. *Down Beat*, December 1942, p. 16.

33. Elliott Grennard, 'Colored Bands Don't Get a Break', *P. M.'s Weekly*, August 24, 1941.

34. *Down Beat*, April 1942, p. 6.

35. Teddy Wilson, transcript of interview for the Jazz Oral History Project, Reel 2, p. 28.

36. Danny Baxter, 'Guitar is Burr in Kirk Band's Pants', *Down Beat*, January 6, 1939, p. 8.

37. *Metronome* report was in the issue of January 1939, p. 17. Kirk's estimate of the band's annual mileage is in Kirk, *Twenty Years on Wheels*, p. 88.

38. '"Clouds of Joy" are Sharp, but Definitely', *Down Beat*, 3 March 1942, p. 6.

39. For a discussion of the politics of Hammond and others, see Stowe, *Swing Changes*, pp. 50–93.

40. 'Negro Hot Jazz Invades Frisco', *Down Beat*, 15 January 1942, p. 9.

41. Freeman, *Crazeology: The Autobiography of a Chicago Jazzman* (Oxford: Bayou Press, 1989), p. 45.

42. For a discussion of the 'revivalist' movement and its values, see Erenberg, *Swinging the Dream*, pp. 218–23.

43. James Lincoln Collier, *Jazz: The American Theme Song* (New York: OUP, 1993), pp. 89–123.

44. For further discussion of *Blues in the Night*, see Chapter 4.

45. Freeman, *Crazeology*, p. 41.

46. Letter from George Schott, of Tarentum, PA., *Down Beat*, 1 January 1942, p. 17.

47. *Down Beat*, June 1937, p. 8.

48. See, for example, Theodor Adorno, 'Jazz – Perennial Fashion', *Prisms* (London: Neville Spearman, 1967), pp. 121–32, and Peter Townsend, 'Vienna versus the Vernacular', *Prose Studies*, Vol. 11, No. 1, May 1988, pp. 69–88. Martin Jay comments that Adorno 'confessed his visceral dislike for the very word jazz', in *Adorno* (London: Fontana, 1984), p. 119.

49. Weldon Kees, 'Muskrat Ramble: Popular and Unpopular Music', in Chandler Brossard (ed.), *The Scene Before You: A New Approach to American Culture* (New York: Rinehart Winston, 1955), p. 230.

50. Otis Ferguson in Dorothy Chamberlain, Robert Wilson (eds), *The Otis Ferguson Reader* (Highland Park: December Press, 1982), p. 108.

51. James Lincoln Collier, *Benny Goodman and the Swing Era* (New York: OUP, 1989), p. 190.

52. *Down Beat*, April 1937, p. 4.

53. Collier, *Benny Goodman and the Swing Era*, p. 194.

54. Teddy Wilson, transcript of interview for the Jazz Oral History Project, Reel 4, p. 10.

55. Schuller, *The Swing Era*, p. 21.

56. Lees, *Singers and the Song*, p. 72. The radio trailer was used in the mid-1990s on the British station Jazz FM.

57. These references all from Schuller, *The Swing Era*, p. 6.

58. *Down Beat*, 8 January 1942, p. 2.

59. Will Wright, *Sixguns and Society: A Structural Study of the Western* (Berkeley: University of California Press, 1975).

60. Stowe, *Swing Changes*, p. 11.

61. Ibid., p. 11.

62. Charles Hersch, '"Let Freedom Ring": Free Jazz and African-American Politics', *Cultural Critique*, Winter 1995–96, pp. 112 and 114.

63. Erenberg, *Swinging the Dream*, p. 250.

64. Hersch, '"Let Freedom Ring"', p. 119, Stowe, *Swing Changes*, p. 73.

65. Erenberg, *Swinging the Dream*, p. 250.

66. Stowe, *Swing Changes*, p. 142. For discussion of swing in the context of the American war effort, see Erenberg, *Swinging the Dream*, pp. 181–210, Stowe, *Swing Changes*, pp. 141–79.

CHAPTER 4

Telling the Story:
The Representation of Jazz

The first three chapters of this book have been concerned with jazz on
its own territory, considered first as music, and secondly and thirdly in
two of its historical-cultural manifestations. The following chapters will
be concerned with jazz seen from the outside, from within other cultural
forms and media, and with how jazz is represented in the wider culture.
Chapter 2 argued that, within the conditions of a particular time and
place, jazz achieved a certain coherence and autonomy as a culture. In
examining the representation of jazz in these other cultural settings, one
is dealing with exactly the opposite situation. Jazz is here subject to
forces which shape its cultural image according to their own interests
and in line with their own practices.

This chapter will review the treatment of jazz in the American cinema
and within literary forms. When jazz becomes involved in a culturally
powerful medium such as film, with its own preformed habits of
representation, it is drawn into a relation in which its identity as a
music, or as a specific culture, has no particular importance. As the lesser
partner in this relation, a jazz culture has a minimal chance of imposing
its identity on the medium, or on the ways in which that medium
represents it. From the cinematic point of view, jazz has no higher status
as subject matter than gunfighting, espionage or teenage romance. Its
representation in film may include some of its significant features, but
primarily those that are compatible with pre-existing cinematic codes, or
that have the value of being photogenic or sensational.

Some films about jazz have a degree of historical and stylistic
accuracy, but on the whole representations of jazz in films have been
on the same level of authenticity as those of the Wild West or the Second
World War. This deficit has been one of the reasons why documentary
treatments of jazz have been so important. Jazz has a tradition of documentary film-making of high quality, in which a committed attempt has
been made to reflect the music and its players, from the 1944 *Jammin' the*

Blues to the 1995 *A Great Day in Harlem.*[1] In the documentary the jazz content of the film is not filtered through the filmic conventions of genre narrative, delineation of the hero and the star system.

These considerations apply equally to other media: when jazz becomes the subject of poetry or fiction it is implicated in the forms, genres, narratives and character typologies current in those modes of writing. As with film, a number of the most highly regarded written texts on jazz are documentary in nature: the numerous jazz autobiographies and the oral histories, exemplified by Shapiro and Hentoff's *Hear Me Talkin' to Ya* and Gitler's *Swing to Bop.* Among musicians' autobiographies, those of Charles Mingus, Mezz Mezzrow and Art Pepper stand out as having literary qualities in addition to the intrinsic interest of the subjects. Musicians' autobiographies and oral histories are not necessarily to be regarded as unmediated truth, but the prominence of non fictional texts in this field reflects a general failure of literary discourse in its treatment of jazz.[2]

These representations, however, remain influential. The treatment that jazz receives in mainstream film is decisive in establishing the ways in which it is perceived in the society as a whole. Jazz is encoded into the cinematic modes and conventions with which a large audience is already familiar and which they have accepted as representing reality. In these circumstances, aspects of jazz such as, for example, the racial identities of its players, or the working life of the jazz musician, are liable to be represented only in those ways in which such subjects are usually treated within the film industry. The black musician becomes just another case of the film characterization of black people, the working life of the musician is remodelled into another instance of the life narrative of the movie hero.

Representations of jazz are more indicative of the ideologies implicit in the medium, whether in film or written literature, than of jazz itself. They are, however, very instructive as to the cultural position of jazz, which is to some extent the product of these powerful media representations. Through the media of film and literature, in proportion to their power, the image of jazz, subject to whatever adjustments are made by these media, is transmitted to a public which may have little or no other experience of jazz as a culture. It is through these transmissions that jazz is interpreted to this wider audience, in the process ceasing to be perceived as a complex and variegated phenomenon, rooted in history, and coming to be apprehended with the simplicity of myth.

Jazz in the American Cinema

Even the first (1977) edition of the most comprehensive listing of jazz in the cinema, David Meeker's *Jazz in the Movies*, ran to 2,239 items.[3] Many of these were short films, soundies (an early video-jukebox format), and features in which jazz was incidental to what was presented on screen. Jazz, however, had been present in films since *The Jazz Singer* (a 1927 film featuring Al Jolson) and *The King of Jazz* (1930, featuring Paul Whiteman), though 'jazz' would have to be understood here in its broadest late-1920s definition.[4] With the high visibility and commercial attractiveness of the Swing phenomenon, jazz music and musicians began to be featured more substantively in films in the late 1930s, though in many cases performers were only 'spotted' (in the sense used in a film review in *Metronome*: 'The Woody Herman band is spotted, and well spotted too').[5]

Some of the better known performers, especially the white big-band leaders such as Shaw, Goodman and Miller, were given speaking parts in movies about musicians not unlike themselves. Miller, for example, played in *Orchestra Wives* a bandleader named Gene Morrison whose musical style and whose musicians were recognizably those of Miller's own orchestra. Benny Goodman had a slightly wider range of parts, though even in *A Song is Born* (1948) he played a Mittel-European musicologist who learns to play jazz clarinet.[6] Swing Era movies increased the visibility of jazz musicians, but men like Goodman and Miller and their bands were required primarily for their celebrity presence and drawing power at the box office. Despite the numerous films of the period in which musicians appear, it is possible to agree with Arthur Knight that by 1944, the date of the short feature *Jammin' the Blues*, 'no worthy tradition of jazz in film existed.'[7] Knight considers *Jammin' the Blues*, which features performances in a stylized jam-session setting by prominent jazz players including Lester Young and Illinois Jacquet, to have initiated a more genuine model for the portrayal of jazz (within the constraints, especially on racial mixing, imposed by Hollywood codes). But the treatment of jazz continued to be spasmodic and unrepresentative.

Generically, jazz has been divided up among the Hollywood story typologies. Its most constant model has been the biopic, of which less 'classically' generic forms have continued to be made, the most important later example being Clint Eastwood's 1988 biopic of Charlie Parker,

Bird. Some jazz films, especially those made in the Swing period itself, are generically musicals, with their emphasis on what Jane Feuer calls 'the ideology of entertainment'.[8] In the 1950s the presence of jazz was an element in late *noir* films like *The Sweet Smell of Success*. Since the 1950s, owing to the decline in the popularity of jazz and the obsolescence of the earlier film genres, the incidence of jazz in movies is less frequent and less generalizable. An association with jazz sometimes appears, as Krin Gabbard points out, as a positive idiosyncrasy in film characters. In films like Coppola's *The Conversation*, for an individual to play jazz gives them, as Gabbard puts it, '*character*, a trait that jazz has been loaning out to American movie heroes in more recent years'.[9]

Many of the early films featuring jazz are indistinguishable from other musicals except in the style of the music. Performances of jazz and swing provide a natural performance setting for the romantic or sentimental themes of the musical. Jazz films share in the self-reflexiveness of the musical, in that they provide shows about putting on a show, or band performances dedicated to putting on band performances. The musical was the preferred genre in which it was possible for black musicians to be seen, in all-black films like *Cabin in the Sky* and *Stormy Weather*, or in cameo appearances in primarily white-performed movies like *New Orleans*.[10]

The framework of the movie musical dominates a film like *Let's Make Music*, giving top billing to the bandleader Bob Crosby, who takes the undemanding lead male role. The plot concerns an elderly schoolmistress, Miss Malvina Adams, who struggles to make the swing-crazy youth of Newton High take an interest in classical music. The students are bored, to an implausible degree, by a classmate's rendition of a Chopin Prelude, and exclaiming 'Boy, is that music corny!', express their ambition of playing in a swing band rather than a symphony. Miss Adams' composition 'Fight On for Newton High' is picked up by a song publisher, featured on radio by the Crosby band, and becomes a hit. Miss Adams' brief moment of fame is too much for her, and she is driven to a state of nervous collapse. However, she then returns to her school, and to a class newly appreciative of her teaching. The film ends with the pupils in Miss Adams' class honouring her with a swing arrangement of her new song 'Central Park'.[11]

Let's Make Music touches upon one of the familiar conflicts of the musical form: the opposition between a stuffy 'high' culture and a vital, youthful popular culture, a division in which the film comes down strongly in favour of the latter. Just as in some of the Astaire musicals, where high culture figures such as ballet dancers and theatre directors are brought to an appreciation of the superiority of American popular entertainment, so in this film European classicism is shown as anachronistic and bloodless.[12] Swing music is used here to connote a youthful, energetic Americanism of the same variety as Mickey Rooney's in *Strike Up the Band*.

Orchestra Wives (1942), featuring Glenn Miller and his orchestra, places the world of the Swing musician closer to the movie's focus of interest. The film is faithful, at least in outline, to the economic facts of the Swing industry. In an early scene, the band rounds off a rehearsal by refusing to go on the road, unable to countenance playing thirty-six dates in a forty-five-day tour (compare this with the itineraries of the territory bands like Andy Kirk's). Morrison, the leader, played by Glenn Miller himself, explains the necessity of tours: 'We make our money and our reputation on the road.' Then he sounds a more idealistic note, appealing not only to his men's financial interests but also to their populist loyalty towards their working-class public: 'It isn't the carriage trade that pays our salaries, boys. It's those kids that put those nickels in those juke boxes all over the country.' A cut to a jukebox out in Middle America then introduces the young heroine destined to fall in love with Morrison's trumpet soloist. Miller/Morrison's words express the sense of a broad national constituency of music fans whom it is the moral, as well as financial, obligation of the band to play for. *Orchestra Wives* was made in early wartime, and its Americanism is evident not only in statements like these but also in the adapted lyric of the song 'People Like You and Me', a phrase which comes to mean, as well as 'lovers like us', 'ordinary patriotic Americans like us': 'Put your Yankee heart and soul into everything you do.'

By contrast with these examples, *Blues in the Night* (1941, directed by Anatole Litvak) is much more a film about jazz and less a genre piece exploiting its popularity. The script of *Blues in the Night* shows signs of being conversant with the jazz media and their concerns. The clarinettist in the band is a serious jazz purist who reads 'everything from *Le Jazz Hot* to *Down Beat*'. The film combines the populism of the other films with a new conception of the jazz musician as tortured genius, taken from Dorothy Baker's novel *Young Man with a Horn* two years earlier. The hero, Jigger Pyne, a talented pianist and composer, wants to write music that will express 'all of the USA in one song', but he is also a serious jazz musician aware of his separation from the world of commercial music. His transgression from his calling, when under the influence of a rich *femme fatale* he takes a job in a 'Mickey Mouse' band, is punished by a display of disapproval by his former bandmates, who come to his gig and stand in a phalanx staring at him like a bad conscience. The film has elements of melodrama, but it also resembles a biopic, in that Jigger is a seeker after a new style for American music, as were, in their movie characterizations, Al Jolson, George M. Cohan and others. But Jigger is a jazz musician: dedicated to music, he has a total lack of interest in money. We see him giving money away, and he remains indifferent when he is robbed. His fellow musicians, however, are in the end truer to their vocation than the more gifted Jigger: while he sells out to a society orchestra, the rest of his group are content to travel America like hoboes or children of nature, playing jazz in boxcars.

Blues in the Night is an early example of a narrative conflict that was to recur in other jazz-related films, and to be one of the most frequent dichotomies in jazz discourse: jazz versus commercialism. It also contains in a muted fashion another antinomy that is very important in jazz films and elsewhere: black and white. Although this antinomy is visible in many jazz films, it is rarely foregrounded before the 1960s. In *Blues in the Night* black musicians are present in two scenes which are typical of the ways in which the black/white antinomy is featured. In an early scene, Jigger and his band are thrown into jail, where they pass the night in a cell adjoining a group of black prisoners who sing, in the style of a spiritual, the song 'Blues in the Night' (in fact, a pop song written for the film by Harold Arlen and Johnny Mercer). The purpose of this scene is inspiration of the hero: Jigger exclaims 'That's the real New Orleans blues!' and is given a further stimulus to creativity.

In the second scene, Jigger and his band are in a cabaret where a black swing band (not identified in the scene, but actually that of Jimmy Lunceford) is performing. A white trumpeter who is auditioning for Jigger's band suddenly stands up and improvises a bravura hot solo over the backing of the band. This burst of brilliance impresses the Jigger Pyne band, but it also draws an immediate sign of approval from the black musicians on the stand. This is in a sense unimportant, since these musicians are not otherwise involved in the story, but a scene in which white musicianship is explicitly approved by black players is a recurrent feature of jazz films. Validation by black players seems to be a necessary function in these narratives, even though the scenes in which this occurs are of minimal length and extraneous to the plot.

Validation scenes occur in several of the bandleader biopics. In a scene in *The Fabulous Dorseys*, the Dorsey brothers suggest to their friends that they go and hear Art Tatum play, establishing his credentials (in addition to the fact that he is black) by stating 'He's a real musician.' At the club where Tatum is playing, the brothers pick up their instruments and join in, demonstrating their ability to operate on the level of expertise vouched for by Tatum's presence.[13] Similarly, in *The Glenn Miller Story*, Miller and his wife attend a club where Louis Armstrong is playing. Armstrong's music and his effusive greeting inspire Miller to take his trombone and join in an impromptu jam session.[14]

The Benny Goodman Story (1954, directed by Valentine Davies) contains two such scenes. In the first the young Goodman, depressed by the uninteresting music he is obliged to play in a society orchestra, wanders aimlessly about the deck of a riverboat, and hears the sound of a jazz band issuing from a dance-room. He strolls up to the bandstand, and after approximately thirty-seven seconds exposure to the first jazz music he has ever heard, picks up a clarinet and begins to improvise with great fluency and skill. The black musicians supporting him are the Kid Ory band, veterans of the New Orleans scene. Goodman receives their encouragement and congratulations. Later, having become the leader of his own orchestra, and on the threshold of fame, Goodman makes a radio broadcast. We cut to a car radio and a black man listening to Goodman's performance. The man drives to the studio, seeks out Goodman and introduces himself as Fletcher Henderson, arranger and former bandleader. He then announces the purpose of his visit, which is to tell Goodman and the band that they 'sure do play good' and to encourage them to continue. This unambiguous endorsement covers what in real life was a very significant role for Henderson in Goodman's success. The film here gives an allusive acknowledgement of this, but the main function of this brief scene, as in other biopics, is to authenticate the music of the white musician by the approval of a black musician (Tatum, Armstrong, Ory, Henderson).

The jazz biopics are in other respects typical of the genre. Similar narrative devices are used, and narrative interest moves along two trajectories which sometimes interact: success and romance. In the biopic the hero is given a wife or partner who fails to understand the nature of the hero's achievement while being aware of its importance to him. It is typical that the future Mrs Glenn Miller is ignorant of jazz until their marriage, that the future Mrs Goodman is indifferent to jazz until their relationship begins.[15] The hero himself, by contrast, is driven, a young man in a hurry, troubled by a discontent that will only be assuaged by the breakthrough that brings success. Miller and Goodman were in real life men who were disliked by their fellow musicians, Miller for his authoritarian attitude towards the business, Goodman for his frosty and withdrawn personality. In the films these traits are assimilated into the biopic archetype of the discontented seeker after the truth.

Biopics on all subjects frequently use the trope of the chance discovery and the lucky break: in *Dr Ehrlich's Magic Bullet*, for example, the breakthrough is made when the scientist's uncomprehending wife mistakenly overheats the cultures he has been preparing, and the application of heat turns out to be the answer to the puzzle.[16] Likewise in the Miller biopic, the 'sound' that Miller has been looking for, and that the screenplay has been harping on, turns up by chance when the lead trumpeter accidentally cuts his lip: in exasperation, Miller tells the clarinettist to play the trumpet part above the saxophones, and the Miller sound is born.

By the nature of the genre, jazz biopics can only show success and achievement individualistically. The biopic hero is in each film a misfit lacking a social or community context for his music. His achievements are of a different order from those of his fellow musicians, to whom he owes little or nothing. This cuts the idea of a community of players, or a shared musical culture, out of the picture. This is also another explanation of the scenes with black musicians: they directly exempt the hero from any sense of obligation towards a pre-existing cultural setting. Krin Gabbard, in the fullest published account of the jazz biopic, reads these scenes as signifying the superiority of the white players over the black originals: in this interpretation Fletcher Henderson, for instance, is giving his blessing as he sees Goodman carry his music to a higher level.[17] In the biopic, moreover, white and black achievement of the same standards are viewed differently: black musicians can do it by nature, automatically, while the skill of the white hero is a mark of individual merit. A further implication of biopic depictions of jazz performance is that skill in the form is, in one way or another, easy. For black musicians it is present without awareness; for the gifted white protagonist it is a trick that can be mastered on the spot. This is a minor implication in the full set of ideological messages in the biopic, but it has important long-term effects on perceptions of jazz performance. It is never shown as the outcome of study or careful preparation, nor as a result of intellect or intelligence: Benny Goodman simply gets it right first time.

The biopic as a genre was finished by 1960, but by then the predominant film representation of jazz had shifted into another kind of film. There was a sequence of films in the mid-1950s in which one or more of the protagonists was a jazz musician. These films as a group share an atmosphere that derives from that of the *film noir* even if none of them strictly belongs in that genre. Even in films in which a connection with jazz was tenuous, a jazz-influenced soundtrack was in the mid-1950s a frequent resource for communicating what Krin Gabbard has called 'contemporary urban disaffection and turbulence'.[18] The epitome of this kind of scoring was Elmer Bernstein's music for *The Man with the Golden Arm* (1955) and *The Sweet Smell of Success* (1957), and Johnny Mandel's for *I Want to Live* (1958).[19] In these films the music sets the moral tone for stories about, respectively, a heroin addict, a corrupt press agent and a woman on Death Row. The jazz elements used are a mix of influences signifying marginality and deviancy, a bluesy and dissonant blend of bebop and the current 'cool' style, with the problematic connotations that those styles had already acquired. Both bebop and cool had been widely linked, as they are in these films, with the subcultures of drug use and antisocial behaviour. Fifties jazz could be a restless, jittery music, and these film scores use it to generate an unstable nervous intensity.

In *The Man with the Golden Arm* Frank Sinatra plays a drug addict, Frankie Machine, who inhabits the fringes of the jazz world by virtue of his ambition to be a drummer. One scene shows his disruptive participation in a rehearsal (in which the jazz musicians Shorty Rodgers and Shelly Manne are shown on camera). The plot deals with his dependency on heroin, leading to a crisis in which he has to undergo the horrors of withdrawal (an ordeal that can apparently be coped with by spending the night lying on top of Kim Novak). Bernstein's score is mostly non-diegetic (that is, not based on any 'real' music source in the situation), but there is a crucial scene in which diegetic music, and jazz, becomes prominent. This occurs when Sinatra, in the throes of cold turkey, arrives at Novak's apartment on the verge of collapse. She turns on a radio, which plays the same kind of dissonant jazz as on the soundtrack. At the peak of Novak's distress, the music enters as an additional stimulus, serving both to symbolize and to intensify her emotions. In a dark urban world of betrayal, corruption and addiction, a form of jazz is considered, as Gabbard points out, the appropriate music. For the Novak character it also represents, by its frenetic dissonance, the pressures that rest upon her: life in the city, and the neurotic, destructive moral atmosphere with which a 'good woman' is forced to struggle.

Sinatra's Frankie Machine succumbs to the world of which jazz is the auditory symbol. His own musicianship, compromised as it is, does not serve to protect him. In *The Sweet Smell of Success*, although urban sleaziness is even more effectively established, the jazz player who is at the centre of the action is incorruptible, and this is linked with his dedication to his music. The guitarist Steve (Martin Milner) has the integrity to remain a committed artist in the midst of the big city stew of blackmail and moral prostitution, and the strength of character to withstand the powerful threats against him.

The film's narrative turns upon a relationship between the press agent Sidney Falco (played by Tony Curtis) and the gossip columnist J. J. Hunsecker (Burt Lancaster) which is reminiscent of the bond between Ben Jonson's Mosca and Volpone. Hunsecker is determined to prevent his sister, with whom he has an incestuous obsession, from forming a relationship with the jazz musician Steve, and to this end he arranges that Steve is accused of being a drug addict and a Communist (the two prime mid-1950s moral outrages), has marijuana planted on him, and has him beaten up so badly that he is hospitalized. Steve's integrity is shown not only in his refusal to buckle under pressure, but also in his art. Several scenes display Steve's talent as a jazz guitarist in a quintet (that of Chico Hamilton) of evident seriousness and good taste. Finally it is the example of Steve's integrity that causes Hunsecker's sister to stand up for herself and to walk out, in one of the film's few daylight shots, into the New York dawn.

Krin Gabbard has pointed out the incidence of 'so many Tony Curtis films from the fifties in which jazz is associated with sociopaths, thieves and satyrs'.[20] *The Sweet Smell of Success* is almost a riposte to this, since it is Curtis who plays the venal press agent whose ethics are thrown into relief by the shining integrity of the jazz musician. As played by Martin Milner, the character of Steve is a reversal of the standard portrait of the jazz musician as drug fiend or moral degenerate: he looks more like a WASP business executive. His musicianship, also, is not freakish or exhibitionistic: he simply gets on with playing the guitar very well.

As the show-business associations left over from Swing fell away, and jazz receded through the 1950s into a minority art form, the status in films of the jazz player rose. There was a resurgence of the antinomy between the values of jazz and those of commerce. The jazz musician came to be seen as confronting problems common to all creative artists in a materialistic society, and in a literary culture affected by the Beat aesthetic, jazz as a culture was in the late 1950s increasingly seen as honourably dissident, expressing by its attachment to a minority form its principled disaffection from conformist American values.

The protagonist of John Cassavetes' 1961 *Too Late Blues* seems to be a later version of Jigger Pyne. He too ends by dismally selling out to the commercialism he has previously resisted. The screenplay, and some extracts from his music, establish Ghost Wakefield as a musician of outstanding talent. Throughout the film Ghost demonstrates a commitment to his music rather than any commercialized substitute, and in this he is loyally supported by the members of his band. Both Ghost and his colleagues state their position clearly: 'We're free thinkers', 'Let us play what we want to play'. The members of the band are subjected to the aggressive prejudices of a drunk in a pool-room, who blames jazz musicians for 'Taking dope – mixing of races – bad things like that.' Ghost in particular is picked out for the drunk's hostility. This incident leads to Ghost's fall from grace, when, after calling him a 'dope fiend' and a 'Romeo with a pocket full of needles', the drunk assaults both Ghost and the band's female singer. Ghost's failure to prevent the assault causes a wave of self-disgust which leads to his walking out on his band into the embrace of an older woman who wants to make him rich and famous. Even then, Ghost is able to say of himself 'I did some weird things, man, but I never sold my soul. I play what I like with no compromises', and, in an ambiguous end to the movie, the band cluster around him while they play one of Ghost's own compositions.

Too Late Blues is more fundamentally a jazz film than any other of this period: the action is placed within the jazz group, and it bears upon their lives in music. The director, John Cassavetes, had earlier worked with the jazz composer Charles Mingus on the film *Shadows*, where the improvisational method of the actors was intended as a counterpart to the music score, and Cassavetes' later work shows a continuing involvement with jazz.[21] In *Too Late Blues*, however, the treatment of race is equivocal. The opening shots of the film seem to be establishing an African-American environment: a crowd of black children listening to music and swaying their feet in time to it. But the band, Ghost and his associates, are white men. The scene is unconnected with anything else in the movie, and its meaning is as ambiguous as the film's ending. It can be read as another 'validation' scene, or, as Jon Panish suggests, as signifying that the real spirit of jazz is being sustained by white players.[22] It can also be read as unresolved, suggesting some kind of transaction between black and white traditions, but not following up the implications of this.

Too Late Blues can be seen as an example of what Gabbard has called 'a tendency in American culture of the 1950s to idealise the white jazz musician'.[23] The white jazz player has an 'outsider' appeal that can be individualized: he can be seen as a type of the existentialist hero, and he chooses to inhabit a high-risk subcultural world which is itself mythologized as unknown and exotic, while still possessing the intellectual cachet of an art form. The white player's life and art can be seen as a matter of choice, and the tribulations he suffers can be dramatized as those of an exceptional individual. The corresponding suppositions about black musicians are very different. In this kind of mythological thinking, black involvement in jazz, and the kinds of problems experienced, are predictable, collective, and not chosen but given. The consciousness of the white jazz-playing protagonist is therefore more fraught with the kinds of trauma that were attractive to filmmakers in the late 1950s. In films like *Too Late Blues* it is the white players whose lives are weighed down with the burden of it all.

From the early 1960s onward, jazz could no longer claim to be influential in the American cinema. Films about jazz musicians have never again been as common as they were in the 1950s, and with the overwhelming dominance of rock after the mid-1960s, jazz to a large extent ceased to be used in film scores. Films about jazz from the 1970s through to the 1990s have been largely the work of individual directors, with a particular, usually retrospective, interest in the music; for example, Martin Scorsese's *New York, New York* (1977), Francis Coppola's *The Cotton Club* (1984), and Robert Altman's *Kansas City* (1996). These films show a commitment to historical authenticity, and this extends to their recreations of the music. Another major director, Spike

Lee, was responsible for the 1990 *Mo' Better Blues*, a film that to some extent reinstated the role of the tortured jazz-playing hero, though it was mixed with elements of other genres, and expressed an unusually deep ambivalence about jazz culture. Two directors, Woody Allen and Clint Eastwood, have, throughout this period, made consistent and highly personal use of jazz in their films. Allen, for instance, has his protagonist in *Manhattan* name, as one of his reasons for living, Louis Armstrong's solo on 'Potato Head Blues'. Eastwood's most substantial project relating to jazz is *Bird*, the 1988 biopic of Charlie Parker.

This group of films reflects the higher prestige that jazz has enjoyed as it has become publicly ratified as part of American cultural history. The life of Charlie Parker contained drug addiction, psychotic behaviour and enforced custody in a psychiatric hospital: *Bird* uses these elements to full effect, but the context of their representation is the biography of a great artist, rather than a late-fifties immersion in hipsterdom. Parker's aberrant behaviour is shown as the response of a complex creative personality to racism, a corrupt music industry and America's philistine indifference to its great artists. As played by Forrest Whitaker, Parker constantly seeks the audience's sympathy. He is in continual physical or psychological pain, and even his stance while playing jazz is agonizingly expressive (as distinct from the impassivity of Parker's real-life playing attitude). *Bird* is a kind of film representation of a jazz musician that could be made for a mainstream audience only at a time when jazz is acknowledged as an art, as a respected product of American cultural history. The greatness of Parker is a given which conditions our interpretation of the events of his life. There is a feeling that the storm and stress around jazz are now a thing of the past, that what remains is to commemorate and celebrate, and to compensate for past neglect.

Jazz emerges in its film treatment at the end of the century as signifying the richness of an American past. For individual characters, it signifies admirable personal qualities: in *A Bronx Tale* Robert De Niro, as the incorruptible Italian-American bus driver, shows his distinction and independence of mind by listening to jazz in preference to the other musics (doowop, rock and roll) available in the neighbourhood; in *Mr Holland's Opus*, in some respects a latter-day version of *Let's Make Music*, the dedicated teacher of music and amateur composer shows his cultural breadth and his spirituality by naming his son after the saxophonist John Coltrane.[24]

Jazz in Literary Fiction

One point of continuity between jazz in film and jazz in written fiction is the qualitative judgement that jazz has not been adequately served by either. This comment, from a jazz bibliography, is more restrained than some: 'It should be said that there are no jazz novels that stand in the first rank of literature and just as the definitive jazz film has yet to be made, they remain to be written.'[25] In his survey of jazz fiction, Richard Albert notes that the reception by jazz critics of jazz in fiction has been 'generally negative', and he cites a review by the record producer Orrin Keepnews which asks 'When is someone who has some knowledge and understanding of jazz ... going to write a novel you can read without squirming?'[26]

These comments are directed primarily at fictional works that are 'about' jazz, that are structured around the music and its players; but, as in films, jazz enters into American fiction at various levels, from the 'jazz novel', through to incidental characters and settings, to work in which jazz has a presence as a cultural hinterland. Philip Roth's *American Pastoral*, for example, identifies a character, Mendy Gurlick, as a type of late-1940s teenage hipster:

It was Mendy Gurlick who'd taken me with him to the Adams Theater to hear Illinois Jacquet, Buddy Johnson, and 'Newark's own' Sarah Vaughan; who'd got the tickets and taken me with him to hear Mr. B., Billy Eckstine, in concert at the Mosque.[27]

J. D. Salinger's Holden Caulfield is as judgemental about jazz music as he is about people:

She kept saying these very corny, boring things, like calling the can the 'little girls' room', and she thought Buddy Singer's poor old beat-up clarinet player was really terrific when he stood up and took a couple of ice-cold hot licks. She called his clarinet a 'liquorice stick'. Was she corny.[28]

Jazz in fiction has had a similar profile to jazz in films. There were peaks during the music's greatest period of popularity during the Swing Era, and in the late 1950s, when it became associated with the prevailing Beat existentialism. From the first period there was Dorothy Baker's *Young Man with a Horn*, Dale Curran's *Piano in the Band*, Eudora Welty's story 'Powerhouse' and others; the second period saw the publication of several novels by Jack Kerouac with substantial jazz content, John Clellon Holmes's *The Horn*, John Williams's *Night Song*, and James Baldwin's *Another Country* and the short story 'Sonny's Blues'.[29]

Literary fiction has never been subject to the tight institutional controls that were exerted on films by the studio system, and jazz fiction is less markedly generic than the films on the subject. Nevertheless, the detective-thriller genre, an equivalent to the *film noir*, has had a long association with jazz-related settings and content. Richard Albert lists eleven novels in this mode, from Harlan Reed's 1938 *The Swing Music Murder* to Julie Smith's *Jazz Funeral*, published in 1993. A series of well-received novels by Bill Moody, *Death of a Tenor Man*, *The Sound of the Trumpet* and *Bird Lives!*, have in the 1990s joined the conventions of the detective thriller with closely specified circumstances of the lives of jazz musicians such as Wardell Gray and Clifford Brown.[30]

Another recurrent structure is also analogous to an equivalent cinematic genre, the biopic: the jazz-related novel or story which narrates the life of an individual musician, though not usually as affirmatively as in the biopic. A theme that is distinctive to jazz fiction is a preoccupation with the lives of a number of real musicians and singers. References to Miles Davis, Jelly Roll Morton and Lester Young are numerous, each of these a musician who projected a certain personal mystique. Michael Ondaatje's *Coming Through Slaughter* uses mixed modes of narration to relate the life of the early New Orleans trumpeter Buddy Bolden. Bolden was a figure on the very edge of jazz pre history, where it falls away into legend: he was institutionalized for the last two decades of his life, only one photograph of him exists, and he made no recordings.[31]

In the view of Vance Bourjaily, the story of Buddy Bolden inaugurates a narrative pattern common to the literary presentation of jazz lives, which Bourjaily calls simply 'The Story'.[32] The elements of this archetype are found throughout jazz fiction, and especially in the large number of texts relating to a group of charismatic, narratogenic individuals: the singer Billie Holiday, the 1920s cornetist Bix Beiderbecke, and the most frequent model of all, Charlie Parker. All of these, as we shall see in the next section, are also the most frequent subjects for poetry. Holiday is subject of, or an important presence in, novels by Elizabeth Hardwick (*Sleepless Lights*, 1979), Kristin Hunter (*God Bless the Child*, 1964), Alice Adams (*Listening to Billie*, 1978), and a number of short stories.[33] Beiderbecke is the disguised subject of, amongst others, Dorothy Baker's *Young Man with a Horn* (1938), one of the most influential jazz novels, made into a film in 1959. Charlie Parker, however, has a special status as hero, model for, inspiration for, symbol in, a very large number of narratives. This is reflected in Richard Albert's survey of Parker fictions, and by the chapter devoted to fictional representations of Parker in Jon Panish's *The Color of Jazz*. Amongst the many works of fiction that draw on Parker's life are John Williams's *Night Song* (1961), and *The Sound* (1961) by Ross Russell, a record producer who was at one time Parker's manager and has written a biography of him.[34]

The prominence of this handful of individuals' lives as the template for so many jazz fictions is itself a sign of the kinds of interest that writers have found in jazz as fictional material. Of the three favourite individual subjects, none lived past the age of forty-four (Beiderbecke died at twenty-eight); all three had problems of alcoholism or drug addiction; all three were pre-eminent in their particular fields but failed to come to an accommodation with the music business; all three lives ended in a tragic death. These characteristics of the real lives of Beiderbecke, Parker and Holiday became key components of the literary 'Story', and subsequently of the mythology of jazz.

Drug and alcohol addiction in the jazz world is prominent in a number of novels, including Al Neil's *Changes* (1976), Garson Kanin's *Blow Up a Storm* (1959), Jeane Westin's *Swing Sisters* (1991) and others. The familiar antinomy between jazz and commercialism is invoked in Dorothy Baker's *Young Man With a Horn*, Robert Oliphant's *A Trumpet for Jackie* (1983), Henry Steig's *Send Me Down* (1941) and elsewhere. Interracial contacts and friendships are prominent in Williams's *Night Song*, Kanin's *Blow Up a Storm*, and others.[35] A motif that keeps recurring, and is exemplified in the fictional use of Parker and Holiday, is the musician-protagonist's 'self-destructiveness'. This is a stereotype that had particular currency in the late 1950s and early 1960s, following the deaths of Parker and Holiday in 1955 and 1959. Dorothy Baker's *Young Man With a Horn* had already produced the more romantic Beiderbecke-based version of 'The Story'. Baker's protagonist, whose influence on cinematic jazz heroes has already been noted, combined dysfunctional personality traits with a sense of having been selected for great talent and exemplary suffering. His early death and his alcohol dependency mirrored those of Beiderbecke, as does the mysteriously beautiful aura of his music. Baker's protagonist Rick also foreshadowed the biopic treatment of the driven, questing jazz musician, in his constant aspiration towards an elusive ideal music that will lift him beyond the normal limits of self-expression and free him from the sordid world of commercial music.

A review of the elements of jazz fiction demonstrates that it has followed not only the historical profile of the jazz film, but also its preoccupations. Through both mediums emerges the same mythological construct of 'the jazz musician'. Pathologized as 'self-destructive', the jazz musician progresses from great talent to an early end, prompted by the artistic temperament working together with self-indulgence, addiction to drugs, the philistinism of the public and the business, and racial prejudice.

Richard Albert lists only three substantial works of fiction on jazz published before 1940. A general cultural image of jazz was, however, already widely distributed through popular culture. An age called, by F. Scott Fitzgerald, 'The Jazz Age', had, according to him, already 'leapt to a spectacular death' in 1929.[36] Matthew Bruccoli has commented that Fitzgerald knew nothing about jazz.[37] This is certainly correct in the current sense of the word jazz, but it cannot be said of a man as active as Fitzgerald in the riotous social milieus of the period that he did not know about jazz in its 1920s sense. Fitzgerald's comments on the origin of the word suggest more than a casual interest: 'The word jazz in its progress towards respectability has meant first sex, then dancing, then music.' He notes the role of early jazz records in the early 1920s breakdown of puritanism: 'For a while bootleg Negro records with their phallic euphemisms made everything suggestive.' For Fitzgerald, jazz was 'associated with a state of nervous stimulation, not unlike that of cities behind the lines of a war',[38] a description which fits the atmosphere of later eras, especially the genesis of bebop in the clubs of wartime New York.

Another meaning of jazz for Fitzgerald was a vulgarity inseparable from its vitality. The scene in *The Great Gatsby* in which 'The Jazz History of the World' is performed on Gatsby's lawn seems intended to parallel the kitsch grandiosity of Paul Whiteman's 1924 Carnegie Hall concert:

'Ladies and gentlemen', he cried. 'At the request of Mr Gatsby we are going to play for you Mr Vladimir Tostoff's latest work which attracted so much attention at Carnegie Hall last May. If you read the papers you know there was a big sensation.' He smiled with jovial condescension, and added: 'Some sensation!' Whereupon everybody laughed.

'The piece is known' he concluded lustily, 'as "Vladimir Tostoff's Jazz History of the World".'[39]

As the bearer of older and more refined cultural values, the narrator, Nick Carraway, adopts a lofty tone towards 'Mr Tostoff's composition', but this is not Fitzgerald's own position. Fitzgerald was as ambivalent about popular culture as he was about the lives of the rich. His attitude towards the cinema was fastidious dismissal alternating with a half-envious fascination. There was a similar tension in his attitude towards jazz and popular music.

Fitzgerald often used the lyrics of popular songs to specify a time or a mood, from the rhythmic ditties of the early 1920s in *Gatsby* ('In the morning, in the evening, ain't we got fun'), through the evocative power of popular songs for Americans in exile in *Tender is the Night* to the romantic lyrics favoured by Cecilia Brady in *The Last Tycoon*. Cecilia is a child of the vital new popular medium, the cinema, and her awareness of jazz is a token of her innate understanding of what interests and moves the American public. She makes mention of Benny Goodman, Paul Whiteman and Guy Lombardo, popular bandleaders with a degree of connection with jazz, and her comments are linked with particular dates, as if she were tracking popular tastes across those years. When Fitzgerald wanted to characterize the creative drive and inventiveness of a movie production team, he turned to another popular art form, jazz, for an analogy: 'Suddenly they were at work again – taking up this new theme in turn like hepcats in a swing band and going to town with it. They might throw it out again tomorrow, but life had come back for a moment.'[40] Fitzgerald's language strikes a false note here, even allowing for the dated slang of 'hepcats' and 'going to town'. The passage was written in 1940, at the height of the Swing boom, and gives an impression of a desire on Fitzgerald's part to sound contemporary, and to use the vocabulary of one popular medium to describe another. As we shall see in Chapter 5, film writing is only one of a number of kinds of creative work for which the improvising jazz musician has stood as an analogy.

In a number of important texts, jazz is used to signify not familiarity but a formidable strangeness. Eudora Welty's well-known story 'Powerhouse' is as much a confrontation with the power of black culture, in

the Southern setting of Welty's fictional world, as it is specifically with
jazz, but the elements of jazz performance are as strongly realized here as
in any fiction. The fictitious 'Powerhouse', a jazz pianist of ominous
presence, is closely based on Fats Waller. Welty's Powerhouse, however, is Waller Africanized and magicalized to the point of becoming
grotesque. Waller's style of playing was characterized by fullness and
power, but in Welty's heightened version, he plays with 'outrageous
force'. The description of Powerhouse is founded upon amazement,
and the language is made up of the superlative and the prodigious. An
element of repulsion is included in the amazement: as well as being 'a
person of joy' Powerhouse is 'a fanatic'. 'Brutality' is mixed with
'delight' in his playing. His rapture when he plays is 'hideous' as well
as powerful, and his open mouth is 'vast and obscene'. The same word
recurs in the description of his posture at the piano: 'He is in motion
every moment – what could be more obscene?'[41]

His expression is likened to a monkey's face, and his fingers compared
to bananas. The elements of racist caricature are present in the text, but
their effect in Welty's story is more like a frank admission of fascination
at this overwhelming manifestation of a black culture. The narrative
tone, from the opening annunciation of his arrival ('Powerhouse is
playing!'), seems designed to register a fearful fascination that at times
gives up on articulation: 'Is it possible he could be this! When you have
him there performing for you, that's what you feel.' The narrator's
confusion and sense of being overwhelmed are due in part to the
interracial nature of the encounter, and an appeal is made, by the use
of the pronoun 'you', to the reader's recognition of this: 'You know
people on a stage – and people of a darker race - so likely to be
marvelous, frightening'.[42]

The second part of Welty's story is an imaginative step into the black
community of the small Mississippi town which welcomes and nour-
ishes Powerhouse. The ambiguity of the story is sustained through
Powerhouse's reaction to the report (by no means certain) of his wife's
death. He seems alternately troubled, heartless and mocking. Afterwards the players return to the bandstand for another demonstration of
their disturbing power, and in the midst of this the story ends. The
music functions as a defensive screen against the pains and vicissitudes
of life. Through their music, the players regain the stance against the
world that will sustain them against their losses, and carry them through
the hundreds of one-night gigs in towns like 'Alligator, Mississippi'.

Welty's story is an attempt to penetrate the masks of Powerhouse and his culture: what it communicates in the end is the conscious failure of this attempt, and a fascinated reinforcement of the mystery of black musicians and their art.[43]

In Carson McCullers's *The Member of the Wedding* another small-town setting comes into disturbing contact with the expressive power of jazz. For McCullers's adolescent protagonist Frankie, the song of a trumpet she hears in the distance, 'the sad horn of some colored boy', serves as a correlative to the complex emotions of a momentous summer:

> The tune was low and dark and sad. Then all at once, as Frankie listened, the horn danced into a wild jazz spangle that zigzagged upwards with sassy nigger trickiness. At the end of the jazz spangle the music rattled thin and far away. Then the tune returned to the first blues song, and it was like telling that long season of trouble.[44]

The music, the blues song and the 'jazz spangle', presumably an improvised cadenza, serves for Frankie as a means of articulating emotions she is not capable of expressing. The music contributes its own qualities, its marginality in a white Southern town, to her emotions. It is explicitly black music, 'wild' and characterized by 'sassy nigger trickiness', as well as a bluesy melancholy. The memory of the music stands as a point of reference to the state of mind which it has distilled and made accessible: 'after the long twilights of this season, when Frankie had walked around the sidewalks of the town, a jazz sadness quivered her nerves and her heart quivered and almost stopped'.[45] Combined with 'jazz' as an adjective, Frankie's sadness is enriched with other properties. it has colour and energy and a suggestion of secrecy, for Frankie's emotions are as invisible to others as the black trumpeter is to her.

These texts, each by white Southern women writers, share a sense of distance from the jazz music that suddenly appears in their environment. These are encounters with jazz at the extreme edges of its social and geographical orbit. For each of them the blackness of the performer is important. The response to jazz and its players is tangential and uncomprehending, and the subjectivity of the response is stressed: jazz is a means of entry to realms of feeling that are beyond the reach and outside the normal context of the people in these stories. It retains the charm and the threat of things perceived at a distance.

The relation to jazz of Ralph Ellison is exactly the contrary. All four of Ellison's published books make extensive reference to jazz, and his occasional essays on jazz, collected in *Shadow and Act* and *Going to the Territory*, contain some of the most independent-minded work by any writer on the subject.[46] Ellison was born and brought up in Oklahoma City, and numbered among his childhood friends such celebrated jazz musicians as the guitarist Charlie Christian and the singer Jimmy Rushing. Before becoming a writer, Ellison had studied music at Tuskegee Institute, and although intending to compose music in the classical tradition, had long experienced jazz as part of a 'total way of life'[47] in the black community of his hometown.

In Ellison's writing about jazz there is none of the sense of strangeness that beset Welty and McCullers. He writes about the Minton's jam sessions as an insider, and about Duke Ellington and Charlie Parker on the basis of personal acquaintance.[48] Among American novelists of any age and background, Ellison was uniquely placed in intimate relationship to jazz. Even in his fiction his approach to jazz was non-mythologizing. Jazz is mixed, in *Invisible Man*, into the illustrative series of episodes that bring Ellison's protagonist to the point of realizing his 'invisibility'. The blues singer Peetie Wheatstraw appears in person in one section, and in another the lyric of a Jimmy Rushing song provides the name Rinehart, the 'personification of chaos'.

The plot of *Invisible Man* puts its hero through a succession of ordeals, the result of which is his realization that his life has consisted of one form of exploitation after another. The hero concludes from his experiences that, as a black man, he is socially 'invisible', and reasoning that in the circumstances he might as well be literally invisible, he decides to go, equally literally, underground. The opening and ending of the novel disclose him inhabiting a subterranean room somewhere under the streets of Manhattan, lit and heated by energy from an illegal power line which also enables him to play over and over a single phonograph record, Louis Armstrong's 'Black and Blue'.

This recording has a number of meanings for Ellison and his hero. It represents pleasure and indulgence, like the warmth, the light and the gin and ice-cream the hero consumes while listening to the record. Its punning lyric addresses the hero's position and his protest explicitly: 'What did I do / To be so black and blue?' The hero's reiteration of this question forms the bridge into the main narrative of his exploitation and disillusionment. The song 'Black and Blue', with words by Andy Razaf to a melody by Fats Waller, and first recorded by Armstrong in 1929, is unusual among popular songs of the time in its direct reference to the experience of racism. Ellison's use of the song, however, is more complex: his narrator evidently revels in the music as a sensuous experience and as an expression of a jazz sensibility. He marvels at the way in which Armstrong 'bends that military instrument into a lyrical beam of sound'. This image reverses and compensates vicariously for the situation of the hero: as he is subject to and acted upon by the white power structure, so he delights in hearing Armstrong impose a black lyricism upon the 'military' instrument, the trumpet.

'Perhaps I like Louis Armstrong' the hero continues, 'because he's made poetry out of being invisible. I think it must be because he's unaware that he *is* invisible. And my own grasp of invisibility aids me to understand his music.' The two men share invisibility, but Armstrong has turned this property into a positive value. Ellison's hero, like many musicians who have spoken of Armstrong, dwells upon his sense of musical time, but for the invisible man, this faculty is indicative of their shared handicap. 'Invisibility, let me explain, gives one a slightly different sense of time, you're never quite on the beat.' The analogy between the two invisible men lies in their need to find a place within the given structures. Ellison's protagonist has found a safe haven in one of the gaps in the social fabric, in a hole in which he can feed off society while being unseen by it; Armstrong, in the invisible man's interpretation, occupies a similar niche in the structures of music: 'you slip into the breaks and look around. That's what you hear vaguely in Louis's music.'[49]

Although his narrator represents Armstrong as 'innocent' and 'unaware', Ellison never questions the power and artistry of his music. Jazz is, it goes without saying, a cultural resource that the black writer can call upon to express ideas of complexity and weight. Ellison, whose narrative structure in *Invisible Man* was influenced by the 'mythic method' of T. S. Eliot's 'The Waste Land', has no difficulty in speaking of jazz on the same level of esteem as this intellectually intricate modernist poem. Ellison is happy to assume the value of Armstrong's music and to make use of its resonance as an important element in the narrative strategy of the novel.

Despite his relaxed acceptance of jazz, Ellison is aware of its persistently stigmatized status, within some black communities as well as in American society generally. In his memoir of his early days in

Oklahoma City, he comments that jazz 'was still regarded by most of the respectable Negroes of the town as a backward, low-class form of expression'.[50] This perspective is consistently presented in the work of James Baldwin. The figure of the jazz and blues musician regularly features, as in *Go Tell It on the Mountain* and *The Amen Corner*, as specifically the antithesis of religious values, and generally the morally delinquent advocate of sensuality and lax habits.[51] Baldwin, who in David Leeming's words 'modeled himself on jazz musicians rather than other writers – especially on Miles Davis and Ray Charles – who "sang a kind of universal blues"',[52] shows some sympathy with these marginalized creative individuals.

In Baldwin's fullest account of jazz performance, the story 'Sonny's Blues', the moral dichotomy appears when the jazz musician Sonny watches a group of gospel singers performing in a New York street. Sonny, whom we see through the eyes of his 'respectable' schoolteacher brother, is a recovering heroin addict, whose career as a pianist has been halted by a spell in prison. The narrator refers back to Sonny's first declaration of his ambition to be a jazz musician and forward to a club performance which is the climax of the story. If jazz is the moral opposite of respectability, the hesitancy of Sonny's declaration to his brother is understandable, but the scene is stressed and extended to an extreme:

> 'Now', he said, very sober now and afraid, perhaps, that he'd hurt me, 'I don't want to be a classical pianist. That isn't what interests me. I mean' - he paused, looking hard at me, as though his eyes would help me to understand, and then gestured helplessly, as though perhaps his hand would help – ' I mean, I'll have a lot of studying to do, and I'll have to study *everything*, but, I mean, I want to play *with* – jazz musicians.' He stopped. 'I want to play jazz' he said.[53]

After the fearful expectancy of the build-up, this final statement comes to the contemporary reader as an anticlimax. Sonny's decision is invested with tremendous significance. This is in part a general effect of Baldwin's style: for example, when Sonny temporarily quits his dedicated practice at the piano, 'the silence of the next few days must have been louder than the sound of all the music ever played since time began'.[54] It is also, though, a function of the tragic-heroic role in which, in many fictions of the period, the jazz musician was imagined. Stories like 'Sonny's Blues' register how far up the scale of significance the image of the jazz player had moved, from the entertainer of the 1930s to the existentialist hero of the 1950s. This shift of persona is also presented here in Sonny's contempt for Louis Armstrong ('that old-time, down home crap') and his admiration for Charlie Parker, hero of a hundred other narratives.

The final section of the story offers a degree of resolution. Sonny is reintegrated into the jazz world, and his brother reconciled to this vocation, through Sonny's comeback performance in a Greenwich Village club. The occasion is important and difficult, but Baldwin loads it with more significance than it can bear. A group of musicians, in conversation in front of the bandstand, are reluctant to step into the lighted area; the narrator reads their attitude as signifying that 'if they moved into the light too suddenly, without thinking, they would perish in flame'. When Sonny improvises he is 'exactly like someone in torment' in the 'fire and fury of the battle which was occurring in him up there'. Baldwin generalizes the activity of the jazz musician in these terms: 'the man who creates the music is hearing something else, and is dealing with the roar rising from the void ... What is evoked in him, then, is of another order, more terrible because it has no words.' It is not only Sonny, struggling with his personal problems, but all the other musicians, to whom Baldwin attributes these agonies of the spirit. 'He and his boys up there were keeping it new, at the risk of ruin, destruction, madness and death.'[55]

There is little sense in Baldwin's fiction of the specifics of jazz as music or as an art of performance. The schoolteacher narrator's stated unfamiliarity with contemporary jazz is also Baldwin's own. Rather than being grounded, like Ellison, in an understanding of how jazz actually functions in practical terms, Baldwin is confined to impressionistic description which seeks its effect in the elevation of the jazz musician into the quasi-religious mode of the sacrificial hero, who suffers on behalf of the community or of humanity: 'I seemed to hear with what burning he had made it his, with what burning we had got to make it ours, how we could cease lamenting.' When Sonny, at the close of the story, places a drink on top of the piano, the narrator imagines, in a strange, vaguely religious phrase, that 'it glowed and shook above my brother's head like the very cup of trembling.'[56]

Baldwin makes it clear that Sonny suffers and triumphs on behalf of a black community. Jon Panish sees a distinction between texts by black writers and those by whites in the fact that in the latter the (frequently white) protagonist is individualized and isolated, while in the former the black protagonist is placed in relation to a community with which he has some sense of identification. However, the rhetorical heightening of the significance of the jazz musician as hero in a manner similar to Baldwin's is found equally in fiction of the same period by white writers. It is consistent, for example, with Norman Mailer's allusions to jazz in his 1957 essay 'The White Negro', and with the emotional atmosphere of novels like John Clellon Holmes's *The Horn*.[57] Some idea of the extravagant dimensions of the role designated for the jazz musician in this period can be got from this comment, by Holmes in a letter to Jack Kerouac: 'All he knows is that something speaks within him and he has been bestowed with the mechanics of prophesy. He threatens at any minute to save the rest of us with his earnest efforts at grace.' For Holmes, it is jazz musicians who 'most perfectly epitomise the sorry, and often fabulous, condition of the artist in America'.[58]

Some sections of *The Horn* liken well-known jazz players to figures from the canon of American literature (Charlie Parker to Melville, and Billie Holiday to Emily Dickinson, for instance). Holmes also likens the jazz musician to Dostoevsky's character Kirillov, whose life was dominated by the search for a moment of spiritual transcendence. In other places, the jazz player is made to symbolize 'the trek of the American across his wastes', in search of 'some intoxicative moment of fruition, some indefinable phrase or note', and facing 'dangers of the journey' such as 'spiritual impoverishment'.[59] Holmes's version of the jazz musician is just as beleaguered as was Baldwin's, but, in line with Panish's thesis, his ordeal is less rooted in a particular culture, and more viable in the realms of high culture established by Holmes's literary analogies.

In *The Horn* the same level of discourse prevails. Holmes presents portraits of two central characters, Edgar Pool and Geordie Dickson, which are easily recognizable as Lester Young and Billie Holiday exaggerated to the point of caricature. Geordie Dickson (Holiday) has a physicality of the same overstated order as the ordeals and terrors involved in playing jazz: her thighs 'shivered in brute, incomplete expression of the pure urge inside her'. When the young saxophonist Walden has the temerity to challenge Pool in a jam session, 'the affront had shocked everyone else, the room was frozen, speechless'. Walden then enters a realm described in terms of Conradian mystery and

Hemingwayan stress upon what men must do: 'But thereby he was placing himself outside their mercy and their judgement, in a no-man's land where he must go alone.'[60]

Holmes's writing shows some signs of a greater circumstantial knowledge of jazz, its performers and history, than Baldwin's, and yet his expression of its importance is similarly unconcerned with anything intrinsic to it as an art or craft. Baldwin has recourse to religious and quasi-religious language; Holmes's strategy is instead to establish the height and depth of jazz by allusion or direct reference to other literature, especially literature in which a spiritual crisis of some magnitude is invoked. It is worth noting, too, Holmes's focus on the same few jazz musicians whose lives had already, in other works, become emblematic of the figure of the troubled, 'self-destructive' artist.

Although Jack Kerouac was the recipient of the letter in which Holmes voiced his vision of the jazzman as transcendent American hero, Kerouac's own uses of jazz are quite differently conceived. Jazz is used for a variety of purposes and effects in Kerouac's writing. Reference to jazz is frequent throughout his work, including the novels *Maggie Cassidy*, *The Subterraneans*, *Desolation Angels* and most famously *On the Road*.[61] However, none of Kerouac's books is specifically about jazz in the manner of *The Horn*. Jazz is not structural, but features instead in short indicative episodes in which description predominates.

In trying to give an account of Kerouac's relationship to jazz, one confronts, as well as the serious criticisms of writers like Jon Panish, the uncritical comments of Kerouac's exponents and biographers. Kerouac himself, as a man and as an image, has become as powerful an icon of an imagined 1950s America as jazz is. Implicated in the influential discourse of 'The Fifties', jazz becomes a stereotypical component of a larger myth. The following kind of representation of Kerouac's writing results from this process: 'Drugs, sex and jazz fuelled the hot-rod go-go prose style because only they were spontaneous and defiant enough and high-octane enough to keep it on the move.'[62] In this instance, jazz has become completely enmeshed in a complex retro cultural image compounded of fragments of Charlie Parker, James Dean and the lifestyles of later rock and roll singers.

Kerouac's biographers have been relatively uninterested in jazz, and have applied to it a conception derived partly from popular myth and partly from Kerouac's work itself. Gerald Nicosia, for example, offers a characterization of bebop and its musicians that owes much to the rhetoric of writers like Baldwin and Holmes: 'many of bop's innovators were extremely tormented men and died early deaths'. On the contrary, it could be argued that the majority of bop's innovators (excepting the iconic case of Parker) were, like Dizzy Gillespie, rather practical men who lived and played on for another forty years. 'In this case,' Nicosia goes on, 'the energy to explore the inexhaustible reaches of soul seems to have come, in large part, from equally inexhaustible stores of anguish.'[63] This comment links the supposed psychological condition of the beboppers with the state of mind Nicosia attributes to Kerouac, but at the cost of accuracy to the facts. The early pioneers of bebop, as African-American artists and citizens, did experience racism, and their reaction to it is encoded in the music, but Nicosia's 'anguish' is too heated and too generalized.

Nicosia's description of the musical practices of bebop gives the impression, through a common confusion about their use of alternative themes over the chords of popular songs, that the beboppers actually invented improvisation:

> In effect, the soloist discarded the melody of the song he was playing and improvised a completely new melody more consistent with his whims of the moment . . . the possibilities of new sound were infinite, and the only limitation the physical stamina of the performer.[64]

For all its brilliance, bebop music cannot be described as opening up 'infinite' or limitless possibilities. Miles Davis made the move into modal playing ten years later to escape some of bebop's limitations. Nicosia's description, which is closely linked with his exposition of Kerouac's prose style, remakes bebop in an image more consonant with the aesthetic of Kerouac and the other Beat writers.

Kerouac himself, however, had long-lasting and close relations with jazz culture. As Jim Burns has shown, Kerouac's references to jazz in his novels in effect document the development of jazz and jazz-related music over a twenty-year period from the mid-1930s, when as a teenager Kerouac began to hear Swing Era music on the radio, up to the mid-1950s.[65] At one stage Kerouac aspired to be a jazz journalist, interviewing Count Basie for a student magazine and submitting an article about Lester Young to *Metronome*. The fact that, despite the exclusivity of the scene, Kerouac was one of those present at Minton's in the early 1940s, suggests, as Burns comments, 'that he was one of a small group of genuine enthusiasts'.[66] Among prominent American novelists only Ralph Ellison (also an attender at Minton's) had an involvement with jazz comparable with Kerouac's, though Ellison had the advantage of being a player as well as a fan. As Burns puts it, 'Kerouac's interest in jazz was lifelong' and this distinguishes and distances him from most of his commentators.[67]

At its best, Kerouac's treatment of jazz is evocative, exact and specific. The portrait he produces of the pianist George Shearing in *On the Road* is as pictorial as the impressionistic writing of a jazz writer like Whitney Balliett: 'a distinguished-looking Englishman with a stiff white collar, slightly beefy, blond, with a delicate English-summer's-night air about him' (compare Balliett on Dizzy Gillespie: 'A mild-mannered, roundish man, who wears thick-rimmed spectacles and a small goatee, and has a new-moon smile and a muffled, potatoey way of speaking'.).[68] Kerouac's descriptions of Slim Gaillard in *On the Road* and the saxophonist Brew Moore in *Desolation Angels* are also effective transpositions of the mood and character of their performances into prose.[69]

The performances of unnamed musicians are also handled with some care and an attempt at empathy. Watching a group of young bebop musicians performing in a saloon in Chicago (a set-up very like the 'roving bands' referred to by Ira Gitler in Chapter 2), Kerouac observes each player in turn and gives a brief description of their physical and mental dispositions: 'The leader was a slender, drooping, curly-haired, pursy-mouthed tenorman, thin of shoulder, draped loose in a sports shirt, cool in the warm night, self-indulgence written in his eyes.' Of the trumpeter, Kerouac writes: 'He raised his horn and blew into it quietly and thoughtfully and elicited birdlike phrases and architectural Miles Davis logics.' The pianist is 'a big husky Italian truck-driving kid with meaty hands, a burly and thoughtful joy'. This group description is split in two by a digression into a one-paragraph history of jazz which contains similar touches of description: the trumpeter Roy Eldridge 'leaning to it with glittering eyes and a lovely smile'; Charlie Parker 'in his early days when he was flipped and walked around in a circle while playing'. There is an extended description of Lester Young's posture changing in parallel with his playing style: 'his horn is held weakly against his chest, and he blows cool and easy getout phrases'. These are pictures evidently based on first-hand observation.[70]

Kerouac's approach even in these passages is nevertheless highly subjective. An element in it is the writer's imaginative projection of his awareness into that of the performers, and this can distort reality in favour of something that Kerouac is happier to believe. The most harmful examples occur when Kerouac attempts this kind of empathy with black musicians. One of the notorious self-gratifying descriptions in *On the Road* is Kerouac's idealized picture of life in the black section of Denver, where he wanders 'wishing I could exchange worlds with the happy, true-hearted, ecstatic Negroes of America'.[71] Jon Panish has described Kerouac's vision of Charlie Parker, who appears a number of times in his work, as 'a white fantasy of a black self.'[72] According to Panish, Kerouac's picture of Parker fixes exclusively upon Parker's status as victim and as subcultural hero.

Another feature is the sacrificial, Christ-like or Buddha-like resignation which Kerouac claims to see in Parker's facial expression. Kerouac's accounts are circumstantial and specific, seemingly based on actual observation of Parker in performance. From *The Subterraneans*, for instance, we are presented with Parker as he 'pursed his lips and let great lungs and immortal fingers work, his eyes separate and interested and humane, the greatest musician there could be and therefore naturally the kindest'.[73] Panish objects that for Kerouac to pick out Parker's 'kindness' is to assimilate him to the gentle, helpful Negro of 'minstrel-like depictions of black people'.[74] However, some details of the picture are striking and graphic, especially the triplet of adjectives describing the look of Parker's eyes while his fingers play: 'separate and interested and humane'. This is as much a product of pure, if subjectivized, description as the portraits of the unknown Chicago beboppers. Kerouac registers what seems to him a revealingly sympathetic expression in Parker's eyes while his mind is fully engaged with the complexities of high-speed improvisation. Kerouac clearly overinterprets what is only a fleeting moment of apparent insight, but the 'kindness' he perceives in Parker is more Buddha than Uncle Tom.

All the same, Kerouac's conviction of a rapport that he shares with black musicians is at times unwarranted, whether on his own behalf or on behalf of the 'hero' of *On the Road*, Dean Moriarty. Dean, who 'had the energy of a new kind of American saint', responds with manic self-involvement to jazz records ('Dean, sandwich in hand, stood bowed and jumping before the big phonograph, listening to a wild bop record') and to players in nightclubs ('Dean was directly in front of him with his face lowered to the bell of the horn, clapping his hands, pouring sweat on the man's keys').[75] Panish views these displays, and Kerouac's sense of a special communion with men like Parker, as fantasies of 'a conduit of empathy and energy flowing from African American performers to particular Euro American audience members'.[76] The nightclub, or the place and time of jazz performance, becomes again the 'utopian' setting which for David Stowe is represented by Swing performance in the 1930s: a special realm exempt from the stresses and exclusions of the wider society, and where, within a limited frame of time, a transracial harmony can be enjoyed. Whether or not this momentary communion was a fantasy is presumably to be decided by the parties involved, but in Kerouac's writing one comes across the same concept in a different form. Jam sessions in a San Francisco nightclub in the 'Negro jazz joints in the oil flats' are equivalent to the raft on which Jim and Huckleberry Finn can enjoy their moment of rapport in temporary seclusion from society on the banks.

The acquisition by jazz of new 'cultural capital' in the late 1980s and in the 1990s has made it once again viable as literary subject matter, and there has been a resurgence of jazz-related fiction. Amongst these texts, one might mention Bill Moody's sequence of jazz detective novels, Bart Schneider's *Blue Bossa* (1998), with its indirect reference to the trumpeter Chet Baker, and Rafi Zabor's imaginative and authentic *The Bear Goes Home* (1997).[77] Zabor's novel manages to refer directly to musical values and to describe jazz performance with a sense of its meaning for its participants.

The most prominent of these texts of the 1990s is Toni Morrison's 1992 novel *Jazz*.[78] By its title Morrison's book might seem to be claiming to be the definitive novel on the subject. However, the book is more accurately seen as a historical gloss upon the semantics of the word 'jazz' and a rediscovery of one of its older meanings for the purpose of recreation of a particular time and place. Morrison is quoted as saying that the book's title might not be ideally appropriate, as jazz functions as a background 'image and metaphor' rather than the substantive subject.[79] The title *Jazz* is metonymic: it names a condition of society, the style and tenor of a particular period, rather than simply denoting the practice of jazz music. Morrison's metonymic use of 'jazz' is not far removed from Fitzgerald's usage in the phrase 'The Jazz Age', and the novel is set in 1926, the exact middle of the period Fitzgerald was referring to. The meaning of 'jazz' becomes the sum total of Morrison's text itself: the lives, the actions, the rhythms and the qualities that the text presents.

The term 'jazz' was used in a related way within the period itself: as an attributive adjective, 'jazz' was used by lyricists and by writers of social comedy, such as P. G. Wodehouse, to refer to things, such as items of clothing, that in their modernity, brightness and eccentricity were somehow expressive of the prevailing culture.[80] Morrison's 'jazz' is not a recreation of this ephemeral meaning, but an extension of the word into the sector of experience her text is concerned with. The milieu of the novel is the 'Renascent' Harlem of the mid-1920s, especially the self-revaluation of the black southern migrants under the impact of the city. Jazz as music and as musical culture is present in a number of places in the text: the Okeh label record that a young woman carries under her arm, the jazz band of the fictitious Slim Bates, the music of the 'rent party' which is described extensively, the rooftop trumpeters and clarinettists. Morrison's text repeats some of Fitzgerald's points of reference: his 'bootleg negro records with their phallic euphemisms' become blues lyrics grafted into the text: 'a knowing woman sang ain't nobody going to keep me down you got the right key baby but the wrong keyhole you got to get it bring it and put it right there'.[81]

As for Fitzgerald, music is associated with release from restraints on sexual behaviour, and for one of the novel's witnesses, Alice, a threatened disruption of all social restraint. In Alice's mind, the race riots in St Louis, the demonstrators on the streets of Harlem, are somehow connected with the music:

> It wasn't the War and the disgruntled veterans; it wasn't the droves and droves of colored people flocking to paychecks and streets full of themselves. It was the music. The dirty, get-on-down music the women sang and the men played and both danced to, close and shameless or apart and wild. Alice was convinced and so were the Miller sisters as they blew into cups of Postum in the kitchen. It made you do unwise disorderly things. Just hearing it was like violating the law.[82]

Music is here a symptom, or even a cause, of destabilizing change, in a way that is reminiscent of Jacques Attali's idea of music's power to predict social transformation.[83] Morrison's treatment of the idea also has common ground with Fitzgerald's analysis of the same mid-1920s years. Both display a movement within American society that may be exhilarating and liberating, but which also threatens to loosen the bonds which have previously held society in place.

Peter Brooker has pointed out that Morrison's *Jazz* is notable for the quantity of documentary detail on 1920s jazz that it leaves out: the location of Joe and Violet's apartment on Lenox Avenue is close to the epicentre of jazz culture at the time, but Morrison does not pick up on this or on other opportunities to reinforce the jazz-historical foundation of the text.[84] It is clear that *Jazz* is not about jazz in any narrow sense, or even in the usual sense in which the word is used. As we have seen throughout this book, the word 'jazz' is polysemous, a floating signifier which is occasionally anchored down to a specific restricted meaning. In this novel, Morrison has generated and defined another meaning. The subject of *Jazz*, and Morrison's meaning of 'jazz', is an ensemble of moods, textures and actions which are produced and elaborated by this text, and which reflect black urban culture of the 1920s.

One of the by-products of some of the jazz fiction discussed in this chapter is that writing about jazz suggests the possibility of writing in a jazz-like way. Jazz provides an attractive alternative model to conventional fictional methods and structures. This is evident in American fiction from Welty's 1941 'Powerhouse' onwards: it may be manifested in Kerouac's writing at the level of prose style and compositional method, and has been claimed as an influence on Morrison's technique.[85] Jazz has been accorded a similar function in poetry, and, as we shall see in Chapter 5, jazz as an aesthetic example or model can be seen as exerting an influence across a wide range of expressive forms, even beyond music and literature, into the visual arts.

Jazz and American Poetry

Jazz is scattered through American poetry in much the same way as through fiction. It figures prominently in the work of individual writers who have expressed an affinity with it, such as Hayden Carruth, and it has served as an occasional subject for many notable American poets, from William Carlos Williams in the 1920s through Frank O'Hara in the 1950s to Dana Gioia in the 1990s. Otherwise, the incidence of jazz-related poetry follows a historical curve distinct from that of fiction but sharing a peak period in the late 1950s. Jazz poetry has also attracted some of the same doubts as to overall quality as we have seen in fiction: 'To my mind, (jazz poems) came across as, at worst, crusty relics of a beatnik sensibility, or, at best, as merely pale imitations of the free flowing energy of a real jazz performance.'[86]

It can be argued, however, that American poetry has had a relation of special closeness to jazz. As well as figuring as subject matter, jazz has been manifested in poetry as an aesthetic example. As poetry is closer than prose to music, it has seemed to some American poets that an American musical idiom should be a natural partner for their poetry. There is also, taking this a step further, the possibility of merging the two idioms in performance, producing 'jazz poetry' in a literal sense. Jazz and poetry have also been linked by their status as minority art forms, bound together by their expression of non-standard attitudes and by their separation, principled or enforced, from commercial interests. Jazz poetry has flourished mostly in the small-circulation magazines, just as much jazz recording has been issued by small record companies.

Poetry is also found in the lyrics of songs that spring from or are allied with the musical culture of jazz. Lyricists like Johnny Mercer and Andy Razaf, co-composer of 'Black and Blue' with Fats Waller, and composer-lyricists such as Mose Allison and Dave Frishberg have produced substantial bodies of verse which derive from the conventions of both jazz and popular music. Among jazz composers, Duke Ellington stands out as a musician capable also of producing vivid and original poetry. Ellington's lyric for 'The Blues', a movement of his 1943 suite *Black, Brown and Beige*, uses a series of striking images to present the blues as a state of bleak *anomie*:

> The blues ain't nothing but a cold grey day
> And all night long it stays that way.
> The blues is a one-way ticket from your love to nowhere,
> The blues ain't nothing but a black crape veil
> Ready to wear.

The traditional blues themselves have provided a source and example of poetic imagery and a form in which to articulate it. The blues poetic tradition has continued uninterrupted in some varieties of jazz. Some jazz instrumentalists have been accomplished singers in the blues tradition, many of them able to improvise verbally as well as instrumentally on the blues form. Among blues-conversant jazz players should be mentioned instrumentalist-singers such as Lips Page, Jack Teagarden, Clark Terry and Eddie Vinson.

Jazz, or one its precursor forms, makes a fragmentary appearance in the 'Shakespeherian Rag' section of T. S. Eliot's *The Waste Land*, a poem whose rhythms were heard by Ralph Ellison as being 'closer to jazz than were those of the Negro poets'.[87] An attempt by Carl Sandburg to include jazz in his Whitmanesque panorama of American life fastens upon the idea of jazz as the prelude to 'rough stuff' among the people:

> you jazzmen, bang together drums,
> traps, banjoes, horns, tin cans – make two people fight
> on the top of a stairway and scratch each other's eyes
> in a clinch tumbling down the stairs.[88]

William Carlos Williams's earliest contact with jazz took place in 1945, and provoked the poem 'Ol' Bunk's Band'.[89] The poem begins and ends with the exclamation 'These are men!', and moves in a percussive monosyllabic rhythm. Williams appears to have experienced the encounter as a revelation of primitive energy and disruptive power:

> the
> ancient cry, escaping crapulence
>   eats through
> transcendent – torn, tears, tempo
>   town, tense,
> turns and backs off whole, leaps
>   up, stomps down,
>   rips through! …

This poem, designated by Hayden Carruth 'the worst poem Dr Williams ever wrote', is reminiscent of Welty's 'Powerhouse' in its awed celebration of the power of black music, but it lacks the self-awareness of Welty's story. In Carruth's view, Williams 'treats Bunk Johnson and the old-time musicians playing with him as if they were some unintelligible anthropological specimens, people from another and distant culture making noises for the mere hell of it or out of animal exuberance'. Carruth laments Williams's inability to establish a meaningful context for the music, or to engage with the Johnson band as individuals involved like himself in the practice of a specific cultural form: 'That they were artists like himself never crossed his mind.'[90] In much of the poetry concerned with jazz there is evidence, as in this poem, of the same problem of distance as is evident in fiction. Jazz, perceived from an external vantage point, is taken as symbolic of primitivism, masculine force, a state of derangement of society. For Williams and Sandburg it is one of the curious life-forms that can be observed in the

interstices of American social structure. Lacking a foundation of familiarity with the culture, these writers can only translate jazz into a
symbol of general qualities such as energy, exuberance and anarchic
force.

These limitations do not apply in the work of Langston Hughes,
whose position in jazz-related poetry is comparable with that of Ralph
Ellison in fiction. Hughes's engagement with jazz was close and long-
lived, from his 'Weary Blues' of 1923 up to the time of his death in 1967.
Jazz crops naturally out of the landscape of Hughes's poetry, which is
largely that of the black communities of Harlem and Chicago, and it
remains fluid in its significance. Hughes's earliest references to jazz, in
poems like 'Jazzonia' and 'Jazz Band in a Parisian Cabaret', acknowl-
edge the exoticism which was customary in the presentation of jazz in
the 1920s, and the novelty which the music still possessed for Hughes
himself:

> In a Harlem cabaret
> Six long-headed jazzers play
> A dancing girl whose eyes are bold
> Lifts high a dress of silken gold.
>
> ('Jazzonia')

This novelty is compounded by a further level of exoticism for the
white visitors to the black cabarets who figure frequently in Hughes's
jazz world. 'Jazz Band in a Parisian Cabaret', for instance, has the band

> Play it for the lords and ladies
> For the dukes and counts
> For the whores and gigolos
> For the American millionaires

and 'Harlem Night Club' pictures 'dark brown girls / In blond men's
arms'. In Hughes's more politically barbed poetry of the 1930s these
comments on white voyeurism harden into his attitude in 'Visitors to
the Black Belt':

> You can say
> Jazz on the South Side –
> To me it's hell
> On the South Side.

At the same time, jazz is one of the threads that make up the fabric of urban life in the 'Harlem Renaissance' period. In a poem entitled 'Heart of Harlem' Hughes places jazz musicians such as Earl Hines and Billie Holiday alongside individuals of the stature of Adam Clayton Powell, Joe Louis and W. E. B. DuBois. Hughes's continuous awareness of the place of jazz in his community enables him to record its scenes and its changes across the decades. 'Lincoln Theatre', a poem published in a collection in 1949, gives a memorably exact rendering of the sort of Swing Era performance, in a Harlem theatre, that was discussed in Chapter 2:

> The movies end. The lights flash gaily on.
> The band down in the pit bursts into jazz.
> The crowd applauds a plump brown-skin bleached blonde
> Who sings the troubles every woman has.

Hughes responded with particular sympathy to jazz of the bebop period, which he saw as having great political significance. 'Montage of a Dream Deferred', published in 1951, is one of Hughes's most substantial sequences of poems, and it is shot through with references to jazz. His editorial note to the sequence explains the stylistic influence of bebop on its composition:

> This poem on contemporary Harlem, like be-bop, is marked by conflicting changes, sudden nuances, sharp and impudent interjections, and passages sometimes in the manner of the jam session, sometimes the popular song, punctuated by the riffs, runs, breaks and distortions of the music of a community in transition.

As Hughes made clear in other places, he heard bebop as an expression of a dissident spirit within the younger black community:

> Little cullud boys with fears
> frantic, kick their draftee years
> into flatted fifths and flatter beers ...

and 'A Dream Deferred' resounds with suggestions, threatening or impudent, that well up in the music, the 'boogie-woogie rumble':

> Listen to it closely
> Ain't you heard
> something underneath.

Bebop affected the forms of Hughes's poetry at the higher architectural levels, dictating the structural rhythm of longer works like 'Dream
Deferred', but otherwise he employed a small range of simple verse
forms that originate in earlier styles of black music. A particular
favourite was a two-stress line rhymed in quatrains, derived from
spirituals, and he also frequently used a looser form drawn from the
12-bar blues. The first of these Hughes was able to use with remarkable
flexibility, considering its brevity. The form is often used for aphoristic
effect, as in 'Motto':

> I play it cool
> And dig all jive.
> That's the reason
> I stay alive.

or in 'Sliver', a comment on the form itself:

> A cheap little tune
> To cheap little rhymes
> Can cut a man's
> Throat sometimes.

What is even more remarkable is the naturalness of its effect in these
diverse contexts. Hughes makes the form serve the purposes of narrative and description just as flexibly as that of comment. It gives
Hughes's verse its idiomatic flavour, so that even where the subject
is not jazz or even music, the verse is still permeated with the qualities
of black musical culture.[91]

The work of Hughes, and of Sterling Brown, whose verse is
stylistically similar to that of Hughes, established jazz as a subject for
poetry in the historical context of the literary and artistic 'Harlem
Renaissance' of the 1920s and 1930s. The second peak in the profile of
jazz in poetry occurred, as with prose fiction and film, in the 1950s. The
1950s presented the strongest upsurge to date of poetry performed with
jazz, a movement into which Hughes was drawn back in the late 1950s,
and which also involved Kerouac and a number of other writers based
in San Francisco, most notably Kenneth Patchen and Kenneth Rexroth.
Kerouac was featured on a number of recordings in which he read his
prose and poetry with accompaniment by a small jazz band. Rexroth
was responsible for setting up a series of poetry readings in San
Francisco in which the practice of reading poetry with jazz was explored

by himself and other writer-performers. Rexroth himself seemed not to have been satisfied by the results of this mode of poetry performance. This he put down to the difficulty of marrying the procedures of the two idioms. Feinstein and Komunyakaa comment that 'Even at the height of poetry and jazz readings, there was significant criticism, much of it justified, that the cross-medium relationship seemed forced – that neither art form was allowed to breathe.' Or, as Rexroth put it more acidly, 'It was ruined by people who knew nothing about either jazz or poetry.'[92] Nevertheless, coupling jazz and poetry in performance has seemed to practitioners of both forms a perennially interesting possibility. There has been evidence in the 1990s of renewed activity in this area, and a revaluation of earlier work, inspired by the resurgence of 'performance poetry' in general.

The third period in which there was a significant movement towards jazz as a subject of poetry occurred in the late 1960s. A reassertion of a distinctively black creative tradition had been evident in jazz music itself from the beginning of the 1960s, and the 'New Black Poetry' was closely identified with this music, its performers, and the politics and philosophy of the movement as a whole. A poet whose experience bridged these two periods is LeRoi Jones (Amiri Baraka), who had been a participant in the poetry and jazz proceedings in the late 1950s and went on to become one of the most prominent voices of the New Black Poetry. Baraka's autobiography states the importance of music for this poetry: he and his colleagues were 'drenched in black music and wanted our poetry to *be* black music'.[93] Stephen Henderson's critical anthology of the New Black Poetry reiterates the centrality of the music in the genesis of the poetry: 'Whenever Black Poetry is most distinctively and effectively *Black*, it derives its forms from two basic sources, Black speech and Black music.'[94]

In the writings of this movement, poetry is caught up in a complex set of transactions between cultural categories: it becomes difficult to separate poetry from music, and music in turn comes under a new and inclusive term 'Black music'. There is a sense, in relations within and between the arts of the period, that ultimately all of these terms come under a single dominant term 'Black art' or 'Black culture'. Baraka's criticism of the time stressed the continuity of a tradition of black music that transcended the confines of 'jazz' and spanned the entire range from Tamla Motown to the avant-garde improvisations of Albert Ayler. In the relations between jazz and poetry (or black music and poetry), there was a similar loss of boundaries: thus, Baraka says, 'we wanted our poetry to *be* black music.' At the same time, jazz musicians were producing and publishing, sometimes on the liner notes of their own albums, their own poetry. Another wave of jazz-and-poetry performance was another of the products of the dissolution of boundaries: Baraka, for instance, made recordings with a number of leading jazz musicians.

The jazz poetry of the late 1960s was explicitly black. Reference to jazz serves in some cases to articulate the political protest which was frequently overt in the poetry and music of the period. Percy Johnston's 'Round About Midnight, Opus 17', for instance, expresses with some force the notion that the deeper meanings of black music, here represented by a Thelonious Monk composition, are not accessible to white experience:

> You can't dig this song
> We play at midnight
> Unless
> Life's feces
> Have bathed your face
> Going to the Apollo or the Howard
> Midnight show
> Won't help you dig this tune.[95]

Lance Jeffers's 'How High the Moon' reads a message of defiance in the sound of jazz improvisation:

> the thin young black man with an old man's face
> lungs up
> the tissue of a trumpet from his deep-cancered corners
> racks out a high and seamy curse!
> Full from the sullen grace of the streets it sprouts:
> NEVER YOUR CAPTIVE![96]

The poetry of this movement is in some respects the formal analogue to the jazz of its time. As in the 1950s Kerouac had aspired to reproduce the cadences of bebop in his prose and poetry, so the writers of the New Black Poetry seemed to emulate the extreme formal liberties of 'Free Jazz' in the highly variegated and irregular use they made of the resources of prosody and typography. Metre and rhyme and the other resources of traditional verse were as inapplicable to its

aesthetic as the conventional 32-bar song was to free improvisers like
Ornette Coleman. There was the same disdain for conventional forms
as Amiri Baraka praised in John Coltrane's 'murder' of the popular
song.[97]

   The figure of the saxophonist John Coltrane exerted over the writers
of the late 1960s a fascination as strong as that of charismatic individuals
like Parker and Holiday over the writers of previous decades. Some of
the poems written about Coltrane, and about his early death in 1967,
have the character of religious invocation, such as Michael S. Harper's
'Dear John, Dear Coltrane' and 'Here Where Coltrane Is', and Baraka's
'AM/TRAK':

> Trane,
> Trane,
> History Love Scream Oh
> Trane, Oh
> Trane, Oh
> Scream History Love
> Trane . . .

Coltrane's importance for writers was, however, different in kind from
that of earlier models such as Parker. In Frank Kofsky's estimation, 'no
single figure in the history of jazz – regardless of style – ever possessed
greater moral authority than John Coltrane'.[98] Coltrane's later music
was avowedly spiritual in intent, and this gave his example a significance beyond the confines of music. Some writers compared him with
contemporary moral and political leaders such as Martin Luther King
and Malcolm X.[99] Coltrane was an inspiration for poetry rather than for
fiction. While his death, at forty, was just as early and as tragic as those
of the earlier mythicized figures, the trajectory of his life was quite
different. Coltrane's musical career was at an unprecedented height at
the time of his death, and it had followed an impressively purposeful
curve upward to his triumphant performances of the 1960s. His life did
not follow, and has not subsequently been fitted into, the pattern of
'The Story'. It is unlikely that a Coltrane biopic will ever be made, or
that such a film will romanticize the tribulations of his life as versions of
jazz lives have so often done for other musicians in the past, and as
earlier sections of this chapter have shown. The jazz poetry of the 1960s
and afterwards stops at the invocation of Coltrane as an example of
black creativity, of spiritual inspiration, of moral leadership.

The literary manifestations of jazz have on the whole remained true to the description given as long ago as 1958 by Hugh L. Smith: a 'set of romantic symbols'.[100] Certain writers – Hughes, Ellison, and to some extent Kerouac – have separated themselves from a purely symbolic treatment, from the received ideas about the music and its culture, and from the conventional narratives which have dominated its presentation. Jazz as a subject in these writers, however, rarely occupies the centre of their intentions.

One can see here a fundamental division of interest. Jazz is a distinctive cultural form; so is the cinema; so is the novel. There is no particular reason to assume that a close and adequate representation of any one of these forms can be given by another. It is only the greater cultural prestige of both the cinema and literature that has made jazz seem a possible subject for treatment by them. Jazz has a different audience, a different 'interpretative community' from literature, and literary-cinematic versions of jazz have had the function of making jazz intelligible to the literary and the cinematic audiences, with their different compositions, perspectives and assumptions. The effects of this process of translation have been seen in this chapter.

Notes

1. *Jammin' the Blues* (1944), directed by Gjon Mili; *A Great Day in Harlem* (1995), directed by Jean Bach.
2. Nat Hentoff and Nat Shapiro (eds), *Hear Me Talkin' to Ya* (London: Penguin, 1962); Ira Gitler, *Swing to Bop: An Oral History of the Transition in Jazz in the 1940s* (New York: OUP, 1985); Charles Mingus, *Beneath the Underdog* (New York: Knopf, 1971); Mezz Mezzrow with Bernard Wolfe, *Really the Blues* (New York: Random House, 1946); Art and Laurie Pepper, *Straight Life* (New York: Schirmer, 1979). On the interpretation of oral histories, see Burton W. Peretti, 'Oral Histories of Jazz Musicians: The NEA Transcripts as Texts in Context', in Krin Gabbard (ed.), *Jazz Among the Discourses* (Durham: Duke University Press, 1995).
3. David Meeker, *Jazz in the Movies: A Guide to Jazz Musicians 1917–1977* (London: Talisman, 1977).
4. *The Jazz Singer* was directed by Alan Crosland, *The King of Jazz* by John Murray Anderson.
5. *Metronome*, April 1942, p. 19.
6. *Orchestra Wives* (1942), directed by Archie Mayo; *A Song is Born* (1948), directed by Howard Hawks.
7. Arthur Knight, '*Jammin' the Blues*, or the Sight of Jazz 1944' in Krin Gabbard (ed.), *Representing Jazz* (Durham: Duke University Press, 1995), p. 28.
8. Jane Feuer, *The Hollywood Musical* (London: BFI/Macmillan, 1982).
9. Krin Gabbard, *Jammin' at the Margins: Jazz in the American Cinema* (Chicago: University of Chicago Press, 1996), p. 228.

10. *Cabin in the Sky* (1942), directed by Vincente Minnelli; *Stormy Weather* (1943), Andrew Stone; *New Orleans* (1947), Arthur Lubin.

11. *Let's Make Music* (1940), directed by Leslie Goodwins. There are some striking parallels in narrative structure between this film and the otherwise very different *Mr Holland's Opus* (1995).

12. For an account of the musical's theme of the superiority of American popular culture over European high culture, see Leo Braudy, 'Genre: The Conventions of Connection', in Gerald Mast, Marshall Cohen, Leo Braudy, *Film Theory and Criticism* (New York: OUP, 4th edn, 1992), pp. 435–52.

13. *The Fabulous Dorseys* (1947), directed by Alfred E. Green. This short scene makes up the whole of Art Tatum's career in the movies.

14. *The Glenn Miller Story* (1953), directed by Anthony Mann.

15. In relation to a number of scenes in biopics involving jazz performance and the partners of jazz musicians, Krin Gabbard has suggested an underlying theme of sexual maturation. See Gabbard, *Jammin' at the Margins*, chapters 2 and 5.

16. *Dr Ehrlich's Magic Bullet* (1940), directed by William Dieterle.

17. See Gabbard, *Jammin' at the Margins*, pp. 64–100.

18. Ibid., p. 134.

19. *The Man with the Golden Arm* (1955), directed by Otto Preminger; *The Sweet Smell of Success* (1957), Alexander Mackendrick; *I Want to Live* (1958), Robert Wise.

20. Gabbard, *Jammin' at the Margins*, p. 127.

21. *Shadows* (1958–9) featured music composed by Mingus and solos by Shafi Hadi and Phineas Newborn, Jr. For a discussion of Cassavetes' films, including his connections with jazz, see Raymond Carney, *American Dreaming: The Films of John Cassavetes and the American Experience* (Berkeley: University of California Press, 1985).

22. Jon Panish, *The Color of Jazz: Race and Representation in Postwar American Culure* (Jackson: University of Mississippi Press, 1997), Chapter 4.

23. Gabbard, *Jammin' at the Margins*, p. 129.

24. *A Bronx Tale* (1993), directed by De Niro; *Mr Holland's Opus* (1995), directed by Stephen Herek.

25. Donald Kennington, *The Literature of Jazz: A Critical Guide* (London: The Library Association, 1970), p. 104.

26. Richard N. Albert, *An Annotated Bibliography of Jazz Fiction and Jazz Fiction Criticism* (Westport: Greenwood Press, 1996), pp. xv and xvi.

27. Philip Roth, *American Pastoral* (London: Vintage, 1998), p. 48.

28. J. D. Salinger, *The Catcher in the Rye* (London: Penguin, 1958), p. 79.

29. Dorothy Baker, *Young Man with a Horn* (New York: Houghton Mifflin, 1938); Dale Curran, *Piano in the Band* (New York: Reynal, 1940); Eudora Welty, 'Powerhouse', first published in *Atlantic Monthly*, June 1941; John A. Williams, *Night Song* (New York: Farrar Straus, 1961); James Baldwin, *Another Country* (New York: Dial, 1962), and 'Sonny's Blues', first published in *Partisan Review*, Summer 1957. Details of texts by Holmes and Kerouac are given below.

30. Harlan Reed, *The Swing Music Murder* (New York: Dutton, 1938); Julie Smith, *Jazz Funeral* (New York: Fawcett Columbine, 1993); Bill Moody, *Death of a Tenorman* (New York: Dell, 1997), *The Sound of the Trumpet* (New York: Dell, 1998), and *Bird Lives!* (New York: Walker, 1999).

31. Michael Ondaatje, *Coming through Slaughter* (New York: Norton, 1976). On Bolden and his legend, see also Martin Williams, *Jazz Masters of New Orleans* (London: Macmillan, 1967), pp. 1–25.

32. Vance Bourjaily, 'In and Out of Storyville: Jazz and Fiction', *New York Times Book Review*, December 1987, 13:1, pp. 44–5.

33. Elizabeth Hardwick, *Sleepless Lights* (New York: Random House, 1979); Kristin Hunter, *God Bless the Child* (New York: Scribners, 1964); Alice Adams, *Listening to Billie* (New York: Knopf, 1978).

34. Richard N. Albert, *An Annotated Bibliography*, pp. ix–xviii; Panish, *The Color of Jazz*, Chapter 3, 'Caging the Bird', pp. 42–78; Ross Russell, *The Sound* (New York: Dutton, 1961).

35. Al Neil, *Changes* (Toronto: Coach House, 1976); Garson Kanin, *Blow Up a Storm* (New York: Random House, 1959); Jeane Westin, *Swing Sisters* (New York: Scribners, 1991); Robert Oliphant, *A Trumpet for Jackie* (Englewood Cliffs: Prentice-Hall, 1983); Henry Steig, *Send Me Down* (New York: Knopf, 1941).

36. F. Scott Fitzgerald, 'Echoes of the Jazz Age', *The Crack-up, with other pieces and stories* (London: Penguin, 1965), p. 9.

37. Matthew Bruccoli, *Some Sort of Epic Grandeur* (London: Cardinal, 1991), p. 153.

38. Fitzgerald, 'Echoes of the Jazz Age', pp. 12, 15.

39. F. Scott Fitzgerald (M. J. Bruccoli ed.), *The Great Gatsby* (1925; London: Abacus, 1992), p. 49.

40. F. Scott Fitzgerald, *The Last Tycoon* (1941; London: Penguin, 1960), pp. 129–30.

41. Eudora Welty, 'Powerhouse', *The Collected Stories of Eudora Welty* (London: Marion Boyars, 1981), p. 131.

42. Ibid., p. 131.

43. Welty's description of Powerhouse, with its stress on the mystery of his expressive power, and on the 'otherness' of his racial identity, is reminiscent of the portrait given by Willa Cather of the black musician Blind D'Arnault in *My Antonia* (1918).

44. Carson McCullers, *The Member of the Wedding* (1946; London: Penguin, 1962), pp. 54–5.

45. Ibid., pp. 32–3.

46. Ralph Ellison, *Shadow and Act* (London: Secker and Warburg, 1967); *Going to the Territory* (New York: Random House, 1986).

47. Ellison, *Shadow and Act*, p. 238.

48. On Minton's, 'The Golden Age, Time Past' in *Shadow and Act*, pp. 199–212; on Parker, 'On Bird, Bird-Watching, and Jazz' pp. 221–32; on Ellington, 'Homage to Duke Ellington on his Birthday', *Going to the Territory*, pp. 217–26.

49. All these references are from Ralph Ellison, *Invisible Man* (1952; London: Penguin, 1965), p. 11.

50. Ellison, *Shadow and Act*, p. 238.

51. James Baldwin, *Go Tell it on the Mountain* (London: Michael Joseph, 1954); *The Amen Corner* (London: Michael Joseph, 1969).

52. David Leeming, *James Baldwin: A Biography* (London: Michael Joseph, 1994), p. 206.

53. James Baldwin, 'Sonny's Blues' (1957), collected in Richard N. Albert, *From Blues to Bop: A Collection of Jazz Fiction* (Baton Rouge: Louisiana State University Press, 1990), p. 189.

54. Baldwin, 'Sonny's Blues', p. 194.

55. Ibid., pp. 203, 204, 205.
56. Ibid., pp. 205 and 206.
57. Norman Mailer, 'The White Negro', *Advertisements for Myself* (Cambridge: Harvard University Press, 1959), pp. 337–58; John Clellon Holmes, *The Horn* (1958; London: Jazz Book Club, 1961).
58. Letter from Holmes to Jack Kerouac, 3 February 1950; quoted in Gerald Nicosia, *Memory Babe: A Critical Biography of Jack Kerouac* (Berkeley: University of California Press, 1994), p. 298.
59. Holmes, quoted in Nicosia, Ibid, p. 298.
60. Holmes, *The Horn*, pp. 12 and 17.
61. Jack Kerouac, *Maggie Cassidy* (New York: Avon, 1959); *The Subterraneans* (New York: Grove, 1971); *Desolation Angels* (London: Mayflower, 1968); *On the Road* (1957; London: Penguin, 1972).
62. Roy Carr, Brian Case, Fred Dellar, *The Hip: Hipsters, Jazz and the Beat Generation* (London; Faber and Faber, 1985), p. 105.
63. Nicosia, *Memory Babe*, p. 125
64. Ibid., p. 125.
65. Jim Burns, 'Kerouac and Jazz', *Review of Contemporary Literature*, 3.2, Summer 1983, pp. 33–41.
66. Ibid., p. 36.
67. Ibid., p. 40.
68. Kerouac, *On the Road*, p. 128; Whitney Balliett, *Dinosaurs in the Morning* (London: Jazz Book Club, 1962), pp. 22–3.
69. Jack Kerouac, *Desolation Angels*, p. 210; *On the Road*, pp. 175–7.
70. Kerouac, *On the Road*, pp. 239–40.
71. Ibid., p. 180.
72. Panish, *The Color of Jazz*, p. 57.
73. Kerouac, *The Subterraneans*, pp. 19–20.
74. Panish, *The Color of Jazz*, p. 59.
75. Kerouac, *On the Road*, pp. 113 and 197.
76. Panish, *The Color of Jazz*, p. 86.
77. For Moody's novels see note. 30, above; Bart Schneider, *Blue Bossa* (New York: Viking, 1998); Rafi Zabor, *The Bear Goes Home* (London: Cape, 1998).
78. Toni Morrison, *Jazz* (London; Picador, 1993).
79. Morrison quoted in Linden Peach, *Toni Morrison* (London: Macmillan, 1995), p. 114.
80. The *Shorter Oxford Dictionary* gives one of the meanings of 'jazz' as being applied to 'fantastic designs and vivid patterns'.
81. Morrison, *Jazz*, p. 60.
82. Ibid., p. 58.
83. Jacques Attali, *Noise: The Political Economy of Music* (Manchester: Manchester University Press, 1985).
84. Peter Brooker, *New York Fictions: Modernity, Post-Modernism, The New Modernism* (London: Longman, 1996), pp. 200–9.
85. For discussion of stylistic and technical influences of jazz upon Morrison's writing, see Chapter 5, below.
86. Ted Gioia, preface to Peter McSloy, *For Jazz: 21 Sonnets* (Lafayette: Hit and Run Press, 1995), pp. 9–11.
87. Ralph Ellison, *Shadow and Act*, p. 160.

88. Carl Sandburg, 'Jazz Fantasia', *Smoke and Steel* (1920), reprinted in Sascha Feinstein, Yusef Komunyakaa (eds), *The Jazz Poetry Anthology* (Bloomington: Indiana University Press, 1991), p. 187.

89. William Carlos Williams, 'Ol' Bunk's Band', in Feinstein, Komunyakaa, *The Jazz Poetry Anthology*, p. 237.

90. Hayden Carruth, *Sittin' In: Selected Writings on Jazz, Blues and Related Topics* (Iowa City: Iowa University Press, 1993), p. 24.

91. All quotations taken from Arnold Rampersad, David Roessel (eds), *The Collected Poems of Langston Hughes* (New York: Vintage, 1995): 'Jazzonia' p. 34, 'Jazz Band in a Parisian Cabaret' p. 60, 'Harlem Night Club' p. 90, 'Visitors to the Black Belt' p. 215, 'Heart of Harlem' p. 311, 'Lincoln Theatre' p. 360. Other quotations are from 'Montage of a Dream Deferred', pp. 387–429.

92. Feinstein, Komunyakaa, *The Jazz Poetry Anthology*, p. xvii.

93. Amiri Baraka [Leroi Jones], *The Autobiography of Leroi Jones/Amiri Baraka* (New York: Freundlich, 1984), p. 237.

94. Stephen Henderson, *Understanding the New Black Poetry* (New York: William Morrow, 1973), pp. 30–1.

95. Ibid., pp. 192–3.

96. Ibid., p. 200.

97. Leroi Jones [Amiri Baraka], *Black Music* (New York: Quill, 1967), p. 174.

98. Frank Kofsky, *John Coltrane and the Jazz Revolution of the 1960s* (New York: Pathfinder, 1998), p. 323.

99. See Kofsky, John Coltrane, pp. 430–2, for the comparison with Malcolm X. Ronald Radano, in *New Musical Figurations: Anthony Braxton's Cultural Critique* (Chicago: Chicago University Press, 1993), likens Martin Luther King to Richard Muhal Abrams and to John Coltrane, 'who provided a new, priestly image for the nation's youth' (p. 81).

100. Hugh L. Smith, Jr, 'Jazz in the American Novel', *The English Journal*, Vol. XLVII, November 1958, p. 468.

CHAPTER 5

'An Analogous Dynamic in the Design': Jazz as Aesthetic Model

The influence of jazz upon the arts in America has not only been through functioning so frequently as subject matter. Jazz has had formal and stylistic influences on the other arts, its procedures translated into the vocabularies of those arts. Practitioners of prose fiction, poetry, painting and film have used, or have claimed to use, procedures drawn from jazz music in their own work in these diverse media. Some, like Jack Kerouac in fiction, have described their creative methods as being modelled on the improvisational activity of the jazz performer. Others have defined their relation to jazz in formal terms, in terms of the qualities of the art itself. 'Jazz rhythm', for example, has been transposed from the field of music to that of painting, with the artist attempting to replicate visually some of the rhythmic effects produced in jazz.

In artists like Kerouac, the jazz influence is supposed to bear on the compositional method, or even the demeanour, of the performer, while for others the attempt is to emulate in some other medium the aesthetic qualities of the music itself. In either case, the process still depends on some representation or interpretation of jazz, either what jazz is or what the jazz performer does. These interpretations differ from one practitioner to another, but they also show some of the main ways in which the properties of jazz are selected, represented, and emphasized as models to be used elsewhere. As we shall see later, the particular elements of jazz practice that have become templates for the other arts are also reflections of the wider cultural image that jazz carries with it.

As with the presence of jazz as subject matter in literary forms, there are certain detectable historical peaks and troughs in its influence on other American cultural and artistic forms. For instance, jazz as a model for literary composition is much used and debated during the 1950s and then virtually disappears from this role through the 1960s and 1970s:

this is the same temporal curve as the incidence of jazz in novels, stories and films. The influence of jazz has been felt in all significant American art forms, even in those which are in theory remote from it, such as cinema and painting. Literature seems to be a middle ground, with some evident formal parallels with jazz music, as well as some equally obvious disparities.

The medium in which the forms and procedures of jazz could be taken up with the smallest effort of translation is, of course, music. Jazz has had a long-standing but fitful influence upon American classical or concert music, stretching back as far as the occasional use of ragtime and other black musical forms by Charles Ives and other composers in the early years of the century. In this early, proto-jazz, period, the black musical styles were enlisted in American music's search for a distinct identity, a late instance of the musical nationalism which had earlier led composers to investigate American Indian music. By the 1920s jazz had already begun to excite the interest of such European composers as Stravinsky, Ravel and Milhaud. In the American 1920s, 'jazz' had become a culturally magical term, and an effort was made to bring some of its contemporary aura into the concert hall. Much of what traded under the name of jazz in the cultural marketplace of the 1920s would afterwards hardly seem to justify the title. In Charles Schwartz's words, 'with jazz a relatively new and exciting phenomenon, all works that smacked of jazz, no matter how tame and conventional they were, almost automatically took on an aura of contemporaneousness and creative boldness they did not necessarily have'.[1]

Jazz made a highly publicized arrival in the concert music repertoire with the 1924 premiere at the Aeolian Hall in New York in which the Paul Whiteman orchestra performed George Gershwin's *Rhapsody in Blue*. Whiteman had for some years been trying to convert jazz into a 'respectable' form for concert presentation, while Gershwin's experience encompassed years of work in the songwriting business and personal acquaintance with many of the Harlem jazz pianists. But Gershwin's ambition pointed, like Whiteman's, towards the transmutation of jazz into a 'higher' form. He is quoted as expressing his dissatisfaction with one of the most fundamental features of the idiom:

There had been much chatter about the limitations of jazz, not to speak of the manifest misunderstandings of its function. Jazz, they said, had to be in strict time. It had to cling to dance rhythms. I resolved, if possible, to kill that misconception with one sturdy blow.[2]

Gershwin renounced the steady beat which has characterized most of jazz performance throughout its history. Classical performance also did not allow for improvisation. Even if one believes that no absolute definition of jazz is possible, it is still apparent that divesting it of two of its most distinctive features puts a limit to the extent of its influence on American concert music. From the point of view of later jazz culture, Gershwin's 'jazz' concert works remain of tangential value compared to his output of high-quality popular songs.

Another composer, Aaron Copland, was affected by the jazz-saturated cultural atmosphere of the 1920s, and to some extent repelled by it. Copland was careful to distinguish between jazz as cultural fad and 'what interested composers ... the more technical side of jazz   the rhythm, melody, harmony, timbre'. Copland's work, for a brief spell in the 1920s and 1930s, made use of some of these musical elements, but, like Gershwin, he was uncomfortably aware of what he perceived as the music's limited scope: 'From the composer's point of view, jazz had only two expressions: the well-known "blues" mood, and the wild, abandoned, almost hysterical and grotesque mood so dear to the youth of all ages. These two moods,' he concluded, 'encompassed the whole gamut of jazz expression.'[3]

A sense of the potentiality of a relation between jazz and concert music revived in the 1950s. The most notable manifestation of this convergence was 'Third Stream', a term devised by Gunther Schuller to denote works which 'synthesize the essential characteristics and techniques of contemporary Western art music and various ethnic and vernacular musics',[4] the latter principally meaning jazz. Schuller distinguished Third Stream music from the 'symphonic jazz' of the 1920s on the grounds that it included improvisation. Third Stream was from the beginning an attempt to fuse the two idioms rather than simply an influence flowing from jazz into classical music. Many of the writers and players who worked within it had track records within jazz, rather than being composers seeking out jazz as a source of new material. The movement was given credence by the fact that some sectors of jazz, notably the Stan Kenton orchestra, were in the 1950s passing through a brief classicizing phase. This, however, was to be swept aside by the turn towards black ethnicity in the music of the early 1960s.

Between jazz and classical music the lines of demarcation are increasingly hard to draw, as older jazz compositions are performed by repertory orchestras dedicated to the faithful recreation of earlier work, and as jazz players receive commissions to write and perform music for ensembles in concert settings. A jazz composer like Duke Ellington worked prevalently in longer forms and emphasized composition over performance as his career progressed, so that he became a creative personality who was, in one his own favourite phrases, 'beyond category'. However, the works of jazz composers like Ellington, Thelonious Monk, Jelly Roll Morton and others are increasingly incorporated into orthodox concert repertoires, and this tendency is likely to become more prevalent in the future.

Nevertheless, the sum total of the influence of jazz upon American serious music has not been especially great, given its importance in the culture as a whole. None of the accepted canon of American composers has been deeply influenced in their musical practices by jazz, and it usually appears as a colour or flavour in the concert repertoire. This may be a result of the fact that all of the canonical composers have been white, but it also has to do with the discrepancy of methods between the two musical domains. Improvisation and a regularly stated beat are alien to the tradition of European-American concert music but fundamental to jazz, and historically this has proved to be an unbridgeable divide.

Music cannot claim or pretend to be using analogies or parallels to jazz; it either uses the same materials or it does not. In the other arts, though, influence must be indirect, passing through some process of transformation of the jazz material into the appropriate material for the art form involved. In literature and the visual arts, as the rest of this chapter will show, the structures and the methods of jazz have been put into use in whatever ways were the available analogies within those art forms. Terms like rhythm, syncopation and improvisation can have meanings within literature and painting which are not entirely different from their meanings in jazz. During the century a number of American artists have devised ways of strengthening the resemblance, in a desire to graft on to their own work some of the properties of jazz. This desire is often indicative of a perception of the freshness or power or importance of jazz, a sense that what it expresses is something deeply American, or definitively modern, or both, a way of renewing or nativizing art forms which lack its grounding in a twentieth-century vernacular culture.

Literature as Jazz

The artefacts that have been influenced by jazz can be placed on a continuum, ranging from those in which the formal or stylistic influence of jazz is apparent on the surface, to those in which the influence of jazz is not manifested in the text, but in the compositional methods of the artist. The strongest form of direct formal influence is imitation. In a literal transposition of jazz devices into another medium, the poet Jerry Ward speaks of his efforts to 'imitate certain sound structures' of jazz.[5] An example of the tendency to use jazz-derived structures when the subject of the piece is jazz itself is Eudora Welty's 'Powerhouse'. Leland Chambers has shown how in this story, which is structurally unique amongst Welty's work, Welty substitutes a literary process (the storytelling of Powerhouse and his colleagues) for a musical one, improvisation.[6]

The structure of Welty's story, aberrant in terms of the usual narrative codes, is accountable instead in terms of the codes of jazz performance. Powerhouse tells three different versions of his wife's death, in a direct parallel to the jazz conventions of theme and variation: each version is a new 'chorus' of improvisation. One might suggest that the total form of the story, in its non-compliance with normal narrative patterns, is an imitation of a full-length jazz performance, with the ending of the story, a return to Powerhouse playing on stage, being a resolution more typical of a jazz piece than of a piece of prose fiction, analogous to the way in which, in jazz, a repeated statement of the original theme conventionally brings a performance to a close.

One step beyond attempts at imitation are the numerous instances in which literary artists have looked for formal analogues to features of jazz in their own modes of writing. Most of these analogues have been based on conceptions of rhythm, although some writers have spoken also of 'melodic' devices and of parallels between poetic organization and the structure of the jazz ensemble. Sterling Plumpp, for instance, mentions the presence in his writing of 'polyphony', presumably after the example of the collectively improvised jazz of New Orleans or of the 'free jazz' style of the 1960s.[7]

Writers using the rhythmic effects of jazz mostly emphasize disruptive or disjunctive qualities rather than a steady rhythmic pulse or flow which, one might argue, is just as representative of jazz rhythm as played. Langston Hughes's note to 'Montage of a Dream Deferred', mentioned in the last chapter, shows this tendency: he acknowledges the stylistic importance to his poem of 'conflicting changes', 'sudden interjections', 'broken rhythms' and 'breaks and distortions'. Hughes is thinking specifically of bebop style, but the same rhythmic character is attributed by others to jazz in general. Sterling Plumpp speaks of its 'quick shifts of emphasis', Alice Fulton of its 'time changes' and 'unconventional dynamics'. Another of Fulton's statements on her work recalls Miles Davis's comment, quoted in Chapter 1, on the drummer Tony Williams: 'I try to write a line with a pushy, impulsive edge, an energetic phrasing that pulls the reader along.' Fulton is writing 'on top of the beat'.[8]

Writers of poetry seem particularly concerned with the parallelism between jazz and poetry in the rhythmic realm of anticipation and delay. Robert Pinsky refers to his use of 'the building and breaking of expectation', and Alice Fulton describes a related procedure in her own work. It is the 'enjambments' of her poetry that are affected by the 'technical questions and resolutions of jazz': 'Just as a jazz singer will stretch one note over several bars . . . I sometimes like to withhold sense until the end of a sentence, using line breaks to indicate underlying meaning and false stops along the way.'[9]

Practices in jazz that can be claimed as parallel to this kind of device are easy to find: as an extreme example, Charlie Parker's trick of 'turning the chorus around', in which he would deliberately fall out of step with the rhythm section and hold back a resolution of this conflict throughout a whole chorus:

> Like we'd be playing the blues, and Bird would start on the eleventh bar, and as the rhythm section stayed where they were and Bird played where he was it sounded as if the rhythm section was on one and three instead of two and four. Every time that would happen, Max Roach would scream at Duke Jordan not to follow Bird, but stay where he was. Then, eventually it came round as Bird had planned and we were together again.[10]

'Syncopation' is a term which has a long history in jazz, and at one time was almost synonymous with jazz rhythm. In Theodor Adorno's hostile polemics of the 1940s, the rhythmic 'trick' of syncopation is, mistakenly, presented as the single rhythmic device available to jazz.[11] Syncopation can be defined as the displacement of an expected stress to an unexpected place. In jazz this can mean displacement to the theoretically 'weak' beats of the bar, or its placement between the beats. The analogies to this in poetry are similar kinds of beat displacement, or the non-coincidence of line endings with units of sense: this is theoretically the case in Alice Fulton's work. The viability of these two kinds of poetic syncopation depends, though, on the poetry: in free verse, where there is no regular pattern of beats, the first kind of syncopation is not available. There is also a fundamental difference between most poetry and most jazz: rhythmic variation in jazz takes place against a regularly stated beat or pulse, providing a constant frame of reference in which the variations are felt and understood. In verse, wherever the rhythm of stresses is broken, interrupted or deviated from, the stable rhythmic context is lost. This means that, except in rare cases, the likeness between rhythmic effects in the two modes, jazz and poetry, can only be analogies.

This situation is compounded in prose, which lacks the formal structures of verse to serve as an equivalent to the musical structures of jazz. Unless a novel or short story were composed in order to be read over the pulsation of a rhythm section, no prose writing can, in a literal sense, use jazz rhythm. As with poetry, the aesthetic resources of jazz can only be exemplars, aspirations, inspirations or models in a diffuse sense. John Clellon Holmes's novel *The Horn*, however, makes explicit use of some jazz structural terms. The fifteen sections of the novel are divided into an alternation of sections labelled 'chorus' and 'riff', with a final section 'coda'. Each chorus and the coda is given to one of the novel's eight main characters, as if each were a soloist in a continuous group performance. As Holmes's prefatory note also indicates, the book, 'like the music it celebrates, is a collective improvisation'.[12] Thus each individual 'chorus' is followed by a collective 'riff' and the performance is closed out by a coda.

It is worth noting, in passing, that Holmes provides a definition of one of his terms: 'A jazz riff – a melodic device, insistently repeated, the primary function of which is rhythmic.'[13] Holmes 'riff' sections are not, however, internally repetitive: the prose in these sections has the same kind of narrative rhythm as the other parts. They are 'riffs' in the way in which they relate to the overall structure of the book, analogous to the way in which riffs in jazz relate to the structure of the performance. The aesthetic influence of jazz is present here at the higher levels of text, in the structuring of the work as a whole rather than in the stylistic texture of the prose.

In the case of Toni Morrison's *Jazz*, the effect of jazz has been claimed to be perceptible at the level of the prose itself. Unlike Holmes's book, there is no explicit linkage of literary and musical features, but the novel's title and some stylistic traits have been taken as an indication that jazz is an important determinant, or even the sole determinant, of its language and structure. The opening of the book, a compressed summation of the narrative which is to follow, suggests that Morrison is setting up, as in Welty's 'Powerhouse', a fictional equivalent to a 'theme statement' or 'head' in jazz performance, to be followed by individual variations on this theme.

Jazz is widely acknowledged in Morrison's writings and public statements. Her study *Playing in the Dark* takes as its starting point her reflection on 'the consequences of jazz – its visceral, emotional and intellectual impact'.[14] She has spoken of jazz as an analogy for her own art as a novelist. A number of writers have suggested that the novel *Jazz*, or the whole of Morrison's work, reflects the influence of jazz, even down to its phrasing and sentence structure. The novel *Jazz* in particular is seen as exemplifying what Henry Louis Gates has called 'the jazz aesthetic'.[15] Other critics have spoken of her 'jazzy prose style' or more generally her 'literary jazz'.[16] Remembering Morrison's own comment that jazz functions in *Jazz* as a general historical metaphor rather than as the subject, Linden Peach suggests that 'we should resist trying to discover a single source for her aesthetics' in jazz itself.[17]

The critical literature on Morrison, however, includes a number of studies which argue for jazz as the primary or sole source of numerous stylistic features of Morrison's work. This critical debate shadows another argument about the presence in her work of two traditions: a 'European' modernist tradition that derives Morrison's literary strategies from writers like Faulkner and Joyce, and an African-American tradition which refers these same strategies to models in black vernacular. Jazz is an important concept here, because the same kind of argument about the relative strengths of European and African elements can be articulated about jazz itself. The question of jazz in Morrison's work is caught up in a larger debate concerning Europeanism and Africanism.

A device that figures prominently in the debate about the influence of jazz on Morrison's style is 'the riff'. The way in which this term has become established in the critical literature is indicative of an important process in the interpretation of jazz in literary-critical contexts. The term 'riff' has been mentioned above in Holmes's definition, which is close to a consensus usage in jazz culture (*Grove* defines it as 'a short melodic ostinato two or four bars long, which may be repeated intact or varied to accommodate an underlying harmonic pattern').[19] The uses of 'the riff' in literary criticism, however, have moved steadily away from its usage in jazz performance. The origin of this gradual remodelling of the term seems to lie in H. L. Gates's reading of the term in an essay by Ralph Ellison, which leads him to make the statement that the riff is 'a central component of jazz improvisation'. Most transcriptions confirm, however, that for jazz musicians the riff is virtually absent from their improvisations, which consist of non-repetitive phrases. Most jazz players consider the riff to be an element of ensemble routine rather than of improvisation.

However, the modification of the meaning of 'riff' has been handed on to other writers who refer to Gates, and this redefinition has become understood within literary-critical discussion as the primary meaning of the term. By this stage 'the riff' has virtually lost contact with its previous applications in jazz. When Morrison's prose style is analyzed in terms of 'the riff' as a component of 'jazz', any genuine relation with a musical basis has already been obscured. 'Jazz' here is not jazz as a musical culture, but an inadvertent reconstruction of the term within literary-critical discourse. The end result of this process is a gradual drift away from a basis in jazz culture itself, and a consequent difficulty in judging, in a case like Morrison's, the nature of the relationship between jazz and any literature that may be influenced by it.

It is not only Morrison's, but also a number of other writers' work whose connection with jazz is obscured by the gradual loss of the empirical basis of the argument. Another contributing process is the succession of writers whose reference to jazz is based on secondary and then tertiary sources, with an increasing thinning out of the source material, like the homeopathic procedure of potentization which eventually produces a dilution containing no molecules of the original substance. It seems that the amount of evidence required in support of assertions about jazz is quite small. One study which largely concerns jazz in Kerouac's fiction contains a reference to only one text on jazz.[20] Even Gates's *The Signifying Monkey* refers to only three sources on jazz, and later writers who take their perspective on jazz from Gates do not add to this. Some of these critics are then cited by others as sources for further generalizations about jazz.

Literary studies of Morrison, and equally of Jack Kerouac, are required to show detailed knowledge of texts and secondary sources: the jazz side of the equation, however, is required to show very little. Comment on the jazz-derived structures and devices in Morrison's prose is casual in its attribution of general features to the whole of jazz : 'In the style of jazz composition, Alice's memories embellish the narrator's description of the women.'[21] 'Jazz composition' is in itself a large and complex subject, taking in the varying practices and techniques of Jelly Roll Morton, Charles Mingus, Duke Ellington and numerous others: in this quotation it is scaled down to a single idea casually attached to a trait of Morrison's prose style.

The same imbalances of evidence arise in discussions of jazz in the work of Jack Kerouac. It has been shown in Chapter 4 how close were Kerouac's connections with the world of jazz, especially during the emergence of bebop. That Kerouac's compositional methods were in some way affected by this is also evident from his own statements. But in Kerouac's critics and biographers there is a severe limitation of understanding of jazz as a product and as a process. As with critics on Morrison, there is a disproportion between detailed knowledge of the writer's work and casualness and confusion in describing the music which is claimed as an important influence upon it. Gerald Nicosia's account of the musical innovations of bebop, already mentioned in Chapter 4, seems to credit the bebop musicians with the invention of improvisation. The same passage continues:

> The bop saxophonist's flight along a variable-noted line had to stop only when he ran out of breath. The possibilities of sound were infinite, and the only limitation the physical stamina of the performer. Bird sometimes extemporised for hours until his audience lost all sense of time and place.[22]

Missing from this description is any sense of the musical factors involved. Improvised phrases do not end solely on account of running out of breath, and improvisation is not best characterized as the pursuit of the limits of endurance.

The image that has here coalesced around the jazz of the 1940s reflects some other cultural setting entirely, the open-ended, exhaustive improvisations of post-1960s rock bands, or the free jazz of the 1960s that led to the transcendent sensations described by Amiri Baraka:

It was a mad body-dissolving music ... rose and stayed there ...
ecstasy of understanding then, evolution. The feeling such men make
is of the consciousness of evolution the *will* of the universe.[23]

1940s bebop, by contrast, was a disciplined and determinate music,
working within a definite set of musical forms and harmonic schemes.
However, such a background does not accord with the psychological
and intellectual atmosphere in which Kerouac's work has been located,
and Kerouac's proponents handle this discrepancy by misrepresenting
the music in which he was interested.

Kerouac's own statements on jazz and his writing have primarily to
do with compositional process, though he also indicates some stylistic
effects. Kerouac's theoretical statements about his work, most notably
his 'Essentials of Spontaneous Prose', contain strategically significant
references to jazz. He compares his own position as a writer with that of
a jazz musician who 'has to get out ... his statement in a certain number
of bars'.[24] Kerouac's prose is not bound, like the improvisation of bop
musicians, by fixed structures such as the 32-bar chorus, but he makes a
loose analogy with 'the page', and with the time constraint generated by
his own practice of writing at speed. He speaks of one of the main
influences upon his work as being 'jazz and bop, in the sense of, say, a
tenor man drawing a breath and blowing a phrase on his saxophone, till
he runs out of breath, and when he does, his statement's been made'
(this comment is perhaps the origin of Nicosia's overemphasis on breath
capacity). The direct application of Kerouac's analogy with jazz is his
method of punctuating his prose: 'That's how I therefore separate my
sentences, as breath separations of the mind.' The dashes that articulate
Kerouac's prose are, for him, equivalent to the jazz saxophonist's pauses
for breath between improvised phrases.

Kerouac also sees himself elaborating on particular images, descrip-
tively or associatively, in the way that jazz musicians decorate or
improvise on specific chords: 'undisturbed flow from the mind of
personal secret idea-words *blowing* (as per jazz musician) on subject
of image'.[25] Here Kerouac broaches the idea of improvisation, in
writing as in jazz, as a means of access to a personal vision and source
of creative imagery. But for some critics, the specific function of jazz in
this philosophy of composition is overplayed. Jon Panish comments
that 'there is nothing inherently musical or jazz-like in Kerouac's
writing. Composing without editing ... replacing standard punctuation

with dashes, and tapping into some sort of essential part of oneself do not necessarily make Kerouac's prose sound like jazz.'[26]

Carruth, in similarly sceptical fashion, comments that the Beat writers of the 1950s 'took to bop as a reinforcement of what they wanted to do in literature' and that they 'understood the music no better than most writers understand most music'.[27] Jazz, and especially bebop, stood to the Beat writers as a suggestive, and historically available, model for their own activity as writers. But it is noticeable that the jazz influence, stronger in Kerouac, was weak or absent in other writers of the Beat period. There were also many other sources for the Beat emphasis on spontaneity. The Beats were inheritors of an American philosophy of composition that descended from Emerson, Whitman and William Carlos Williams. Whitman stressed the need for the poet to be 'the free channel of himself', and Williams spoke of the usefulness of 'headlong composition'.[28] These elements in the creative philosophy of Whitman and Williams directly affected, and reinforced as the example of jazz did, the ways in which Kerouac, Ginsberg and the Beat writers approached composition. The forces pushing the Beats towards a belief in unrestrained spontaneity were numerous; as well as their own pre-existing compositional methods, developed independently of theories about jazz, there were the Zen and other spiritual practices, the uses of hallucinatory drugs, Surrealism, and the work of other writers around them, such as Cassady and Burroughs.

Jazz, and in particular bebop, nevertheless continues to be seen as the most influential model upon the Beat writers. The textual evidence for this in, for example, Kerouac's novels, is not very great, despite his love of the music. As with Morrison, there seems to be a widespread preference for jazz as the decisive influence. In Kerouac's case the reasons for this seem to have to do with the historical foreshortening that happens as the 1950s recede into the past. It provides a convenient historical handle upon the distant days of the fifties to tie in Kerouac's writing with the rest of the mythologies of the period. Thus, for W. T. Lhamon, Kerouac and bebop are components of the postwar gestalt of speed; for Daniel Belgrad, Kerouac and bebop are participants in a 'culture of spontaneity' that defines the arts in postwar America.[29]

These historical generalities, however, can be constructed only by cutting corners in the description of jazz itself, and by avoiding close examination of its supposed influences on other art forms. One of the ways in which the narrative of jazz is reshaped to fit in with these mythological overviews is the misrepresentation of the relation between bebop jazz of the 1940s and 1950s and the jazz styles that came before it. A crude distinction is set up between the earlier music, described as 'corporate', 'regimented' and 'commercial', and bebop, which is presented as the intellectually revolutionary inversion of all of these. All bebop players, however, began their musical lives in the 'regimented' big band formats, and some, like Dizzy Gillespie, went frequently and happily back to it. Bebop, as the presumed counterpart to Beat literary culture, is naturally represented as intellectually weighty, spontaneous and subversive beyond all comparison with earlier forms of jazz. Yet Kerouac's autobiography contains passages like this, set in the pre-bebop year of 1940:

> I'm sitting in an easy chair in the frat lounge playing Glenn Miller records fullblast. Almost crying. Glenn Miller and Frank Sinatra with Tommy Dorsey 'The One I Love Belongs To Somebody Else' and 'Everything Happens to Me'.[30]

Nevertheless, jazz of the bebop era and later has been represented, especially by recent writers, as virtually the only style of jazz worthy of keeping intellectual company with artists in other fields. It seems to have come as an embarrassment to writers on Jackson Pollock, another spontaneous, improvising quasi-Beat artist, that his preferred musical ambience was not bebop at all, but consisted largely of earlier jazz, including Swing, Dixieland and what one expert referred to as 'schlock'.[31]

The ascription of a jazz influence to other artists is, as cases like these show, not necessarily an inference from known facts and observed features. In some cases it is more indicative of a mythology of jazz from which supposed qualities of the music are 'borrowed' for transference elsewhere. The charisma of jazz musicians, their status as 'romantic outsiders', their subculturalism, their ethnicity, and their prowess as 'natural' and 'spontaneous' creators of art serve to make jazz a powerful set of images with which other artists have found it congenial to identify themselves. For the Beats, the claimed emulation of jazz is part of their drive towards counterculture, the romantic identification with marginalized groups that caused Kerouac to say that he wished he were a Negro.

It sometimes happens that there is cultural capital to be gained by proximity to jazz. This has made for hasty and ill-founded accounts of its influence on certain writers, with such side-effects as the strange afterlife of the word 'riff' in literary-critical writing. The influence of jazz upon American writing is best described as a general awareness of its presence, occasionally swelling into efforts to take on some of its aesthetic qualities or its improvisatory attitude.

Jazz and the Visual Arts

Arts that represent music visually, within a frame or as a physical object, are one step further removed from music than arts that use language. Poetry, for instance, has in common with music that it unfolds in time, that it is sequential, whereas in painting or sculpture the element of time is missing. Nevertheless, many American visual artists have taken jazz music not only as subject matter but also, again like the literary artists, as a model for their work. As with the art forms discussed in the previous section, we find jazz operating in the visual arts as a source of stylistic adaptations and borrowings. Visual artists have attempted to devise ways of translating the perceived qualities and energies of jazz music into the currency of their own arts. Among these, again as with literature, the two fundamentals of rhythm and improvisation are prominent.

Jazz as subject matter was widespread through the visual arts in America from the 1920s onwards. Among the important early artists were painters like Aaron Douglas, who was also the illustrator for some of Langston Hughes's poetry, and Archibald Motley. In Motley's work, jazz culture appears as naturally as it does in Hughes's verse, as an occasional presence in a panorama of the life of Harlem. Motley's best-known paintings with jazz subjects are *Syncopation* (1925), and *Blues* (1929), a scene drawn from a jazz cabaret in Paris. In later artists, jazz was treated with greater abstraction, from Piet Mondrian's *Broadway Boogie-Woogie* (1942–3), a network of lines and rectangles of bright, kinetic colours, through Stuart Davis's *Swing Landscape* (1938), to Franz Kline's 1958 *King Oliver*. What we see in this succession of art works, as well as a historical drift towards abstraction, is the influence of jazz expressed indirectly, through the application of what Stuart Davis called 'analogous dynamics in the design'[32] – transpositions of the properties of jazz as music into equivalent forms in the language of visual art.

Jazz has performed this function for visual artists since their earliest awareness of it. Douglas's work of the 1920s and 1930s, most notably his mural 'Aspects of Negro Life', is described by Peter Wollen as finding a pictorial equivalent to jazz in his 'stylized silhouettes and undulating bands of colour'.[33] Though Wollen does not explain the basis for the equivalence of these visual elements to elements of jazz, it has come to be understood in theoretical discussion that the visual space of the canvas constitutes the ground in which 'rhythm' is represented in ways designed to reproduce the energies of rhythm in jazz.

In this way, Motley's cabaret scene *Blues* is animated by a visual rhythm across the canvas, making the composition parallel its subject. The rhythm of the painting is compositionally 'interrupted': it has a crowded, jostling design, the backs and heads of dancers dividing the frame vertically into seven segments which are breached by the arm of a woman, the protruding bell of a clarinet. For Richard Powell, the picture is an 'orchestrated study of improvisational pattern under the guise of a genre scene', its jazz design being as significant as its jazz subject. In Powell's account, the basis of the shift from musical to visual language is 'anticipated shapes' and 'recurring intervals'.[34] The ideas of anticipation and syncopation are as prominent here as in jazz-influenced poetry. Motley's work can be seen as an ideal example of what Powell called 'the blues aesthetic', typified by 'constant use of hot, bold colours and improvised compositions, with syncopated rhythms of accentuation and suspension, push and pull'.[35]

A similar interpretation of the visual uses of jazz is apparent in the work of Stuart Davis. Jazz was important to Davis:

> Some of the things which made me want to paint . . . are . . . fast travel by train, auto and aeroplane which brought new and multiple perspectives . . . movies and radio, Earl Hines 'hot piano' and Negro jazz music in general . . . the quality of these things plays a role in determining the character of my paintings.[36]

Like Jackson Pollock after him, who had jazz playing day and night in his studio, Davis says of jazz that 'I almost breathed it like air.' Davis had a particular admiration for the pianist Earl Hines, and maintained that he had learned to carry over into his painting Hines's 'intervals'. Earl Hines was a 'stride' piano player with a rhythmically complex style, his left hand playing lines almost as elaborate as those of his right. 'Intervals' in Davis's statement means not only pitch differences, but also the gaps and spaces in Hines's rhythmic texture. Davis responded not only to Hines, but also to what he called 'the numerical precisions of the Negro piano players'.[37] He admired, for the purposes of his painting, the 'objective order' he found in the work of these musicians. It is unusual, as we can see by contrast with earlier examples, for any artist to stress the qualities in jazz of precision and structure rather than primitivism and spontaneity.

Davis encouraged other artists, such as Romare Bearden, to recognize the value of these qualities for compositional purposes. In Davis's 1938 mural *Swing Landscape* there are design principles at work which are not unlike those of Motley's *Blues*: the large surface of the work is divided by three abstract vertical shapes overlaid with brightly coloured fragments of a harbour scene, producing, in Robert Hughes's words, 'a riotous, almost chaotic frieze in which his passion for finding visual analogies to jazz syncopation gets full play'.[38] As with Motley, 'syncopation' is visually realized by the composition, in which the spatial divisions of the canvas correspond to the musical divisions of time. Against this visual 'beat' the smaller shapes within Davis's design set up tensions and overlappings, like the anticipations and delays of jazz phrasing, and this is further heightened by the energetic colours. The mural almost overcomes the non-sequentiality of painting, creating a series of 'cells' across its surface that become successive, almost temporal.

Romare Bearden was Davis's pupil for a short time, and, like him, 'lived and breathed the music', during his many years residence in Harlem.[39] Bearden's career passed through a number of stylistic phases, but in the early 1960s he began to work in collage, using an approach that made use of a creative relation with jazz. Bearden's technique consisted of using cut-out fragments of photographs and printed materials against painted backgrounds. In a work like *Carolina Shout* (named after a stride piano piece by James P. Johnson) there is again a rhythm of verticals across the frame. In a 1964 piece, *The Dove*, a trail of cut-out fragments, mostly of the faces of black men, twists irregularly across a background of verticals representing houses in a street. Bearden's irregular foreground pattern, with its 'sudden abutments, breaks and repetitions', works, in Robert Hughes's words, 'as a visual equivalent to the jazz he loved'.[40]

The same kind of compositional analogy with jazz is presented in the work of Jimmy Ernst, one of the Abstract Expressionist school of artists based in New York. Mona Hadler has argued that jazz was an important contributory influence on the work of this school, affecting such artists as Franz Kline, Robert Motherwell and Jackson Pollock.[41] Ernst took the notion of structure in jazz just as seriously as did Davis and

Bearden. In his *Riff* (1946), there is the same use of a series of verticals progressing across the canvas in a repetitive but slightly varying pattern. The lower half of the canvas presents an irregular honeycomb of shapes that can be read as another set of variations against the rhythmic pattern of the upper section, the 'syncopation' principle that Robert O'Meally has identified as a central trait of Bearden's style: 'When Bearden divides his canvas into three sections on one side and two on the other and says it's his version of 3/4 time working with and against 2/4 time, as in jazz, we'd better pay attention.'[42]

In Jackson Pollock's relation to jazz, what many commentators have stressed is his use of improvisation. This makes Pollock the counterpart to Kerouac in fiction, and both are enlisted into Belgrad's aesthetic of spontaneity on this account. Cultural historians consistently draw Kerouac and Pollock together with figures like Charlie Parker and James Dean into a mythology of the period which dwells on the resemblances between these artist-heroes and plays down the differences. Pollock is especially qualified for this by being one of the triumvirate of charismatic martyrs of the years 1955 and 1956. Pollock and Dean died in automobile accidents, Parker while watching a variety show on TV, but Parker's death can be assimilated into this myth as an absurd version of the more heroic extinctions of Pollock and Dean. These four men (with Kerouac) are taken to exemplify the same set of values, embodying a love of extreme experiences and an improvisatory attitude towards art and life. A contemporary report on Parker's death illustrates the perception of a common cause:

> Together with Jackson Pollock, Dylan Thomas, and James Dean [Parker] became a symbol of protest for a whole generation. It is easy to see how these four artists shared the same rebellious mind and desperation, expressed so clearly in their work in different arts. And it is still easier to find the common ground in their death: Pollock and Dean through a mania for speed, Thomas and Charlie Parker through alcohol and drugs.[43]

Pollock's method, during a brief period of his career, of dripping paint vertically on to a canvas while moving freely about its space, justifies considering him an improviser. It is also known that jazz records were played continuously in his studio as he did this. If this jazz were bebop, a close likeness to Kerouac would be clinched, and many critics have stated or assumed this to be so. 'Lee Krasner has asserted the profound influence of bebop on Jackson Pollock's painting during the crucial year, 1946, when he developed his gesture-field style of painting.'[44] Another critic states that 'Pollock even painted to the music of Charlie Parker.'[45] In fact, as was mentioned in the previous section, Pollock's ambient music was made up of older styles of jazz. These styles, however, do not carry the intellectual cachet of bebop. Pollock's musical inspiration, at least, does not confirm his kinship with Parker or with Kerouac.

Pollock has been likened not only to Parker but also to the radically 'free jazz' saxophonist Ornette Coleman and to Thelonious Monk. The latter resemblance is developed by Peter Wollen, who nevertheless spells out 'basic differences' between the fields in which these improvising artists worked.[46] One of the difficulties in tracing the influence of jazz improvisation on other art forms is the definition of 'improvisation' itself. In jazz, the term stands for a particular kind of musical creativity taking place in the conditions described in Chapter 1. But in its loosest possible usage, 'improvisation' can be used to denote any situation in which an outcome is not wholly preplanned: the Oxford English Dictionary gives one of its meanings as 'anything done on the spur of the moment'.

It is not unusual for practitioners conscious of jazz to claim their own 'improvisation' as equivalent to that of the jazz performer. Hence Clint Eastwood's comment on his own directorial style: 'I think the free flow of jazz and its improvisational aspect has definitely had its influence on my directing. When I make a film, I'm never locked in note-for-note on sheet music, as it were.'[47] Likewise there is a pressure for other improvisational media to be likened to jazz: Pollock's painting; Method acting; the standup comedy of Lenny Bruce; Kerouac's prose; and photography, as in Roy De Carava's comparison: 'the jazzman and the photographer have to react at the moment'.[48]

Improvisation in each of these fields, however, is technically different from the others. Peter Wollen distinguishes Pollock's improvisation from what happens in jazz: 'Jazz improvisation consists of virtuoso embroidery around a given theme or rhythm, breaking it up, complicating it, pushing it to its limits. Pollock's automatism starts out with a void and then fills it with its own web of forms.'[49] Pollock's themeless improvisations, like Kerouac's open-ended prose excursions, are anticipatory of the 'free jazz' approach which was to arrive in jazz a decade or more later. Ornette Coleman, one of the leaders of that style, in choosing one of Pollock's paintings for the cover of his album *Free Jazz*, remarked that Pollock had worked 'in the same state I was in and doing what I was doing.'[50] The jazz of the bebop era, with which Pollock is routinely and mistakenly linked, was by comparison a constrained style, using complex pre-set harmonies usually derived from popular songs and regular 12- and 32-bar forms.

Another important distinction to be drawn is that in these other art forms, improvisation was a transitory phenomenon related to a particular stage of the game. In jazz it is permanent, or in Paul Berliner's phrase, 'infinite'.[51] Jackson Pollock's career as an improviser spanned the four years 1947–51. 'Method' acting for a time used improvisation as a training technique. In jazz, improvisation has been the principal focus of performance, theory and learning from the 1920s through to the end of the century. The enlistment of jazz in an early-1950s turn towards an improvisatory culture across all of the arts seriously underplays the centrality and the longevity of improvisation in the economy of jazz itself.

More significantly still, this type of generalization across a range of arts ignores the specific origins of jazz as one of the improvisatory modes based in black vernacular culture. A statement like that of the theatre director Julian Beck demonstrates the difference of perspective: 'Jazz is the hero, jazz which made an early break into actual improvisation.'[52] This implies a united front of 'the arts', engaged in a common cause, with jazz happening to be the first to make a particular strategic advance. But the origins of jazz improvisation share a more relevant commonality with a black vernacular art like dance than with the 'high' arts. Improvisation in jazz is not an avant-garde development, or the theorized response to a particular art-historical situation: it grows directly out of the African-American culture in which it has had its roots.

Jon Panish has made this point in relation to the ways in which improvisation is represented in different traditions. Jack Kerouac's version, in Panish's words, 'primitivising' jazz improvisation, portrays it as an accomplishment 'that requires almost no training, skill or education: just pick up a horn, tap into your emotions and "blow"'.[53] More generally, Panish contrasts the view of improvisation promulgated by 'Euro-American' writers, 'a universal experimental technique – not tied to any particular cultural tradition', with the view among African-Americans which 'saw improvisation as part of a specific cultural lineage', with a corresponding emphasis upon a community of improvisers as a opposed to a single individual.[54] Black writers, in Panish's view, stress the continuity of a rooted culture; in white writers, improvisation is seen as a disruptive, individualistic break away from a common culture.

In any case, for the improvisation of artists like Kerouac and Pollock there are numerous precursor movements in the twentieth-century trajectories of their respective arts. Both take their direction from tendencies towards modes of art in which conscious control over the creative process is diminished. Improvisation is only one of the manifestations of this, together with a faith in automatism, aleatory techniques, the use of 'headlong composition', and psychotropic drugs to sidestep the inhibiting functions of the mind. The techniques of both Pollock and Kerouac are products of this stream of influence more than of the example of the jazz musician.

The model of the jazz improviser is, however, often invoked. The motivations for this are implicated with factors in the period in American culture in which these artists were working. As was shown in Chapter 4, the 1950s was one of the prime periods for the literary and cinematic representation of jazz. Jazz culture was also, to Kerouac at least, of interest for its identification with black America. As Daniel Boorstin has pointed out, an important impulse in modern American society has been a search for spontaneous experience in a highly organized and predictable social order: jazz was one of the obvious places to look.[55]

Last, and most important, of the factors promoting the idea of jazz as an influence at this time is the mythological status of the jazz musician. One of the concurrent products of this mid-century phase of American culture was a new type of hero, a new self-image of white masculinity. Kerouac has Dean Moriarty, a hipster, a speedster, a virtual outlaw, a sexual adventurer, a creative artist, an improviser, a Westerner (from Colorado) and lover of jazz. In the association of Jackson Pollock with bebop, there is the construction of an almost exactly similar archetype: Pollock too was a Westerner (from Wyoming), a sexual adventurer, a speedster (who died at the wheel), a creative artist. To complete the archetype, Pollock too needed to be an improviser and lover of jazz, preferably bebop. 'Pollock's image', as Ann Gibson puts it, 'could be compared not only to the cowboy, but also to the jazzman, another heroic American image.'[56]

In this kind of view of jazz and its players, one is evidently dealing with a culturally constructed myth: 'the jazzman' as a version of the hero comparable with 'the cowboy', these two models being combined in figures like Pollock and Neal Cassady. The next chapter will deal with the broader repertoire of myth from which these archetypes are drawn, which has surrounded jazz throughout its history, and which in many cases has come to be its most powerful representation in American culture.

Notes

1. Charles Schwartz, *Gershwin: His Life and Music* (London: Abelard-Schuman, 1974), p. 71.
2. Schwartz, Ibid., p. 77.
3. Charles Hamm, *Music in the New World* (New York: Norton, 1983), p. 439.
4. Gunther Schuller, in Barry Kernfeld (ed.), *New Grove Dictionary of Jazz* (New York: St Martin's Press, 1994), p. 1199.
5. Sascha Feinstein, Yusef Komunyakaa (eds), *The Jazz Poetry Anthology* (Bloomington: Indiana University Press, 1991), p. 275.
6. Leland Chambers, 'Improvising and Mythmaking in Eudora Welty's "Powerhouse"', in Krin Gabbard, *Representing Jazz* (Durham: Duke University Press, 1995), pp. 54–69.
7. Feinstein, Komunyakaa, *The Jazz Poetry Anthology*, p. 270.
8. Feinstein, Komunyakaa, Ibid., p. 257.
9. Ibid., p. 257. Pinsky's comment is on p. 299.
10. Miles Davis, quoted in Ian Carr, *Miles Davis: A Critical Biography* (London: Paladin, 1984), p. 40.
11. Theodor Adorno, 'Jazz – Perennial Fashion', *Prisms* (London: Neville Spearman, 1967), pp. 121–32. For a critique of these views, see Peter Townsend, 'Adorno on Jazz: Vienna versus the Vernacular', *Prose Studies*, Vol. 11, No. 1, May 1988, pp. 69–88.
12. John Clellon Holmes, *The Horn* (London: Jazz Book Club, 1961), unnumbered page.
13. Ibid., Contents page.
14. Toni Morrison, *Playing in the Dark: Whiteness and the Literary Imagination* (Cambridge: Harvard University Press, 1992), p. viii.
15. Henry Louis Gates, Jr, *The Signifying Monkey: A Theory of African-American Literary Criticism* (New York: OUP, 1988).
16. See, for example, Robin Small-McCarthy, 'The Jazz Aesthetic in the Novels of Toni Morrison', *Cultural Studies*, Vol.9, No.2, May 1995, pp. 295–300, and Alan J. Rice, 'Jazzing It Up a Storm: The Execution and Meaning of Toni Morrison's Jazzy Prose Style', *Journal of American Studies*, 28 (1994), pp. 423–32. For a differing view, see Alan Munton, 'Misreading Morrison, Mishearing Jazz: A Response to Toni Morrison's Jazz Critics', *Journal of American Studies*, 31 (1997), 2, 235–51.
17. Linden Peach, *Toni Morrison* (London: Macmillan, 1995), p. 114.
18. *New Grove Dictionary*, p. 1047.

19. Gates, *The Signifying Monkey*, p. 105.
20. Regina Weinreich, *The Spontaneous Poetics of Jack Kerouac: A Study of the Fiction* (New York: Marlowe, 1995).
21. Peach, *Toni Morrison*, p. 123.
22. Gerald Nicosia, *Memory Babe: A Critical Biography of Jack Kerouac* (Berkeley: University of California Press, 1994), p. 125.
23. Leroi Jones [Amiri Baraka], *Black Music* (New York: Quill, 1967), p. 137.
24. Kerouac quoted in George Plimpton, (ed.), *Writers at Work: The Paris Review Interviews*, 4th series (New York: Penguin, 1974). All references here are to p. 378.
25. Jack Kerouac, 'Essentials of Spontaneous Prose', *Evergreen Review*, 2, No. 5, Summer 1958, p. 72.
26. Jon Panish, *The Color of Jazz: Race and Representation in Postwar American Culture* (Jackson: University of Mississippi Press, 1997), pp. 136–7.
27. Hayden Carruth, *Sitting In: Selected Writings on Jazz, Blues and Related Topics* (Iowa City: Iowa University Press, 1993), pp. 178–9.
28. William Carlos Williams, *Selected Essays of William Carlos Williams* (New York: Random House, 1954), p. 230.
29. W. T. Lhamon, Jr, *Deliberate Speed: The Origins of a Cultural Style in the American 1950s* (Washington: Smithsonian Institution, 1990); Daniel Belgrad, *The Culture of Spontaneity: Improvisation and the Arts in Postwar America* (Chicago: Chicago University Press, 1998).
30. Jack Kerouac, *Vanity of Duluoz: An adventurous education 1935–46* (London: Quartet, 1973), p. 58.
31. Pepe Karmel, curator of the Museum of Modern Art in New York, quoted in *Jazziz*, April 1999, Vol.16, No.4, p. 14.
32. Stuart Davis, 'The Cube Root' (1943), in Diane Kelder (ed.), *Stuart Davis* (New York: Praeger, 1971), pp. 130–1.
33. Peter Wollen, *Raiding the Icebox: Reflections on Twentieth-Century Culture* (London: Verso, 1993), p. 110.
34. Richard J. Powell, *The Blues Aesthetic: Black Culture and Modernism* (Washington: Washington Project for the Arts, 1989), pp. 26 and 27.
35. Pamphlet for *Rhapsodies in Black: Art of the Harlem Renaissance*, exhibit at the Corcoran Gallery of Art, Washington DC, June 1998.
36. Stuart Davis in Kelder, *Stuart Davis*, p. 130.
37. Davis quoted in Robert Hughes, *American Visions: The Epic History of Art in America* (London: Harvill, 1997), p. 431.
38. Hughes, *American Visions*, p. 437.
39. For discussion of Bearden's work, including its relation to contemporary musical culture, see Calvin Tomkins, 'Putting Something Over Something Else', in Robert G. O'Meally, *The Jazz Cadence of American Culture* (New York: Columbia University Press, 1998), pp. 224–42.
40. Hughes, *American Visions*, p. 520.
41. Mona Hadler, 'Jazz and the New York School', in Krin Gabbard (ed.), *Representing Jazz* (Durham: Duke University Press, 1995), pp. 247–59.
42. O'Meally, *The Jazz Cadence*, p. 176.
43. *Orkester Jornalen* (Sweden), quoted in Ross Russell, *Bird Lives!* (London: Quartet, 1973), p. 363.
44. Belgrad, *The Culture of Spontaneity*, pp. 194–5.

45. Ann Eden Gibson, *Abstract Impressionism, Other Politics* (New York: Yale University Press, 1997), pp. 31–2.
46. Wollen, *Raiding the Icebox*, p. 113.
47. Eastwood quoted in *Jazz Times*, September 1995, p. 32.
48. O'Meally, *The Jazz Cadence*, p. 177.
49. Wollen, *Raiding the Icebox*, p. 113.
50. Ornette Coleman, quoted in Mona Hadler, 'Jazz and the Visual Arts', *Arts Magazine*, June 1983, p. 97.
51. Paul Berliner, *Thinking in Jazz: The Infinite Art of Improvisation* (Chicago: University of Chicago Press, 1994).
52. Beck quoted in C. W. E. Bigsby, *A Critical Introduction to Twentieth Century American Drama* (Cambridge: Cambridge University Press, 1982), p. 78.
53. Panish, *The Color of Jazz*, p. 139.
54. Ibid., p. 120.
55. Daniel Boorstin, *The Americans: The Democratic Experience* (London: Cardinal, 1988), pp. 403–8.
56. Gibson, *Abstract Impressionism*, p. 31.

CHAPTER 6

'A Tamed Richness': Jazz as Myth

China is one thing, the idea which a French petit-bourgeois could have of it not so long ago is another.

Roland Barthes

Most new art forms attract attention through their most external aspects.

Gunther Schuller[1]

In the preceding chapters of this book, the ideas of 'myth' and 'mythology' have cropped up in a number of the contexts of jazz. The senses in which these words have been used here are those established by Roland Barthes's *Mythologies*, a study of popular culture published in the 1950s. Barthes gave the name of 'myth' to implicit ideological messages carried by the products of contemporary society. The purpose of the 'language' of myth is, according to Barthes, to lend an appearance of naturalness, of inevitability, to the social status quo. One of the principal ways in which this happens is that the historical origins and causes of the things we see around us are obscured: myth creates an ahistorical world in which social structures and products are simply *there*, as if by nature, or as if part of a timeless order.

Myth in this sense involves a reshaping of the complexities of any phenomenon into a simpler and more controllable form. As the first chapters of this book have shown, jazz is a diverse and complicated subject: considered purely as music, it contains a multitude of different styles and schools and individual departures, as well as being in a continuous state of change throughout the twentieth century. The forms it has taken as a culture are equally diverse. Its relation to the world of commercial music, to take only one aspect, is in itself a complex study. To use one of Barthes's phrases, 'it is a complex product which has its determination at the level of a very wide history'.[2] It is just the kind of historical 'complex product' that jazz is that requires and generates myth. The purpose of myth is to find a comfortable niche for any phenomenon within the established social order by imposing a mythic interpretation upon it. Jazz, like other complex historical creations, has needed to be placed within the usual categories of understanding without disrupting fundamental assumptions and ideologies. There are factors within the history and constitution of jazz that have been difficult to square with these assumptions: one is its relation to race, another is its challenge to an orthodox model of culture. Jazz does not fit easily into the pre-existing categories by which cultural formations are usually dealt with. The mythology that has developed around it therefore has its own distinctive features, but it has worked upon jazz in the ways that Barthes describes: by decontextualizing, dehistoricizing and naturalizing it.

To study jazz closely in a specific historical context is to begin to demythologize it. It was pointed out in Chapter 1 that an examination of improvisation, for example, can be disappointing to anyone who has previously bought into its myth of full-blown spontaneity. To look closely at one of the historical locations of jazz, as in a study such as Kenney's history of the Chicago scene, is to dispel some of the romantic exoticism that clings to it. Kenney's description of the environment of Chicago jazz in the 1920s takes in the roles of recording, the popular music industry, dance halls, the local framework of business and the law, interactions between black and white professional musicians, and so on. The picture that is established differs greatly from the stereotype of hoodlums, speakeasies and alcoholic doomed jazzmen that constitutes 'Chicago jazz' in its mythic form. Likewise, Scott Deveaux's examination of the full complex of circumstances from which bebop emerged works against the facile mythology of a cadre of musical revolutionaries turning jazz upside down. 'Chicago jazz' and 'bebop' are not simple constructions reducible to a handful of images or attitudes, but this kind of reduction is what myths accomplish.

As Barthes puts it, myths 'economise': they allow the conviction of having grasped the essence of a phenomenon, by a simple manoeuvre. 'Chicago jazz' (hoodlums, speakeasies, Bix Beiderbecke) provides an 'instantaneous reserve of history' which is much more easily graspable, though much more distorted, than Kenney's compilation of interlocking, overlapping, detailed circumstances. The myth does not include or subsume these facts and details, it transcends them, substituting for them a repertoire of images. In Barthes's words, '[myth] abolishes the complexity of human acts, it gives them the simplicity of essences'.[3]

The 'essence' of jazz is, in its turn, definable mythically. The first part of this chapter will look at some of the mechanisms by which 'jazz' is fixed in its various mythic forms. As with many other aspects of culture, 'jazz' is a composite myth, constructed out of a number of sub- or micro-myths. A composite myth of jazz, taking as many of these as possible into account, might be summarized as follows:

1. Jazz has the quality of being indefinable. It has an essence, but it is mysterious and elusive. Not everyone 'gets it'. If you have to ask what it is, you don't get it (a quotation that can be attributed to Louis Armstrong, Duke Ellington or Fats Waller).
2. Jazz can not be learned or taught. The ability to play it is given to a select few, who simply produce it naturally. Jazz is both difficult and easy: difficult to understand, it is easy to play for those who are predisposed to it.
3. Many African-Americans can play jazz well, and all can understand it, by instinct, as can all black people of whatever national origin.
4. Most white Americans can neither play jazz well nor understand it. Certain white hipster geniuses, however, relate to jazz readily, though their apprehension of it is more intellectual than instinctual.
5. Jazz originates in certain bordellos in New Orleans. This kind of place is still its natural home.
6. The lives of jazz musicians are tragic. Jazz musicians frequently suffer from drug addiction, and die young.
7. Women in general do not participate in jazz, except as singers. The abilities of female singers are improved by unhappy and abusive love lives.
8. Jazz musicians share none of the tastes or attitudes of the American public, whom they despise. They are contemptuous of popular music, but are often obliged to play it.

The propositions of this composite myth, separately or joined in various combinations, generate a large proportion of the discourse of jazz in journalism and fiction. They also provide ways of making swift judgements of value without reference to musical criteria or elements within jazz culture. The purpose of myth is in general to blot out complexity and division within the object of discussion and to reduce it into a term which can then be available in the overall language of myth; so that jazz, radically simplified in this way, can be compared or contrasted with other cultural 'essences', other forms of music, other cultures. Jazz, as was pointed out in Chapter 1, thereby becomes a 'second-order' term: expressed in its entirety in the form of a myth, it is available as an element of larger generalizations.

As Barthes also points out, 'the fundamental character of the mythical concept is to be *appropriated*.[4] In these various mythic conceptualizations of jazz we see a series of attempts to lay claim to its essence, to appropriate it on behalf of cultural formations that lie outside it. Jazz seems to pose an interpretative problem to other parts of the culture: how to place it, how to make sense of it, in terms of received concepts and categories. The remaining sections of this chapter will deal with some of the attempts to reshape jazz from the outside, to fit jazz into the various ideological categories, or to reaffirm its portrayal as myth.

Jazz and Photography

Jazz has been thoroughly documented in photographs, firstly in publicity material and personal portraiture, latterly through individual photographers who have brought their work to a point at which photography has come to be considered as a partner art to jazz. Grauer and Keepnews' *A Pictorial History of Jazz* gives good coverage of the photographic record from the beginning up to the 1960s.[5] Changes in the iconography of jazz can be traced, from the freakish Jazz Age poses, with whole bands brandishing instruments in the air, to the resplendency of the Swing Era portraits, the players in neat rows and glossy uniforms. Later photography concentrates on the expressive individual shot, seeming to confirm Hayden Carruth's perception of a shift in jazz culture from a music of 'coalescing sensibilities into a panorama of limited but separate romantic privileges'.[6]

A number of distinguished photographers have devoted their careers largely to the representation of jazz. Some of these can be considered as recorders and chroniclers of the scene, others more as expressive artists in their own right. Among the latter might be mentioned William Claxton, William Gottlieb, Roy De Carava, Herman Leonard, Carole Reiff, Lee Tanner, Milt Hinton and Herb Snitzer. Each of these has developed what is referred to in film theory as 'personal style', although, like many film artists, jazz photographers have sometimes been constrained by the economics of the profession. A number of them have done much of their work in journalism and on commission from publicity departments and record companies. Nevertheless, personal styles are apparent: Carole Reiff's work has an expressive rawness,

Claxton's photographs display the well-being of the world of jazz, Leonard's develop an aesthetic of darkness.[7]

The interest of much jazz photography lies in the identity of the subjects, but some images can be read as implicit statements about jazz. One highly significant image, for instance, a photograph by William Claxton, serves as a metaphor for the off-centre, half-perceived place of jazz in American life. It shows the trumpeter Donald Byrd in a subway carriage, causing some disturbance and an almost hostile curiosity among the other passengers. Read metaphorically, it shows jazz as a powerful but exotic and distanced presence in the life of urban America.

Jazz photography, in its starkness and simplicity, grows out of the American documentary tradition of photographers like Edward Steichen and Robert Frank, but it has become a considerable body of work in itself, and is given increasing prominence in the contemporary culture of jazz. Eric Hobsbaum regards photography as being the only art form which 'has taken jazz seriously and on its own terms'.[8] Jazz continues to exert a strong attraction upon photographers, with the result that excellent photographs exist of virtually all well-known performers, and the documentary record also provides visual memory of places, occasions and atmospheres. Some jazz photographs also preserve those collateral details that Barthes refers to as the 'punctum': flashes of random detail that open up a sense of a reality outside the frame of the image itself, the faces of people in crowds, names on billboards, objects in dressing-rooms.[9]

Part of the reason for the current high standing of jazz photography and its practitioners is, however, its mythologizing function. Barthes's comment that 'the great portrait photographers are great mythologists'[10] is applicable to jazz photography too. The way in which performers like Chet Baker and Billie Holiday have been photographed has tended to further the mythologies that surround them. Jazz photography is typically, almost exclusively, in black and white, like documentary film and photography of the past, and like *film noir*. Images of present-day performers are, by this set of stylistic associations, carried back into a mythologized past, into the same visual realm as images made in the 1930s and 1940s. Susan Sontag speaks of the universal tendency of photography to 'turn the past into an object of tender regard, scrambling moral distinctions and disarming historical judgements by the generalised pathos of looking at time past'.[11] This is very close to a description of the operation of myth in general.

The power and success of photography has created for jazz a kind of visual trademark, which in some interpretations even takes on the burden of embodying the 'essence' of jazz itself. A *New York Times* article by Barry Singer separates out the visual ingredients from which this essence is compounded: its 'combination of perspiration and elegance', 'rich shadows, incandescent light and the romantic filtering properties of cigarette smoke'. One of Bill Gottlieb's pictures of Billie Holiday is credited by Singer with capturing 'the essence of jazz – a quality, outside sound, that only a camera can capture'. It is worth noting how definitively this statement places the 'essence of jazz' outside of music.[12]

In these comments one can see the working of myth: the effacement of history in the glamour of images, the consolidation of a timeless 'essence' out of mythologized visual details. The motif of cigarette smoke (what Gary Carner calls the 'Marlboro man in jazz' motif[13]) is particularly interesting: it links jazz with a particular set of postures, from movies and fashion photography, and sustains the underworld exoticism jazz has been coupled with ever since the 1920s.

The concentrated attention of jazz photography upon certain individuals is comparable with the same process in jazz fiction, except that in certain cases the visual potential, the photogenicity, of individuals predominates over their status in the musical culture. The clearest case of this is the trumpeter Chet Baker, whose resemblance to James Dean has made him the subject of entire books of photography.[14] Jazz photography has also tracked the pathos of the decline of its performers, most notably Billie Holiday. Holiday is seen, for instance, in a study by Carole Reiff, taken in rehearsal at Carnegie Hall in 1956.[15] It is a full-shot of Holiday, whose head is lowered, with light coming from below in such a way as to pick out her brow and cheeks, leaving her eyes in shadow. It is a beautiful image, the body, elegant despite the sense of fatigue, perfectly framed in the darkness. All the same, the image plays upon the mythology of the tragic female jazz performer, here seen near the end of her story.

Whatever the excellence of this and other photography, it seems perverse to suggest that visual images best convey the essence of a culture based on music. For Singer, these 'iconographic images come to define the music itself'.[16] In a cultural and technological world in which the visual media predominate over other modes of experience, what we see here is a case in which this has produced an inversion of values. The visual elements attached to jazz (the looks, dress and demeanour of musicians on the stand, for example) may be important, but 'what jazz looks like' is surely not, as Arthur Knight puts it, 'crucial' or even primary.[17]

John Corbett has argued, using Laura Mulvey's essay on visual pleasure in the cinema, that there is something 'fetishistic' about listening to recorded music: listeners are obliged to fantasize a visual presence in order to compensate for the 'disembodied' nature of their listening.[18] This, again, is a strange inversion. Mulvey's essay is about visual, not auditory, experience, and she specifically emphasizes the fetishistic potential of visual media, using examples like Sternberg's static shots of Marlene Dietrich. It is the visual medium which has the power to produce this stasis, the fixity of gaze in which the spectator enjoys power over the person receiving the gaze.

In jazz, it is still in the visual mode that this experience is possible. The music itself moves on in real time, whereas the countenance of Chet Baker, the wardrobe of Miles Davis, the decay of Billie Holiday, can be fixed in the gaze of the spectator. Moreover, since the mythology persuades us that a photographic image or pose 'is jazz', or 'the essence of jazz', one 'knows' jazz in possessing the image. 'Jazz' is reduced to the message that can be read off the image of its charismatic performers, or of its typical visual motifs. As with other mythological operations, this one allows for swift appropriation without the need to engage with the contradictions and ambiguities of history, the complications of the subject, and in this case, even to listen to the music.

Barthes, in his description of contemporary myth, was obliged to invent neologisms like 'Italianicity' and 'Sinity' (or 'Sininess') to denote the constructs of Italian or Chinese identity that he found in advertising imagery.[19] By analogy, it can be argued that what the composite visual mythology of jazz delivers is not 'jazz' but 'jazzness' or 'jazzity'; that is to say, the construct resulting from the ensemble of visual signs (among instruments, saxophones and double basses typically signify jazz), iconic personalities and cool composition that comprise the myth of jazz, and which have come to assume, through use in album covers and magazine photography, the position of the very essence and identity of jazz:

> For me, much of the disembodied music will always look like Francis Wolff's photographs of outrageously cool black musicians with their cigarettes and dark glasses as they appeared on the many Blue Note albums that I began collecting in the 1960s.[20]

Jazz and Cultural Categories

Jazz photography may, as Hobsbaum commented, deal with jazz on its own terms, but both the photography and jazz itself are part of the second-order language in which jazz is articulated in the mythologies of the wider culture. In fiction and in the cinema, jazz is placed and made intelligible to an uncommitted audience by being drawn into the orbit of pre-established narrative genres. Within the wider society, jazz has been expressed through cultural genres, categories of meaning and value whose origins lie outside of jazz culture and which predate and subsume it. Jazz as a set of cultural formations may have its own ways of representing itself, but it is inevitably implicated within the ideologies embedded in the culture as a whole.

An approach to understanding another art form, cinema, within an 'American ideology', has been made by film writers such as Robin Wood.[21] Wood lists twelve components of such an ideology, embracing economic principles, gender roles and attitudes towards nature and the land. A similar exercise might place jazz ideologically as Wood does film genres. One approach used within film studies, under the inspiration of the structuralist principle of binary oppositions, is the use of 'antinomies', as applied by film writers like Peter Wollen.[22] In this approach the work of specific film artists, and film genres, are defined in relation to choices within a series of opposed values. American film has been analyzed in terms of binary oppositions such as these:

civilization	wilderness
society	individual
East	West

The whole list of antinomies could be said to define the value system of the American cinema, and choices between the various antinomies would indicate what is distinctive about genres or individual filmmakers. John Ford, for instance, would differ from Frank Capra in terms of 'Society/Individual'.

Inevitably, jazz too has been described and conceptualized through various combinations of binary distinctions. Some writers on jazz have set out, for particular periods within its history, the antinomies that were in play. In the most systematic attempt at this, Bernard Gendron has described the new discourse of 'jazz as art' that emerged during the 1940s as being structured around this series of binaries:

art   commerce
native   European
authentic   artificial
affect   technique

Around and between these distinctions, as Gendron explains, the lines of conflict were set up between the 'traditionalists' and the 'modernists' contending for the soul of jazz. Lawrence Gushee, similarly, has described three specific antinomies that define the position of the 'serious composer' in jazz. Charles Nanry has pointed out the importance of the antinomy 'urban'/'rural' in the history of jazz.[23] Other important binaries which recur in the literature of jazz include 'written'/'improvised', 'collective'/'individual', and the numerous oppositions in which 'jazz' is itself one of the terms placed in opposition to others: 'popular music', 'classical', 'swing', and so on.

Taking all of these categories together gives a sense of where jazz is placed among the terms that are current in the culture. But by the same process, it becomes clear how frequently the categories that are available do not fit the specific case of jazz. For Charles Nanry, the instances in which jazz fails to be easily accommodated to these antinomies are evidence of its cultural marginality. He gives an example: 'Jazz defies the stereotyped notion of folk art because of its complexity; yet it does not fit into the equally stereotyped notion of "high" art as formalistic.'[24] Other writers use the same kind of argument when confronted with the need to locate jazz in the familiar binary framework. Peter Wollen shows how, during its vogue in the 1920s, jazz was linked with the contradictory values of both absolute primitivism and the machine age. Krin Gabbard writes of the 'precarious' positioning of jazz between a 'hegemonic monoculture' and a 'polyglot diaspora'. Nanry uses the phrase 'on the cusp' to state the position of jazz between 'serious' and 'popular' music.[25]

Numerous other examples of a lack of fit between jazz and the received cultural categories can be found in jazz literature. The division between 'improvisation' and 'composition' illustrates some of the problems that emerge. In any assignment of musical idioms to one of these categories, jazz, before all other American musical forms, would be identified with improvisation. Jazz is the prime, even the stereotypical, example of an improvisation-based music. When composition appears in jazz, it is therefore problematic because of its designation into the opposite category. Compositions like some of

Duke Ellington's, which do not provide openings for improvisation, throw descriptions of jazz into confusion. In fact, the existence of composers like Ellington provokes a whole series of mismatches with categories (hence Ellington's own dislike of categories of any kind[26]). Ellington's experience, as a composer, bandleader and performer, somewhere between jazz and 'serious music', had a wholeness and unity which defy the theoretical problems of category that swarm about it. Ellington's case illustrates perfectly the ways in which the actualities of jazz, the normal activities and purposes of people participating in the music, are fragmented and made problematic by the antinomic concepts that are applied to them.

The most important categories of all are those concerning race. The division between 'black' and 'white' is, of course, of enormous social and historical importance in American society at all levels. What Lawrence Gushee calls 'the quintessentially American polarity of black (or brown or beige) and pink'[27] is of great significance also throughout the history of jazz, and continues to be a source of contestation in discussion of the music up to the present day.

The whole phenomenon of jazz in all its forms is rooted in black culture. As was argued in Chapter 1, it is an instance of the improvisatory African-American cultures that have produced a succession of hugely influential idioms of dance, verbal art and music throughout the last two centuries. All of the performers whose work has deeply affected the course of development of jazz have been black. African-American culture has been definitive of the form of jazz, its values and its very existence. Nevertheless, jazz in America has not been simply coextensive with black culture, and the simple polarity of 'black' and 'white' has screened out some of the historical complexity of jazz. Like cultural phenomena in all fields it overlaps, it has shifting boundaries, and it has been involved in complex historical relations with many other cultural formations, from the popular music business to social institutions to contact between cultural groups.

The antinomy in jazz writing of 'black' and 'white', however, has tended to create in the discourse of jazz a musical-cultural universe which is divided into two mutually exclusive sectors. In this scenario, black individuals encounter and appreciate only 'black' culture (in this case music) and respond to 'white' culture only as a contamination. Some writers on jazz interpret musical performance by projecting on to black musicians this kind of antinomic consciousness, as though, in all musical situations, performers were continually keeping a tally of 'black' and 'white' elements and responding accordingly.

The most prevalent form of this approach concerns the relation between jazz and the popular song form. Writers on jazz have tended to regard the standard song as a culturally inferior product in need of redemption by jazz, and to assume that the same attitude exists in the performers. A 'black' musician (say, Lester Young) playing a 'white' standard song (say, 'All of Me') must therefore hold the song in contempt, and demonstrate this by mocking or subverting it. H. L. Gates's theory of 'signifyin'' is introduced into the argument at this point: artists like Young must be 'signifyin' on' (mocking, parodying, ironizing) standard songs by various tactics in their performance. Even the fact of improvisation itself can, in this argument, be seen as a form of signifyin' subversion, since, by definition, it alters the original form of the song.[28]

The scenario that is proposed by this kind of argument is of whole generations of black jazz musicians continually playing songs which they secretly despise, and expressing this view only by covert signals in their performances. Hence, Coleman Hawkins's repeated revisitings of the song 'Body and Soul' were so many expressions of his distaste for it. Charlie Parker depised, but frequently played, 'Out of Nowhere'. Clifford Brown likewise for 'Ghost of a Chance'. John Coltrane constructed complex modal improvisations on the Broadway song 'My Favourite Things' in order to express his contempt for Rodgers, Hammerstein and Julie Andrews.[29] And so on, through all the hundreds of thousands of performances and recordings of popular songs made by black jazz musicians from the time of the First World War to the end of the century.

This kind of argument springs from the combined action of two of the antinomies applied to jazz: 'black' as an exclusive category is coupled with 'jazz'; 'white' as an exclusive category is coupled with 'popular music'. In the logic of this position, no black musician can have truck with popular music on its own terms. However, this is evidently not the case. From the beginnings of the popular music industry in the late nineteenth century, the popular song has, for better or worse, circulated throughout the whole of American society. A black radio listener in the 1930s could listen to Bing Crosby or Kate Smith and hear the songs of Kern and Berlin just as a white listener could hear Fletcher Henderson and Cab Calloway. These were not hermetic musical universes. Black musicians such as Eubie Blake, Duke Ellington and Fats

Waller have been composers of songs and musicals that have been produced and marketed in the usual way. Hit songs like Waller's 'Ain't Misbehavin'' and Ellington's 'Satin Doll' function in the domains of both pop and jazz in exactly the same way as songs by Gershwin, Berlin and Carmichael. Moreover, there are numerous statements by black jazz musicians of several generations in praise of the material created by popular songwriters. 'In those days', Teddy Wilson commented in an interview, 'we were just crazy about the new writers, Rodgers and Hart, and we played 'Dancing on the Ceiling' and 'You Took Advantage of Me ... they wrote some lovely songs.'[30]

Deprecation of the popular song form has been endemic in jazz writing, in part because of the cultural antinomies that determine an aesthetic segregation into black and white, jazz and popular. André Hodeir, for instance, while paying tribute to Charlie Parker's transformation of its melody, calls Gershwin's 'Embraceable You' 'vapid', despite the fact that Parker found the material interesting enough to return to in a variety of guises.[31] A more complex example occurs in Jon Panish's explication of a jazz performance in Baldwin's story 'Sonny's Blues'. The black musicians in Sonny's band begin to play the song 'Am I Blue'. The interpretation that Panish places on this is that the song represents what Baldwin has earlier referred to as 'the void'. 'The void' is clearly intended to be a metaphysical or existential term: the void of existence, the void that is only overcome by personal action. Yet Panish reads the word as referring to a vacuous type of popular song represented here by 'Am I Blue': 'the musicians take this hollow standard (the 'void'), which has co-opted the basic element of African American music in its title (the blues) ...'[32] 'Am I Blue', a song first published in 1929, has not been too 'hollow' to have been performed by a long succession of African-American musicians ever since then, including Jimmy Noone, Kid Ory, Erroll Garner, Jay McShann, Earl Hines, James Moody and the singers Ethel Waters, Billie Holiday and Jimmy Rushing.

Black and white musicians have not inhabited separate and reciprocally hostile musical universes. Many white musicians have attained great skill and a profound identification with the values of jazz. Black musicians have been capable of valuing structural and harmonic detail in popular songs, the harmonies of 'What's New', the dynamics of Cole Porter's 'Love for Sale', and so on. Black musicians have had an awareness of American popular culture, from movies to sports to television, and as wide and, in Ingrid Monson's term, as 'polymusical' a range of reference as anyone else. John Coltrane, whose music of the 1960s represents a conscious and powerful assertion of blackness, was fond of singing (as Lewis Porter adds, 'believe it or not') 'O Sole Mio'.[33] When Charlie Parker paid tribute to the lyricism of one of his mentors, Johnny Hodges, he likened him to the operatic soprano Lily Pons.[34] The favourite singer of many jazz musicians was the Italian-American interpreter of popular songs, Frank Sinatra. There are thousands of available examples of black musicians playing 'white','popular' material without any evident intention of trashing it: to take a single case, the numerous superb recordings made by the black guitarist Wes Montgomery of standard ballads, from 'Gone with the Wind' to 'Yesterdays'.[35]

In the deprecation of popular material in jazz, one is primarily reading the high art attitudes of the writers, many of whom come to jazz from a literary-critical perspective unaccustomed to the anomalous position of jazz, poised between 'high' and 'popular' culture, between all the other antinomies that have been discussed in this section. The difficulties of describing just where jazz fits into these conceptual schemes is an overall indication of the peculiarity of its position within American culture. Jazz always seems to lie somewhere outside of the binaries, or across them, on the cusp. To cite yet another metaphor, Scott DeVeaux places jazz on the 'fault line' of race relations in the USA.[36] Its location across a series of 'fault lines' is a factor in the continuing marginality of jazz in American culture. Perhaps recalling Ralph Ellison's novel, Gary Giddins has referred to 'jazz's invisibility in its native land' – invisible not only because of its distance from the economic mainstream, but also because of its resistance to the familiar antinomic vocabularies of American culture.[37]

Jazz as Cultural Capital

This section will primarily address the function of jazz as 'cultural capital' in the 1980s and 1990s, though jazz has sometimes performed a similar function in the past. 'Cultural capital' refers to cultural possessions that substitute for actual capital (money) in determining social prestige. Cultural capital is sometimes intangible, consisting of knowledge of, appreciation of or taste for some product which is considered to enhance social standing. Kinds of cultural capital form a hierarchy, with some items being more highly esteemed than others: a taste for and knowledge of opera, for instance, carries more value than a taste for and knowledge of bluegrass music; classical theatre outranks contemporary cinema; the literary novel has a higher cultural capital value than pulp fiction; and so on. For Pierre Bourdieu, the theorist of cultural capital, writing about configurations of taste in France in the 1970s, jazz was one of the 'middle-ground' arts equivalent in prestige to the cinema.[38] Since the middle of the 1980s, in the USA as elsewhere, the cultural profile of jazz has risen to a point where it has become, as Krin Gabbard puts it, a 'signifier of elegance and affluence, an association the music seldom if ever carried before the early 1980s'.[39]

'Elegance' and 'affluence' therefore become the latest concepts to be signified by jazz in its undulating progress through the century. For the 1920s jazz was exoticism, novelty, youthful energy; for the 1950s it connoted non-conformity and urban anxiety, and at the end of the century it presents a more amenable face altogether, configured among the other possessions that constitute the cultural capital of affluence. It is noticeable that in these forms as well as in myth, the inner content of jazz is secondary: it is what meaning jazz can be made to carry, as a second-order term, that gives it a social role. In certain circumstances it can enter into one of the homologies of taste that crystallize into identifiable 'lifestyles'. Joan Didion here identifies the place of a certain type of jazz in an earlier socio-cultural setting:

> there were Ben Shahn posters on the walls, and the gesture towards a strobe light was nothing that might interfere with 'good talk', and the music was not 1968 rock but the kind of jazz people used to have on their record players when everyone who believed in the Family of Man bought Scandinavian stainless-steel flatware and voted for Adlai Stevenson.[40]

In the 1990s jazz, as a component in personal style, co-ordinates with a new configuration of products. The image of jazz in this connection is based largely upon a selection of personal and musical styles that are associated with the notion of 'cool'. 'Cool' originated in black slang around 1940, and was first prominent in the terminology of jazz style a few years later, with the 'Birth of the Cool' recordings of Miles Davis and the Californian 'Cool School' musicians. 'Cool' reached the mainstream through films and journalism by the mid-1950s. A report in the *Daily News* in 1957 provides an example: 'The night club's lights were low, good-looking chicks were around and the jazz was cool, man, cool ...'[41]

By the late 1980s 'cool' was resurgent through the fifties-retro element in contemporary style, and by the late 1990s 'cool' is more prevalent than ever in slang and in the style discourse of the media. To take one example among thousands: a jazz website advertising byline reads 'More Artists. More Music. More Cool.' The dominance of the cool ethos also affects the selection of jazz that is played by some radio stations: cool icons from the 1950s, Chet Baker and Miles Davis, can be programmed among more contemporary styles, while earlier 'hot' forms of jazz are liable to be excluded.

Jazz is seen in the company of other items that signify cultural capital. The leading jazz magazine, *Jazz Times*, which has expanded from a twenty-page foldout paper in the early 1980s to 160 glossy pages by the late 1990s, carries advertising for hi-fi systems, automobiles, whisky and cognac alongside record companies, instruments and distributors. There has been a rapid growth of upmarket jazz festivals, the larger of which are sponsored by communications companies, airlines, hotel chains and investment banks: 184 jazz festivals were listed for the 1999 season in the USA alone.[42]

What it is that jazz contributes by its presence in advertising or in sponsorship schedules can be seen by looking at some of the ways in which it is featured in these contexts. The advertisement image for an Yves St Laurent perfume called 'Live Jazz' shows a young, multiracial crowd of style models posed in a simulacrum of a New York avenue. The word 'jazz' appears sixteen times in the photograph, placed on wall-posters, illuminated signs, on an upturned instrument case, and almost subliminally embroidered into the inconspicuous parts of the image. The jazz crowd includes a young trumpeter whose look and posture recalls jazz photography of the 1950s. The association of jazz with the image here seems insistent and simplistic, as if designed for a market for whom the word 'jazz' is itself a sufficient signal.

Other advertising copy is more conversant with the internal discourses of jazz. Lorus watches, which has sponsored an annual jazz festival, has an advertisement that draws a parallel between the combination of tradition and innovation in jazz and in the craft of watch manufacture. An advertisement for a website design company seems more 'inside' still, with its claim that it will do for your website 'what Bird did for bebop'. This statement begs a lot of questions about the magnitude of the achievement of Charlie Parker (referred to by a nickname) as compared with that of a website supplier, but, more significantly, it places jazz in a specific field of consumer behaviour. An individual in the late 1990s (like the one in the accompanying photograph) can experience jazz as part of a seamless lifestyle continuity with a range of commercial products. These products are then putatively hip, or cool, by association with the world of bebop and 'Bird'.

Jazz contibutes a certain kind of 'outsider' appeal to products that might otherwise seem conventional; it lends 'character' to consumer products in just the same way as, in Gabbard's description, it does to people in films. The language of jazz, its names and images, have spread across the media since its return to fashion in the mid-1980s. The photography and cover design of Blue Note records has been visually cloned by a series of pop artists seeking some of its mystique. Jazz has increasingly been provided as background music in malls and restaurants, and its imagery has spread into many sectors of the economy. In Manchester, England, there were in the 1980s and 1990s, within a few blocks, businesses called 'Jazz', 'Blue Note' and (after a classically 'cool' Miles Davis album) 'Kind of Blue'. Certain varieties of jazz have become, for an affluent and style-conscious demographic, one of the musical forms furnishing their environment.

What has been promoted to this public is a selection of jazz that co-ordinates with pre-existing tastes and with notions of style that are extramusical. Programming on some radio stations concentrates on a narrow range of recorded jazz, with a strong concentration on singers (especially female) and on a small number of specialized instrumental styles, stretching from the 1950s cool of Davis and Baker to contemporary neo-bop. An emergent and controversial idiom in the late 1990s is what radio and record programmers have labelled 'smooth jazz'. Often performed by musicians with no previous track record in other jazz styles, and sharing many of the features of contemporary pop, 'smooth jazz' has considerable commercial potential, and may in the future stretch the already extended definition of 'jazz' still further.

Jazz in the Academy

Compared with that of rock and popular music, the impact of jazz upon contemporary culture is limited. Measured in record sales, jazz as a category accounts for no more than 2.8 per cent of the US market.[43] Even with the advantage of its iconic status in style and design through the 1980s and 1990s, it is still the music of a minority audience; and the market percentage of some of the traditional styles must be minuscule.

Market forces are not likely to favour the long-term survival of the pre-1950s jazz tradition, nor of the more adventurous contemporary styles.

A potential countervailing influence to this is the increasing presence of jazz in the academy. The study of jazz in the academy occurs in two forms: one, the training of jazz musicianship, the acquisition of jazz skills through formal education rather than through the informal learning community of the past; and, two, the new and as yet unformed subject called 'jazz studies'. Jazz made appearances within college syllabuses as early as the 1940s, and established a foothold with the inauguration of a 'stage band' tradition at institutions like the University of North Texas in the 1950s. Collier cites a figure of about 100 colleges and universities offering courses in jazz in 1990; by 1998–9 this figure had doubled to 204 for the USA and Canada.[44] Collier also cites a figure for 1990 of 15,000 secondary school programmes in jazz, and this has presumably also increased since then.

Many of the university level courses are long-established and have distinguished jazz musicians among the faculty: Charlie Haden at Cal Arts, Clark Terry at New Hampshire, Frank Foster at NYU, and many others. Some of the longer established programmes, such as North Texas and the Berklee School in Massachusetts, have a worldwide reputation, and number many prominent contemporary jazz players among their former students. The existence and the recent expansion of jazz education has had a number of positive effects, among them the provision of respectable employment for a large number of jazz musicians. Standards of technique among young players have never been higher, and students on jazz programmes are introduced to the study and playing of material from jazz tradition that they would never otherwise encounter.

However, there has also been plenty of adverse comment on this development. Collier, for instance, claims that the improvised solos of university-trained jazz students 'tend to sound much the same' because, in his opinion, they are taught 'more or less the same harmonic principles'.[45] The same kinds of comment are not infrequently heard from professional jazz players. Speaking in the early 1970s, the pianist Mary Lou Williams referred to the danger of 'losing the feeling in jazz' if it ceased to be a 'self-taught music'.[46] A 1996 interview with the saxophonist Joe Henderson and guitarist John Scofield found them agreeing on the pitfalls of academic jazz education. Scofield commented 'Everybody plays the same licks because they have the same books', and

Henderson 'these days, everybody is doing the same thing and sounding the same, you don't get that individual fingerprint like you used to among players'. Henderson's comment identifies a particular concern among the older jazz community that, with the possible curtailment of individuality in the institutionalization of jazz, one of its cardinal virtues will be lost.[47] On the other hand, it is difficult to see how the existence of large numbers of highly trained young musicians with an interest in jazz and some knowledge of its traditions can be *prima facie* a bad thing. This critical mass of technique and knowledge has to go somewhere, though it is unlikely that it will ever go towards the personal idiosyncrasies of style and sonority and attitude to music and the world of individualists like Lester Young, Joe Nanton, or Thelonious Monk.

The other arm of the reach of jazz into the academy, or vice versa, is what is coming to be called 'Jazz Studies'. Like Cultural Studies, of which Jazz Studies may be seen as a sub-branch, Jazz Studies has not yet established a distinct identity, or a sense of what its aims are. As was pointed out at the start of Chapter 2, jazz is also being studied in an empirical, historicist way by writers such as Ogren, DeVeaux and Kenney. This kind of detailed research, done by writers with academic affiliations, is the successor to the work of earlier historians and students of the music such as Marshall Stearns, Barry Ulanov, Dan Morgenstern and Nat Hentoff, whose approach was that of the unaffiliated freelance, the enthusiast of jazz recording its qualities and achievements.

The term 'Jazz Studies' is coming to be used to refer to an approach to jazz which brings literary and cultural theory to bear on it. From one perspective, this movement can be seen as a symptom of the expansionism of these approaches, homing in upon jazz as a field as yet untouched by theories that have been applied to a huge range of other subject matter. If the full array of analytical techniques available to literary and cultural studies can be successfully extended to cover film, advertising, television, rock and pop music and all types of cultural ephemera, then there is no obvious reason to insist that jazz can not come under the remit of these disciplines. Hence there are studies like Robert Walser's on Miles Davis, Krin Gabbard's on the jazz trumpet, and Michael Jarrett's on Sonny Rollins's album *Way Out West* whose methods will be familiar to those with literary or cultural studies backgrounds. Gabbard, for instance, applies neo-Freudian theory to the understanding of the 'phallic' jazz trumpet and the 'hyper-phallic' (perhaps because larger) baritone saxophone.[48]

Jarrett's essay on the Sonny Rollins album *Way Out West* may be taken as an indication of the new directions and their possibilities. The album is studied in a wide sweep of different perspectives: its title, the iconography of the cover photograph, its relation to the myths of the West, the legend of the non-presence of African-Americans in the old West, the iconography of the saxophone, interpolated personal anecdotes, and so on. The essay is twenty-two pages in length, despite the absence of discussion of the music on the album. It can be seen from this example that the scope of 'jazz studies' is virtually limitless. If one album can be the occasion for such an array of theory, reference and allusion, this kind of approach, if applied to the entire back-catalogue of jazz recording, suggests many millions of potential pages of writing around jazz. One could say, after Sterne's *Tristram Shandy*, that jazz, like life, takes longer to write about than to experience. There is a possible vision of the future of jazz studies as a nightmare Shandean pursuit, jazz itself racing ahead while teams of scholars retrospectively scrutinize note choices, titles, cover art, photographs, and the swathes of cultural history that are connected with any of these things.

Theories and methods derived from literary and cultural studies are not necessarily useful everywhere, and in relation to jazz in particular. As Henry Louis Gates has pointed out, every literary tradition 'at least implicitly, contains within it an argument for how it can be read',[49] and this is just as true for jazz as for literature. Jazz has generated, over many decades, its own means of understanding. Gates's own theory of 'signifyin'' has been applied to the analysis of jazz performance with limited success: some of the musical gestures of jazz, but not all of them, can be understood in those terms. The mere fact of inventing a variation on a tune falls short of the full meaning of signifyin', unless Rachmaninov was signifyin' on Paganini, Beethoven was signifyin' on Diabelli, and so on. Likewise the literary concept of 'intertextuality' does not entirely work in a jazz context. In this case, fleeting musical references or quotations are treated by critics exactly as if they were allusions in a literary text. In this perspective, Dizzy Gillespie's quotation from 'We're In the Money' at the start of his solo on the 1946 'Anthropology' can be read as a complex instantaneous reference to the relation between jazz and the movies, the integrity of jazz against the artificiality of Hollywood, as an ironic statement on the inequities of the music business or on post-Second World War capitalism.

Faced with the unfamiliarity of the methods and values of jazz, writers whose background is literary and cultural, and whose allegiance is to the eventual construction of a 'discipline', typically convert the alien vocabulary into the currency in which they are accustomed to dealing. Jazz, its language, its customs and methods, its implicit rules and understandings, is converted into 'text'. In this form it becomes more amenable to the techniques that have been developed to deal with the analysis of other cultural settings. As 'text', jazz is available for the usual operations of literary-cultural studies to be performed on it.

There is here a fundamental parting of the ways in the study of jazz. The new forms of 'jazz studies' would assert that jazz has no autonomy as a culture, that it is not 'about' music, but 'about' the same values and concepts that are discovered in the description of other cultures and subcultures. Krin Gabbard, for example, comments that 'Most jazz isn't really about jazz, at least not in terms of how it is usually consumed. Jazz is usually about race, sexuality and spectacle.'[50] As jazz moves along what Gabbard calls 'the arduous path to institutionalisation',[51] the issue of the significance of jazz as music comes to the forefront. 'Preprofessional' critics (like Gunther Schuller) might reassert that the music itself is of overwhelming importance, but 'jazz studies' may more and more insist that it is not. Gabbard, for instance, sets out the prospect of the visual presence of the artist assuming much greater importance. 'Repressed' by the 'current ideology of jazz writing', the self-display of the jazz artist will be recognized for what it is worth 'as poststructuralist discourses of the body make their way into jazz studies'.[52]

Reprise: Jazz as Music

Music is a good thing; and after all that soul-butter and hogwash, I never see it freshen things up so, and sound so honest and bully.
                                        Mark Twain, *Huckleberry Finn*

The issue of 'spectacle' may be one of the specific locations of future debate about the nature of jazz, among musicians as well as critics. The avant-garde multi-instrumentalist Anthony Braxton, for example, expresses a disdain commonly held among the community of players for the 'external' aspects of the music: 'By the very nature of the system we live in, once something creative is established, they find a way to turn it into a spectacle.'[53] For Braxton, as for many others, within and without the community of jazz players, it is self-evident that the music itself retains an absolute centrality in the culture. As Ingrid Monson comments, 'In jazz, the music itself is anything but peripheral to the construction of cultural meaning.'[54]

The second half of this book has examined a number of the ways in which jazz is represented in the wider culture. Narratives involving jazz, descriptions of it, and its various literary and cinematic representations were followed in Chapter 5 by versions of jazz as models for creativity in the other arts. The present chapter has examined further perspectives in which jazz has been viewed: firstly through the composite, widely distributed mythologies generated around it, secondly its placement as a commodity, and finally the ways of looking at it that are being formulated by academic disciplines.

Jazz may or may not be 'about' race, sexuality and spectacle. One limitation of this view is that, in a society dominated by media and the power of the visual, everything else, from sport to politics to television, is also 'about' race, sexuality and spectacle. That this can be argued for jazz too is in the circumstances one of the least interesting things that can be said about it. It misses what is distinctive about jazz, its culture and its values, in the context that it finds itself in. Jazz is an anomaly: as we have seen, it falls into a gap between many of the familiar categories of ideology. What is even more distinctive about it, in comparison with other contemporary cultures, is that it has held on to a specific and unusual set of values of its own. 'Jazz music', as Ted Gioia comments on one of its aspects, 'more than most modern art forms, retains an adherence to old-fashioned standards of technical proficiency.'[55]

Jazz has established a musical language and standards of value which are *sui generis*; they are not immediately amenable to public perceptions trained on the taste for photogenicity, sensation and instantaneous access. Although, as Ralph Ellison says, 'there's no inherent problem which prohibits understanding but the assumptions brought to it',[56] jazz requires at least a minimal process of familiarization, a gradual internalizing of the rules of the game. This is anomalous, even anachronistic, in the midst of a mediatized and mythologized culture. It is as though the activities of a craft community, like the musicians of North India discussed in Chapter 1, were suddenly subjected to the attention of a mass public not conversant with the community's practices and values. There are ways of dealing with the interpretative challenge that such a culture presents: mystifying it, dwelling upon the way it looks, turning it into a symbol of the exotic, the secretive, the heroic, the subversive, even the abnormal. All of these strategies have been used upon jazz, the American instance of such a culture.

Jazz is one of the great musical cultures of the world. If one were dealing with the European classical tradition, the idea that a certain respect was required, and that a little time needed to be invested, would not cause such difficulties (or, in Duke Ellington's words, 'if they'd been told it was a Balkan folk dance'[57]). But jazz is not simply a form worked on, perfected and exchanged by a community developing its own methods and values: it stands also in the full glare of the worlds of art and entertainment, and under the gaze of a public unaccustomed to a culture that works according to its own inherent principles. Jazz is still answerable to a set of standards and values that are not immediately transparent to a casual witness. In jazz, in Ralph Ellison's words, 'the condition of artistic communication is, as the saying goes, hard but fair'.[58]

It is a broad, diverse and complex cultural field of its own. 'Jazz' is comparable in both depth and magnitude to such an entity as 'American Literature' or 'English Literature', consisting of a multitude of voices, accents, regions, schools, conventions, typologies, achievements and personalities. To insist that, as Hayden Carruth says, 'we must point out, determinedly and repeatedly, that music is music'[59] is to state the anomalous adherence that jazz still has to a self-generated set of values. To say this is not to insist upon expert knowledge, or a Hemingwayan *aficion*, but simply to suggest a reasonable level of familiarity with what goes on in the music – equivalent to the sort of familiarity that a baseball fan would have of the game of baseball.

There always has been this kind of audience for jazz, consisting of people who have somehow been in a position to acquire a certain basic level of understanding. Ralph Ellison's figure for this, for a public capable of appreciation and understanding, is 'the little man at Chehaw Station'. Ellison describes how he acquired this figure from his piano teacher at Tuskegee Institute:

'All right', she said, 'you must *always* play your best, even if it's only in the waiting room at Chehaw Station, because in this country there'll always be a little man hidden behind the stove.'
    'A *what?*'

She nodded. 'That's right', she said. 'There'll always be the little man whom you don't expect, and he'll know the *music*, and the *tradition*, and the standards of *musicianship* required for whatever you set out to perform.'[60]

From the musicians' point of view, the story is simply that, in Jim Hall's words, 'we listen to each other, and keep the language going'.[61] The musical 'language' of jazz is its continuity and its core, the point of origin of its meanings, its innovations, the richness that in Barthes's words is 'tamed' by its myth. The language continues to be used, modified, extended and added to, just as in a natural language, in the practice of hundreds of thousands of musicians, on a nightly basis, all over the world.

In this sense, jazz is a discourse on itself. It does not stand in real need of any of the discourses of art, literature, analysis or myth. None of these alternate languages contains the past of jazz, its future, its depth and its power. As against the images and legends of a small repertoire of heroes, glamorous and dysfunctional, against the rest of the myths of jazz as they are refracted through the media of publicity and consumption, there is the invention, the force and the eloquence, of the thousands of American musicians who have used the resources of this black vernacular musical form to express an identity within the matrices of its forms and its language. What Greil Marcus said of Elvis Presley is also true of jazz: 'the myth is unsatisfying, because the truth is richer than the myth'.[62]

Notes

1. Roland Barthes, *Mythologies* (1957; London: Paladin, 1973), p. 121; Gunther Schuller, *Early Jazz* (New York: OUP, 1968), p. 54.
2. Barthes, *Mythologies*, p. 124.
3. Ibid., p. 143.
4. Ibid., p. 119.
5. Orrin Keepnews, Bill Grauer (eds), *A Pictorial History of Jazz* (London: Spring Books, rev. ed 1968).
6. Hayden Carruth, *Sitting In: Selected Writings on Jazz, Blues and Related Topics* (Iowa City: Iowa University Press, 1993), p. 11.
7. Examples of the work of these photographers include collections such as: William P. Gottlieb, *The Golden Age of Jazz* (London: Quartet, 1979); Carole Reiff, *Nights in Birdland* (London: Simon and Schuster, 1987); Milt Hinton, *Over Time: The Jazz Photography of Milt Hinton* (San Francisco: Pomegranate, 1991); William Claxton, *Jazz Seen* (New York: Taschen, 1999).

8. Francis Newton [Eric Hobsbaum], *The Jazz Scene* (London: Penguin, 1961), p. 141.

9. Roland Barthes, *Camera Lucida: Reflections on Photography* (London: Cape, 1982).

10. Ibid, p. 34.

11. Susan Sontag, *On Photography* (London: Penguin, 1979), p. 71.

12. Barry Singer, *The New York Times*, 27 April 1997, p. 30.

13. Gary Carner, 'Jazz Photography: A Conversation with Herb Snitzer', *Black American Literature Forum*, Vol. 25, No. 3, Fall 1991, p. 587.

14. See, for example, William Claxton, *Young Chet* (London: Schirmer, 1993).

15. Reiff, *Nights in Birdland*, p. 96.

16. Singer, *The New York Times*, p. 30.

17. Arthur Knight, '*Jammin' the Blues*, or the Sight of Jazz 1944', in Krin Gabbard, *Representing Jazz* (Durham: Duke University Press, 1995), p. 13.

18. John Corbett, 'Free, Single and Disengaged: Listening Pleasure and the Popular Music Object', *October* 54, (1990), pp. 79–101. Laura Mulvey's essay, first published in *Screen* in 1975, is reprinted in Gerald Mast, Marshall Cohen, Leo Braudy, *Film Theory and Criticism* (New York: OUP, 4th edn.1992), pp. 746–57.

19. Barthes, *Mythologies*, p. 121. For 'Italianicity', see Barthes, Stephen Heath (ed.), *Image-Music-Text* (London: Fontana, 1977), p. 35.

20. Krin Gabbard, *Jammin' at the Margins: Jazz and the American Cinema* (Chicago: University of Chicago Press, 1995), p. 5.

21. Robin Wood, *Hitchcock's Films Revisited* (London: Faber and Faber, 1989), pp. 289–92.

22. Peter Wollen, *Signs and Meaning in the Cinema* (Bloomington: Indiana University Press, 1972).

23. Bernard Gendron, '"Moldy Figs" and Modernists: Jazz at War (1942–46)', in Krin Gabbard (ed.), *Jazz among the Discourses* (Durham: Duke University Press, 1995), pp. 31–56; Laurence Gushee in Mark Tucker (ed.), *The Duke Ellington Reader* (New York: OUP, 1993), pp. 423–4; Charles Nanry, *The Jazz Text* (New York: Van Nostrand, 1979), p. 10.

24. Nanry, *The Jazz Text*, p. 10.

25. Peter Wollen, *Raiding the Icebox: Reflections on Twentieth-Century Culture* (London: Verso, 1993), pp. 109–14; Gabbard, *Jazz among the Discourses*, p. 155; Nanry, *The Jazz Text*, p. 4.

26. See, for instance, the section headed 'Categories' in Duke Ellington, *Music is my Mistress* (London: W. H. Allen, 1974).

27. Gushee in Tucker, *The Duke Ellington Reader*, p. 424.

28. Henry Louis Gates, Jr, *The Signifying Monkey: A Theory of African-American Literary Criticism* (New York: OUP, 1988).

29. There is a curious 'paper trail' of references to this song in literary criticism. It may originate with Henry Louis Gates's reference (Gates, *The Signifying Monkey*, p. 104) to Coltrane's 1960 recording as an 'inversion' of the Julie Andrews version (although the latter was not recorded until four years later). Robin Small-McCarthy ('The Jazz Aesthetic in the Novels of Toni Morrison', *Cultural Studies*, Vol. 9, No. 2, May 1995, p. 298) comments on the 'vapidity or ridiculousness' of the 'original version', which Coltrane's improvisation manages to 'expose'. Coltrane himself, however, said of the song to Francois Postif that he 'would have loved to have written it, but it's by Rodgers and Hammerstein' (quoted in Lewis Porter, *John Coltrane: His Life and Music* (Ann Arbor: University of Michigan Press, 1998), p. 182.

30. Teddy Wilson, transcript of interview for the Jazz Oral History Project, Reel 1, p. 51.

31. André Hodeir, *Jazz: Its Evolution and Essence* (New York: Grove, 1956), p. 83.

32. Jon Panish, *The Color of Jazz: Race and Representation in Postwar American Culture* (Jackson: University of Mississippi Press, 1997), p. 83.

33. Lewis Porter, *John Coltrane: His Life and Music* (Ann Arbor: University of Michigan Press, 1998), p. 178.

34. Charlie Parker, in an interview in *Metronome*, 1948, reprinted in *Down Beat*, 11 March 1965, p. 32.

35. Montgomery recorded 'Gone with the Wind' on 26 or 28 January 1960, 'Yesterdays' on 5 or 6 October 1959. Among many other standard ballad songs, many drawn from Broadway musicals, Montgomery made recordings of 'The Girl Next Door', 'Falling in Love with Love' and (from *My Fair Lady*) 'I've Grown Accustomed to her Face'.

36. Scott DeVeaux, *The Birth of Bebop: A Social and Musical History* (Berkeley: University of California Press, 1997), p. 17.

37. Gary Giddins, 'The Evolution of Jazz', in David Baker (ed.), *New Perspectives on Jazz* (Washington: Smithsonian Institution, 1990), p. 41.

38. Pierre Bourdieu, *Distinction: A Social Critique of the Judgement of Taste* (London: Routledge, 1984), p. 87.

39. Krin Gabbard, *Jammin' at the Margins*, p. 102.

40. Joan Didion, *The White Album* (1979; London: Flamingo, 1993), p. 87.

41. 'Village Basement Dive gets Hot Killing with Cool Jazz', *Daily News*, 16 February 1957.

42. 'Jazz and Blues Festival Guide', *Jazz Times*, May 1999, pp. 183–204.

43. Figure for record sales in 1997, *Jazz Times*, August 1998, p. 20.

44. James Lincoln Collier, *Jazz, The American Theme Song* (New York: OUP, 1993), p. 145; figures for 1998–9 come from *Jazz Times 1998–99* Jazz Education Guide.

45. Collier, *Jazz, The American Theme Song*, p. 155.

46. Mary Lou Williams, transcript of interview for Jazz Oral History Project, p. 5.

47. Interview with Henderson and Scofield in *Jazz Times*, December 1996, pp. 68 and 65.

48. Robert Walser, '"Out of Notes": Signification, Interpretation and the Problem of Miles Davis', in Krin Gabbard (ed.), *Jazz among the Discourses*, pp. 165–88; Gabbard, 'Representing the Jazz Trumpet', in Gabbard, *Jammin' at the Margins*, pp. 138–59; Michael Jarrett, 'The Tenor's Vehicle: Reading *Way Out West*' in Gabbard (ed.), *Representing Jazz*, pp. 260–82.

49. Henry Louis Gates, Jr, *The Signifying Monkey*, pp. xix–xx.

50. Gabbard, *Jammin' at the Margins*, p. 1.

51. Gabbard, *Jazz among the Discourses*, p. 18.

52. Gabbard, *Jammin' at the Margins*, p. 8.

53. Braxton quoted in Ronald Radano, *New Musical Figurations: Anthony Braxton's Cultural Critique* (Chicago: Chicago University Press, 1993), p. 179, footnote.

54. Ingrid Monson, 'Doubleness and Jazz Improvisation: Irony, Parody and Ethnomusicology', *Cultural Inquiry*, 20, Winter 1994, p. 313.

55. Ted Gioia, *The Imperfect Art: Reflections on Jazz and Modern Culture* (New York: OUP, 1988), p. 45.

56. Ralph Ellison, interview for *Paris Review*, reprinted in George Plimpton (ed.), *Writers at Work*, 2nd series (London: Penguin, 1977), p. 327.
57. Ellington quoted in Mark Tucker (ed.), *The Duke Ellington Reader*, p. 223.
58. Ralph Ellison, *Going to the Territory* (New York: Random House, 1986), p. 6.
59. Carruth, *Sitting In*, p. 178.
60. Ralph Ellison, 'The Little Man at Chehaw Station', *Going to the Territory*, p. 4.
61. *Jazz Times*, August 1999, p. 34.
62. Greil Marcus, *Mystery Train: Images of America in Rock 'n' Roll Music* (New York: Plume, 1997), p. 138.

Select Bibliography

The musical basis

Berliner, Paul F., *Thinking in Jazz: The Infinite Art of Improvisation* (Chicago: Chicago University Press, 1994).

Hodeir, André, *Jazz: Its Evolution and Essence* (New York: Grove, 1956).

Kernfeld, Barry, *What to Listen for in Jazz* (New York: Yale University Press, 1995).

Levine, Mark, *The Jazz Theory Book* (Petaluma: Sher, 1995).

Nettl, Bruno, 'Thoughts on Improvisation: A Comparative Approach', *The Musical Quarterly*, Vol. LX, No. 1, January 1974, pp. 1–19.

Owens, Thomas, *Bebop: The Music and its Players* (New York: OUP, 1995).

Jazz history and theory

Adorno, Theodor, 'Jazz – Perennial Fashion', in *Prisms* (London: Neville Spearman, 1967), pp. 121–32.

Collier, James Lincoln, *The Making of Jazz* (New York: Delta, 1978).

Collier, James Lincoln, *Jazz: The American Theme Song* (New York: OUP, 1993).

Gabbard, Krin (ed.), *Jazz among the Discourses* (Durham: Duke University Press, 1995).

Gabbard, Krin (ed.), *Representing Jazz* (Durham: Duke University Press, 1995).

Gennari, John, 'Jazz Criticism: Its Development and Ideologies', *Black American Literature Forum*, Vol. 25, No. 3, Fall 1991, pp. 449–523.

Giddins, Gary, *Visions of Jazz: The First Century* (New York: OUP, 1998).

Gioia, Ted, *The History of Jazz* (New York: OUP, 1997).

Gioia, Ted, *The Imperfect Art: Reflections on Jazz and Modern Culture* (New York: OUP, 1988).

Jones, Leroi [Amiri Baraka], *Black Music* (New York: Quill, 1967).

Lees, Gene, *Singers and the Song* (New York: OUP, 1987).

Malone, Jacqui, *Steppin' on the Blues: The Visible Rhythms of African American Dance* (Urbana: University of Illinois Press, 1996).

Monson, Ingrid, 'Doubleness and Jazz Improvisation: Irony, Parody and Ethnomusicology', *Cultural Inquiry*, 20, Winter 1994, pp. 283–313.

Nanry, Charles, *The Jazz Text* (New York: Van Nostrand, 1979).

Newton, Francis [Eric Hobsbaum], *The Jazz Scene* (London: Penguin, 1961).

O'Meally, Robert G. (ed.), *The Jazz Cadence of American Culture* (New York: Columbia University Press, 1998).

Radano, Ronald, M., *New Musical Figurations: Anthony Braxton's Cultural Critique* (Chicago: Chicago University Press, 1993).

Sidran, Ben, *Black Talk* (London: Payback, 1971).
Schuller, Gunther, *Early Jazz: Its Roots and Musical Development* (New York: OUP, 1968).
Schuller, Gunther, *The Swing Era: The Development of Jazz 1930–1945* (New York: OUP, 1989).
Stearns, Marshall, *The Story of Jazz* (New York: OUP, 1956).
Townsend, Peter, 'Adorno on Jazz: Vienna versus the Vernacular', *Prose Studies*, Vol. 11, No. 1, May 1988, pp. 69–88.
Zwerin, Michael, *Close Enough for Jazz* (London: Quartet, 1983).

Jazz in particular periods and locations
Collier, James Lincoln, *Benny Goodman and the Swing Era* (New York: OUP, 1989).
DeVeaux, Scott, *The Birth of Bebop: A Social and Musical History* (Berkeley: University of California Press, 1997).
DjeDje, Jacqueline, and Meadows, Eddie S., *California Soul: Music of African Americans in the West* (Berkeley: University of California Press, 1998).
Erenberg, Lewis, *Swingin' the Dream: Big Band Jazz and the Rebirth of American Culture* (Chicago: University of Chicago Press, 1998).
Gioia, Ted, *West Coast Jazz: Modern Jazz in California, 1945–1960* (New York: OUP, 1992).
Kenney, William Howland, *Chicago Jazz: A Cultural History 1904–1930* (New York: OUP, 1993).
Kofsky, Frank, *John Coltrane and the Jazz Revolution of the 1960s* (New York: Pathfinder, 1998).
Ogren, Kathy J., *The Jazz Revolution: Twenties America and the Meaning of Jazz* (New York: OUP, 1989).
Russell, Ross, *Jazz Style in Kansas City and the Southwest* (Berkeley: University of California Press, 1971).
Stewart, Rex, *Jazz Masters of the Thirties* (London: Macmillan, 1972).
Stowe, David W., *Swing Changes: Big-Band Jazz in New Deal America* (Cambridge: Harvard University Press, 1994).

Biographies, studies of individual musicians and oral histories
Barker, Danny (Alyn Shipton, ed.), *A Life in Jazz* (London: Macmillan, 1986).
Büchmann-Møller, Frank, *You Got to be Original, Man!: The Music of Lester Young* (New York: Greenwood, 1989).
Davis, Miles, with Quincy Troupe, *Miles: The Autobiography* (London: Picador, 1990).
Ellington, Duke, *Music is my Mistress* (London: W. H. Allen, 1974).
Gitler, Ira, *Swing to Bop: An Oral History of the Transition in Jazz in the 1940s* (New York: OUP, 1985).
Hentoff, Nat, and Nat Shapiro, *Hear Me Talkin' to Ya* (London: Penguin, 1962).
Kirk, Andy, with Amy Lee, *Twenty Years on Wheels* (Oxford: Bayou Press, 1989).
Mezzrow, Mezz, with Bernard Wolfe, *Really the Blues* (1946; London: Corgi, 1961).
Pepper, Art, and Laurie Pepper, *Straight Life* (New York: Schirmer, 1979).
Porter, Lewis, *Lester Young* (London: Macmillan, 1985).

Porter, Lewis, *John Coltrane: His Life and Music* (Ann Arbor: University of Michigan Press, 1998).

Russell, Ross, *Bird Lives!* (London: Quartet, 1973).

Tucker, Mark (ed.), *The Duke Ellington Reader* (New York: OUP, 1993).

Cultural and theoretical backgrounds

Baker, Houston, A., Jr, *Blues, Ideology and Afro-American Literature* (Chicago: Chicago University Press, 1984).

Barthes, Roland, *Mythologies* (1957; London: Paladin, 1973).

Barthes, Roland, *Image-Music-Text* (London: Fontana, 1977).

Barthes, Roland, *Camera Lucida: Reflections on Photography* (London: Cape, 1982).

Belgrad, Daniel, *The Culture of Spontaneity: Improvisation and the Arts in Postwar America* (Chicago: Chicago University Press, 1998).

Boorstin, Daniel J., *The Americans: The Democratic Experience* (London: Cardinal, 1988).

Bourdieu, Pierre, *Distinction: A Social Critique of the Judgement of Taste* (London: Routledge, 1984).

Brooker, Peter, *New York Fictions: Modernity, Post-Modernism, The New Modernism* (London: Longman, 1996).

Gates, Henry Louis, Jr, *The Signifying Monkey: A Theory of African-American Literary Criticism* (New York: OUP, 1988).

Lhamon, W. T., Jr, *Deliberate Speed: The Origins of a Cultural Style in the American 1950s* (Washington: Smithsonian Institution Press, 1990).

Powell, Richard J., *The Blues Aesthetic: Black Culture and Modernism* (Washington: Washington Project for the Arts, 1989).

Sontag, Susan, *On Photography* (London: Penguin, 1979).

Wollen, Peter, *Raiding the Icebox: Reflections on Twentieth-Century Culture* (London: Verso, 1993).

Jazz, literary texts and film

Albert, Richard N., *From Blues to Bop: A Collection of Jazz Fiction* (Baton Rouge: Louisiana State University Press, 1990).

Baraka, Amiri [Leroi Jones], *The Autobiography of Leroi Jones/Amiri Baraka* (New York: Freundlich, 1984).

Bourjaily, Vance, 'In and Out of Storyville: Jazz in Fiction', *New York Times Book Review*, 13:1, December 1987, pp. 44–5.

Carruth, Hayden, *Sitting In: Selected Writings on Jazz, Blues and Related Topics* (Iowa City: Iowa University Press, 1993).

Ellison, Ralph, *Invisible Man* (1952; London: Penguin, 1965).

Ellison, Ralph, *Shadow and Act* (London: Secker and Warburg, 1967).

Ellison, Ralph, *Going to the Territory* (New York: Random House, 1986).

Feinstein, Sascha, and Yusef Komunyakaa, *The Jazz Poetry Anthology* (Bloomington: Indiana University Press, 1991).

Gabbard, Krin, *Jammin' at the Margins: Jazz in the American Cinema* (Chicago: University of Chicago Press, 1996).

Henderson, Stephen, *Understanding the New Black Poetry: Black Speech and Black Music as Poetic References* (New York: William Morrow, 1973).

Holmes, John Clellon, *The Horn* (1958; London: Jazz Book Club, 1961).

Hughes, Langston, (Rampersad, Arnold, and David Roessel, eds), *The Collected Poems of Langston Hughes* (New York: Vintage, 1995).

Kerouac, Jack, *On The Road* (1957; London: Penguin, 1972).

Kerouac, Jack, *The Subterraneans* (New York: Grove, 1971).

Kerouac, Jack, 'Essentials of Spontaneous Prose', *Evergreen Review*, Vol. 2, No. 5, Summer 1958, pp. 72–3.

Morrison, Toni, *Jazz* (London: Picador, 1993).

Morrison, Toni, *Playing in the Dark* (Cambridge: Harvard University Press, 1992).

Nicosia, Gerald, *Memory Babe: A Critical Biography of Jack Kerouac* (Berkeley: University of California Press, 1994).

Panish, Jon, *The Color of Jazz: Race and Representation in Postwar American Culture* (Jackson: University of Mississippi Press, 1997).

Smith, Hugh L., Jr., 'Jazz in the American Novel', *English Journal*, Vol. XLVII, No. 2, November 1958, pp. 467–78.

Welty, Eudora, *The Collected Stories of Eudora Welty* (London: Marion Boyars, 1981).

Weinreich, Regina, *The Spontaneous Poetics of Jack Kerouac: A Study of the Fiction* (New York: Marlowe, 1995).

Zabor, Rafi, *The Bear Goes Home* (London: Cape, 1998).

Reference

Albert, Richard N., *An Annotated Bibliography of Jazz Fiction and Jazz Fiction Criticism* (Westport: Greenwood Press, 1996).

Feinstein, Sascha, *A Bibliographic Guide to Jazz Poetry* (Westport: Greenwood, 1996).

Kennington, Donald, *The Literature of Jazz: A Critical Guide* (London: The Library Association, 1970).

Kernfeld, Barry (ed.), *The New Grove Dictionary of Jazz* (New York: St Martin's Press, 1994).

Meeker, David, *Jazz in the Movies: A Guide to Jazz Musicians 1917–1977* (London: Talisman, 1977).

Index

NOTE: The titles of films, literary texts and musical works and the names of places are listed only when they are the subject of substantive discussion.